WHAT WOMEN WANT

For Debbie and Susie, young women of the new century.

WHAT WOMEN WANT

BY

EDWINA CURRIE

AND OTHERS

SIDGWICK & JACKSON LIMITED

LONDON

First published in Great Britain in 1990 by Sidgwick & Jackson Limited

ISBN 0-283-06017-4

Typeset by Rowland Phototypesetting Limited
Bury St Edmunds, Suffolk
Printed by Mackays of Chatham plc, Chatham, Kent
for Sidgwick & Jackson Limited
1 Tavistock Chambers, Bloomsbury Way
London WC1A 2SG

Contents

Acknowledgements

Thanks are due to many people, not least to the contributors who put up with my nagging and phone calls and interruptions to their weekends for months on end with cheerful patience and enthusiasm.

Thanks also to William Armstrong, Hilary Davies, Ruth Baldwin and Morven Knowles at Sidgwick & Jackson for their encouragement and professionalism; to Hilary Rubinstein, supportive as ever; to Clare Whelan, Christine Heald and Jane Lea for all their assistance; and to the brilliant staff of the House of Commons library who know all the answers.

Most of all I would like to thank my husband, Ray, and two teenage daughters, Debbie and Susie, for whom this book is written.

Edwina Currie
May 1990

INTRODUCTION:
The Demographic Timebomb
by Edwina Currie MP

The chamber of the House of Commons was busy, noisy, urgent, as it always is just before Prime Minister's Question Time. The green leather benches, which look so smart on television but in reality are creased and a little shabby, were nearly full of sober-suited men and the occasional woman. The junior ministers at the dispatch box, whose fate today it was to be the opening act before the Prime Minister, were harrassedly attempting to answer questions on their speciality, but no one was listening. The Prime Minister herself was already in her place. She held her briefing notes spread out, fan-like, as an experienced poker player might hold a hand of cards, and muttered to herself, brow furrowed, glancing occasionally at the front bench opposite as the moments ticked away.

I had no question on the order paper that day, so it would require a little indulgence to get called. I went quietly to the Speaker's chair and stood on the right-hand side by the arm. When he looked down, I bowed respectfully and said, 'I have a constituency issue I should like to put to the Prime Minister. May I try to catch your eye?'

He's good and decent. As well as being Speaker, Jack Weatherill is a dapper, elegant man, the MP for Croydon North-East and was formerly a junior minister; I like and respect him.

'Well, Edwina,' he said with a twinkle, 'You are looking very nice today, so maybe you'll have a chance.'

Why did I feel vaguely irritated? I turned away with a sigh and decided to find another way of putting my constituent's point. Puzzled at my own reaction, I walked out of the chamber.

Now I never used to feel that way; heaven help us if charm and terms of endearment were banned from everyday life. The efforts of the dafter local councils such as Derbyshire to ban the use of 'pet' and 'dear' have met quite rightly with hoots of derision. Yet there I was, asking the Speaker to assist me, as any other MP might, and getting a different reply from the one the majority of my colleagues might receive. Imagine his words said to one of the young male MPs.

Attitudes have shifted, and we now sometimes regard comments as discriminatory, even when well-meant, where we might not have done before. Perhaps I have become more sensitive. Or perhaps I notice now what I should not have ignored or denied previously.

Let me give you another example. I served under four secretaries of state in government. A reporter put a question to one of them: 'And is Edwina after your job, then?'

My boss roared with laughter. 'Of course not,' he said. 'Why should she be after my job?'

He thought he was being kind, protective, friendly, but I felt upset and angry. The feeling would not go away, but it took some time and a bit of a struggle before it dawned on me why that remark was so hurtful. Why shouldn't I be after his job? Doesn't anyone worth their salt want improvement and promotion? Then the truth hit home: he wouldn't have said it about a young male minister. It would not have sounded right about John or Mark or Michael. It would not even have occurred to him – instead the remark would have been turned into a true compliment, possibly on the lines of: 'Of course he's after my job. He's very good. But it's not vacant just at present . . .'

This book owes its origins, then, to two factors: first, my own growing awareness that women are different – that there is a gap between what women want and what many good, decent, kindly people, who are all for equality and would be horrified to be called sexist, believe women want; and second, my concern about the effects of the impending explosion of the 'demographic timebomb'. I will explain each in turn.

All my life I have worked in a male-dominated world, whether teaching at a college of further education and in the civil service, or in politics. My connections with other women, educated, professional or otherwise, have always been rather sparse. Even at university, while I was resident in a women's college (there was no choice then), most of my time was spent at the Oxford Union, then as now dominated by the chaps.

My understanding of women's differing needs grew when, in September 1986, I was made responsible for women's health in this country, becoming the first government minister so designated in the United Nations. As I described in my first book, *Life Lines*, it was obvious from the start that women felt differently about many health issues; the Health Department always had a good press and a lot of support, when tackling such problems as breast cancer for example, and not just from people sympathetic to the government. On many occasions, speaking at a banquet or an official lunch, I would be pursued into the Ladies by a bunch of chatty, smartly dressed women, anxious to tell me their views on a host of 'female' subjects – but not in front of the men!

Women of every age and background expressed to me their pleasure that a woman minister was handling these matters, even though men had initiated some of the projects and were giving full support. In a world of real equality and understanding it shouldn't matter who is tackling these topics provided they are competent; but during the eleven months of 1989 when the Department of Health had no women ministers, the style changed and there was a feeling that these issues had been put on the back burner, in contrast to the approval expressed at the eventual appointment of Virginia Bottomley and Baroness Hooper in November 1989.

There was another aspect which bothered me, as I started to plough through the shelf on 'women' in the House of Commons library. Nobody seemed to be speaking for me, or for people like me. Most of the writing about women's issues in the last twenty years has come from the left. Feminism in both Europe and in the USA has been corralled by people with whom, on the whole, I could not agree on any other issue.

A leftish political bias will, of course, influence a writer's perspective and, while appealing to many, may cut her work off from others, including me. On the other hand, journalists such as Mary Kenny, writing about women from a more traditional position, are very few, and sometimes (as in Mary's case and that of many right-wing American women) tend to take a strong line against abortion or embryo research in any form, whereas I am willing to vote in favour. There are right-wing men and groups producing pamplets on 'family policy', but they seem to want all of us women back in the kitchen – and I don't agree with them either.

One or two of the best women writers make no effort to hide their homosexuality, and indeed may point out that their attraction to the cause derives precisely from their sexual orientation. This is fine for them, but it is bound to colour their writing and makes them frankly unrepresentative of the bulk of women in this country.

We may have the highest divorce rate in Europe, but we also have the highest marriage rate, though much remarriage is clearly the triumph of hope over experience.

It was time, therefore, to try to fill that gap. However, perhaps lacking the confidence to declare myself typical (or any evidence that my feelings might be shared by anyone at all), I decided against recording just my personal views. Instead I invited a group of friends, and others whom I had not met but whose work had impressed me, to show how women's position in society is changing and how attitudes are shifting, and to offer some of their professional knowledge of what women want in the 1990s.

There is a lot of diverse opinion here. Gordon Heald, Managing Director of Gallup Polls, describes to us how women are now giving strikingly different answers from men when asked questions by pollsters. Patricia Mann of J Walter Thompson, the international advertising agency, shows how advertising has changed, both in its depiction of women and in its appeal to them as consumers and the difficulties which remain for women working in the business. Writer and teacher Sue Dicks gives a personal view of the hilarious and hurtful ill effects of unguarded discriminatory language on the rueful female listener; I shall never write 'his' again when meaning 'his or hers', and indeed went through some of the texts sent in by my contributors, correcting their own unconscious sexist language.

I love the changes in advertising, especially on TV. In the latest Ariel ad, the shirts are being ironed by a boy – and competently, too. According to Virginia Matthews, writing in the *Daily Telegraph* of 24 January 1990, the latest advertisement for the Volkswagen Passat, made by the ad agency BMP DDB Needham, offers what the company calls 'family values'. I greatly enjoyed her description:

> Filmed in New York and entirely in black and white, 'God Bless the Child' is a moody story of a small child's first encounter with the hostility of adult street life. Clutching the protective hand of her father tightly, the child walks the streets of the busy metropolis to a cacophony of alarm bells, sirens and horns, with a backdrop of fearsome-looking skyscrapers. Just as the scene is beginning to look threatening and the child terrified, her mother draws up in the family's saloon, the sleek-looking Passat. The child and her father clamber inside and they drive away through the city streets without any further fear.

BMP tells me that this represents a move away from the conspicuous consumerism of the Eighties to the family values of the Caring Nineties. This may or may not be the case, but any commercial with a soundtrack of Billie Holiday singing 'God Bless the Child' can't be all bad.

Father instead of mother; mother instead of father. Little girl, come to think of it, instead of little boy. Nice, that. I hope it sells lots of cars for them. What a contrast with the old 1970's ad for the little Fiat: 'If this car was a lady, it would have its bottom pinched'. Underneath, written with cold fury: 'If this lady was a car, she'd run you down.'

Some people are making a real effort for the cause of equality. As I was bashing away at the word-processor writing this book, an envelope arrived from Conservative Central Office. Would I please give a reference to a young man of my acquaintance, who would like his name entered on the approved candidates' list in time to fight the next election? I obliged, trying to remember the details of his personal background, any politically wayward views and whether he had any funny habits.

Then question 7 made me sit up: 'To what extent will his wife and family be a help or a hindrance to him as an MP?'

'You sexist lot!' I wrote on the form. First, the constituency has the right to expect a lot from the MP, but not from his family, if any; the spouse may well want to stay out of politics (as mine does). Second, it was a bit much being asked only about the 'wife'. I phoned and complained.

The voice at the other end was ultra-smooth. 'Oh yes: we know. Actually we have two forms. The other one asks, "To what extent will her husband and family be a help or hindrance . . .?" '

As for the contributors to *What Women Want*, I should emphasise that each person writing here is offering their own point of view. In most cases I've no idea whether they are members of my party, or indeed any party; I haven't asked them. It is not intended to be a political book. What is more important is that the ideas expressed in it should command an audience and generate some thinking, some debate. That is what *this* woman wants.

There is, however, another reason, besides my growing awareness that women exist and are different from men, why a book on what women want is timely. This second issue is much less subjective and easier to quantify. The 'demographic timebomb' which is hitting this country in the 1990s will force more women – and more equality – on British employers, whether they like it and plan for it or not.

What is the 'demographic timebomb'?

I was born in 1946, one of the great surge of European post-war babies. My younger brother, one of the second surge, was born in 1949. As our generation left school and headed for college in the mid-1960s, a revolution in contraception (then euphemistically dubbed 'family planning') was taking place: for the first time in history, women had the power effectively and relatively safely with the Pill to limit their fertility, and did so by the million with sighs of relief. Numbers born in Britain reached their peak in 1964 and then began to plummet. The nadir came in 1977; by then the birth rate was insufficient to replace the number who died and the population was shrinking. By 1980 the number of births was climbing again, as the peak of the early sixties reached childbearing years, but we will not see a rise in the total number of schoolchildren until close to the start of the next century.

The population pattern of this country will be savagely affected by these peaks and troughs for decades to come. For example, as the post-war baby boomers in this country and in many other developed Western nations reach retirement age around the year 2015, the retired age groups will have become a much larger proportion of the population than they are now. At the same time the numbers of those in the working age groups will then be sliding downwards fast. If my generation does not provide now for our future financial needs, we may find a considerable reluctance on the part of the young workers of the twenty-first century to pay our pensions for us. Don't rely on the grandchildren: complacency now will mean poverty in future.

During the 1980s there was no shortage of young people – rather, a tragic glut, with far more workers than jobs. The young men and women born in the early and mid-1960s, when the birth rate was at its peak, were coming on to the job market in large numbers at a time of world recession. The overall numbers available for work climbed rapidly just when we needed them least. A million more jobs were needed just to keep unemployment steady at its three million peak. Youth unemployment was stubbornly high – until YOPS and YTS it was higher than adult unemployment. In poll after poll the British people declared that unemployment was the most important problem facing us as a nation, a view that persists even as many areas get close to effectively full employment. It would have seemed cruel and laughable then to suggest that quite quickly the situation would be reversed – that we would be short of skilled workers and acutely short of young recruits – but that is now the position.

This book is concerned with a short and urgent time scale, the next five years or so. The number of young people entering the job market is now dropping alarmingly fast. In 1988 there were some 800,000 school leavers; by 1993 the number is expected to fall as low as 625,000. Between now and 1995 the number of sixteen-to-nineteen-year-olds in Great Britain's workforce will drop by 23 per cent – almost a quarter. At the same time an unusually large number of people will reach retirement age and require replacement at work. According to the Department of Employment, *by 1995 four out of five new jobs created in this country will have to go to women*; there won't be any spare men around to do them, for everyone of working age employable and available for work can expect to be working.

Don't get me wrong – the country isn't going to grind to a halt. Growth is still possible, and likely. In Britain the overall size of the workforce will rise by about a million or so between now and 1995 – much more slowly than recently.

It is only the number of *young* people entering the job market that will fall. The number of teenagers in the workforce – that is, sixteen-to-nineteen-year-olds – will fall to about two million from its recent almost three million. The number of twenty-to-twenty-four-year-olds in the workforce is projected to decline from 3.7 million in 1987 to 2.6 million in 1999. This isn't guesswork: forecasters can speak with some confidence because they know how many are already coming through the pipeline. Putting the two groups together: in 1989 there were around 7.8 million people in Britain aged sixteen to twenty-four. By the year 2000 that will fall to just over 6.1 million. It will be close to the next century before the number of teenagers available starts to creep upwards again.

The fall in the potential teenage workforce over the next few years will mean that for every five workers in that age group in 1987, there will be no more than four by 1995. As far more of them will be staying on at school, or entering full-time education, this figure (based on the numbers of bodies) almost certainly overestimates the numbers looking for a pay packet. At present only 15 per cent of Britain's eighteen- to nineteen-year-olds are in full-time education, but if the Department of Education and Science has its way, and its predictions are correct, that figure is set to rise substantially. There will be regional differences, too, with falls of 20 per cent or more in Wales and the north of England, and in my own area of the East Midlands. These falls will be only partly due to continued migration to areas with higher earnings and more jobs; the main cause will be that equivalent numbers of people of childbearing age simply haven't been living there in recent years – fewer parents means fewer kids.

Further projections way into the twenty-first century suggest that the number of young people in the workforce will *never* return to the level we are used to. The days of many eager young workers, of young recruits earnestly filling in application forms for choosy employers, are at an end in Britain. More to the point, the adaptations we need to make to cope with this change are not temporary: they need to be worked through as permanent. It will be so long before there is any upturn in the numbers of young recruits – and that upturn will still be at lower levels than in recent years of abundance – that taking on more women and giving them a bigger role in the workforce and promotion stakes, cannot be regarded as transient or a mere fad.

The culture change required to cope with the 1990s is made harder by some lamentable traditions in this country. Many engineering businesses train only on entry to the firm, often still through the age-limited system of apprenticeships. Reach the age of twenty or twenty-five without a City and Guilds certificate and the odds are you have missed the boat. In the dire days of the 1980s many businesses cut their training schemes altogether: they were the first 'extras' to go. This has turned out to be a dreadfully short-sighted policy, and now the same employers are screaming that there is a serious shortage of skilled manpower in Britain. Worse, we are left with a large rump of youngish and middle-aged undertrained men and women, especially in manufacturing industry where the skills shortage is most painful now.

These daft training policies are found elsewhere too. Look at the National Health Service, for another example, with the biggest payroll in Western Europe. In this country the NHS is the largest employer of women – over half a million of them in nursing and midwifery alone. Year by year it takes in thousands of young women from school and college. In 1986 roughly one third of all suitably qualified eighteen-year-old girls in Britain went into the NHS, not just for nursing but for all the other occupations – physiotherapy, laboratories, secretarial work – where women predominate and numbers are increasing; by the early 1990s, it has been estimated, the figure will have grown to half. Do you think that is realistic? No, neither do I, not with all the other opportunities open to able young women now.

Typically we train a nurse for three years, then we expect her to work for a while and leave to start a family. Many hospitals make absolutely no effort to keep nurses or even maintain contact, let alone persuade them to return to work part-time. The attitude is: 'We'll just wait till the next batch of new recruits leave the nursing school.' We have not come much further since the days when a nurse was expected to resign her post on marriage. It takes four and a half years to train a midwife, and she will stay with the NHS on average another four and a half years before resigning. That kind of wastage seems to me criminal, and would have to be tackled even if we were not heading for a shortage of young people. One of the contributors to this book, Barbara Young, the General Manager of Parkside Health Authority and past President of the Institute of Health Service Managers, tells us how the problems are being faced – not just for nurses – in her health authority in the heart of London.

I doubt if there are any answers in the form of immigrants from overseas as there were last time we were short of bodies, in the 1950s. In those days the Department of Health and London Transport put advertisements in the West Indian newspapers to persuade people to come here, an invitation accepted eagerly by large numbers of hard-working people. Immigration laws now prevent further large-scale movements into this country. Nor should we expect much migration to these shores from other European countries, for most of our big European Community partners face a fall in their working populations in the next few years. They will tend to suck away some of our best workers rather than the other way round. Only West Germany has experienced a big rise in the number of people seeking work as a million refugees flooded in during 1989, with another million expected in 1990; for political reasons they will no doubt stay put in Hamburg and Dortmund, and will not consider trotting along to Hammersmith and Dorchester.

The level of understanding about the picture in Britain is woefully, scandalously low. The National Economic Development

Office/Training Agency survey, *Defusing the Demographic Time Bomb*, published in November 1989, found that most employers knew something about the problem, but most – three out of four – were contenting themselves with efforts to be more attractive to young recruits. NEDO found it hard to identify *anyone* in manufacturing who had come to terms with the changes; most of the innovations were happening in the services sector. That is probably a reflection of the fact that in the 1980s manufacturers sloughed off large numbers of workers, mostly male, while the services sector 'growed' like Topsy, taking on several million people, mainly women.

It is all part of a long-term social change which has been taking place under our noses. By June 1989 total male employees, compared with 1971, had fallen from 13.4 to 11.7 million, nearly a million of whom were part-time; while the numbers of women employees had grown from 8.2 to 10.2 million, with more than half full-time. The number of women working part-time during those two decades leapt from 2.7 to 4.3 million and is still rising. Self-employment – much more popular in Thatcherite Britain – adds 2.2 million men and three quarters of a million women to these totals today. The working pattern of men as well as women has changed. Getting an increase in productivity out of all these people, the women especially, is now exercising some smart minds.

The NEDO survey found that one company in five had not made any attempt at all to change its strategy in any way and was not intending to do so. Some 47 per cent of businesses were responding by improving youth training and over one third were in the process of changing pay and benefits: competing harder, in other words, and in a truly inflationary way to boot. Only 7 per cent looked at job sharing and a miserable 3 per cent had considered childcare arrangements.

The prospects for the country if every employer tried to increase pay would be disastrous. The public services can beat us all at that game without batting an eyelid. Nurses' regrading in 1989 added 18 per cent to their NHS pay bill and lifted £2 billion from the Exchequer. During much of the winter of 1989/90 the Department of Health was trying to persuade ambulance crews to accept a pay rise between 9 and 16 per cent over 18 months with most of the British people, according to the polls, wanting them to 'give 'em the money'. The dispute was settled at an even higher figure. It is, of course, our money that is being handed over; the only pocket which is bottomless is the taxpayer's. If pay rises of that kind continue, if other employers join in the expensive game of competing for scarce young recruits with ever fatter pay cheques, that way lies only one thing – inflation.

It has happened before. When I was a young college lecturer in 1974, I received the Houghton pay award, promised by the hard-pressed Wilson government trying to retain and pacify teachers in the course of the election campaign: 30 per cent – great!! The next year, other employers had to follow suit, putting up their prices to compensate, and inflation touched 28 per cent. We discovered that we had been paid in paper money. Worse, the uncompetitiveness so created shoved Britain further into decline and unemployment. We can do that all over again if we try hard enough in the coming years of scarce workers – the unions are just flexing their newly discovered muscles, atrophied during the years of mass unemployment, to attempt it.

If the number of young people is set to fall, and there will be a spate of retirements, how come the number of people in work will grow, albeit more slowly than before?

We know that the numbers in the workforce aged thirty-four to fifty-four will tend to rise. But according to the Department of Employment's White Paper of December 1988 entitled *Employment for the 1990s*, 'two-thirds of the labour force growth in the 1980s was made up of women, and by 1995 the projected increase in the size of the female labour force is some three quarters of a million, over 80 per cent of the total'. Speaking in the Commons on 13 February 1990, Michael Howard, Secretary of State, said that the proportion of new jobs to be filled by women by the year 2000 will be 90 per cent. There is a distinct feeling that our time has come.

In Great Britain from now till 1995, as we see the fall by 23 per cent in the sixteens-to-nineteens, the thirty-five-to-fifty-four-year-olds will increase by 7.2 per cent and the number of women aged twenty-five to fifty-four will grow by 7.9 per cent. That's my age group – the baby boomers. Some regions show even sharper differences: in East Anglia, where more than half the employers already report problems in recruitment, the number of women goes up over 13 per cent; in the East Midlands over 10 per cent. We are here if you want us.

The only other group available is the retired – but enjoying their garden, their gas share dividends and their Saga holidays, they might just be somewhat reluctant to come back into gainful employment. According to another survey, for the CBI in 1989, only one in ten of the retired over-fifties were definitely interested in a return to the labour market, and most of those were in their fifties. Still, from 1989 pensioners can collect a pay packet without losing any of their state pension, now that the earnings rule has been abolished. In terms of flexible hours and a responsible attitude to those with caring and family responsibilities, their needs if they are to be wooed may be much the same as those of non-working women.

Above all there will be new opportunities for women. We are the only workforce still available in large numbers and under-employed in this country. The working pattern, as you would expect, is determined mainly, but not entirely, by the number of their children. The 1988 General Household Survey showed what was happening.

Among women with little children – youngest child under five – in 1988, around one in three (36 per cent) were working, and about 5 per cent registered unemployed. Two thirds of those in work were working part-time, but even with all the problems outlined by the contributors to this book, one woman in ten with little children (11 per cent) was working full-time.

Once the children go to school the activity rate (defined as employed plus registered unemployed but available for work) rises very sharply, with two thirds (65 per cent) working and only 4 per cent unemployed. That gives an activity rate of around 70 per cent. The figures do not change much as the children get older. Where the youngest child is aged ten or over, the figure rises only a little – to 76 per cent. By this time one family in three has a full-time working mother and nearly half (43 per cent) have a part-time one. Working mothers are the majority, not an oddity or minority. *Most of us work.*

Somewhere along the line it is clear that employers are not delivering what women want. Among women with *no* dependent children, 72 per cent were in work – roughly two thirds full-time, one third part-time – and 5 per cent were registered unemployed. Add the two groups together: at 77 per cent, that activity rate is only 1 per cent higher than the figure for women with school-age children, the main difference between the two being the switch from mainly part-time to mainly full-time work. Nevertheless, it suggests that there are plenty more women around who could convert from part-time to full-time. To persuade them, employers will certainly have to figure out what these women want!

Compare the activity rate among men, which in Great Britain is around 88 per cent. We would not expect it to reach 100 per cent, and indeed it is falling as more teenagers stay on at school and college. But see page 39: about one woman in eight without dependent children is currently choosing not to work at all. They are mostly women in the over thirty-five age bracket – my generation again, the 'older women'. Could they be tempted back to part-time or full-time work, given the right terms and conditions? In Sweden and several other Scandinavian countries they think the activity rate of their women will move closer to the men's, with the differences disappearing by the end of the century. It could happen here too.

The projections are for further change in the same direction. When I left university, only half the women in this country were in paid work; half were choosing to stay at home, do voluntary work, care for a sick relative, make jam, look after the baby. Now, for all women of working age, the figure for those choosing to work hovers around 70 per cent. By the end of the century it is expected to be about 74 per cent, but I think that is an underestimate. If women's choice is increased, I believe more of them will choose to work, with all the attendant companionship and mental stimulation, plus the pay packet bringing those lovely feelings of both independence and being able to contribute substantially to the family budget. Most women are not working for pin money. If the women I meet are anything to go by, they work for a sense of identity, a sense of worth, as the microwave and the freezer and the self-cleaning oven reduce both the necessity of and the satisfaction in staying at home.

At the time of writing a very large part of our female workforce is already collecting a pay packet. It follows that tremendous efforts will be needed, as the 1990s unfold, to encourage the others at the margin, the women who are currently choosing to stay at home, or work part-time, to play a bigger part in the economy.

Women will have a lot more choice in the next few years: whether they work or not and, if so, where – at home or in an office; and for whom – for the boss who understands the problems of fetching the kids from school and is helpful, or the one who regards it as nothing to do with him. In increasing numbers women will opt to work for themselves. In many parts of the country we women will have you guys over a barrel: you have been warned. Some businesses are already trying hard to attract more women employees and finding it much trickier than they first supposed. A few may attempt to ignore the inevitable. But if companies do take some notice of these exhortations, if they are to be successful in recruiting more women, and in retaining the services of the women so painfully acquired, they will have to be much more aware of what women want.

In Chapter 6 of this book Dr Clare Baggott, computer specialist, describes what it is like for her being a working mother in Wokingham (no joke), and how that rare bird, the well-organised working parent, can try to make it all happen at once. Margaret Jackson, a formidable lady and long-standing employee of BP, gives us a view from industry: the board may be all in favour of equality, but wait till you try it on the boys on the oil rig. Come to think of it, when will there be a woman on the BP board? The question has been asked at shareholders' meetings, with no answer as yet. Another contributor, Diana Balsdon, is in charge of equal opportunities employment at the National Westminster Bank. The finance sector has made more effort than most, but still finds real equality elusive. If keen people like this find it tough, don't underestimate the effort required when starting from scratch.

And we call the book *What Women Want* because that will be much more important in future. If these jobs are to be filled by women returners, or by women with young children currently at home, or by persuading women staff to go on improvement courses and seek promotion, we are by definition dealing with people who currently face barriers, who find it too hard at the moment. They obviously want something not available at present. I think it goes deeper than that. So much current thinking, as both Joanna Foster and Anthony Clare point out, assumes, as Freud did, that women really want to be men. I wonder if Sigmund asked any women about it? George Bernard Shaw made the same assumption. There is Eliza Doolittle, trying so hard to remove her imperfections and weaknesses, to be more like the horrible Professor Higgins; even she accepts, at least for a time, that such is her role in life, with much of the plot depending on her varying success.

I venture to suggest, however, that most modern women don't want to be like men. Often they have a try and don't like it and refuse to compete any further – going off, not always back to the sink, but to run their own show in a different atmosphere. I think they want to be themselves, not imitation chaps. The conclusion is the same – most employers are not giving women what they want, which is why so many, even without onerous family responsibilities, choose not to work, or to work only part-time.

Many companies congratulate themselves on their efforts to get more women into higher positions, then wonder why they don't seem to stay long. Women have dubbed this the 'glass ceiling', in that you can see where you want to go but prejudice stops further progress. Perhaps it is more complicated. A company might try to eradicate the difficulties women employees face in becoming more like their male colleagues by say, providing childcare. Women employees are seen as having 'problems' which the company must solve. At least that is better than no help at all, but it begs a more fundamental question: how can the company get the best out of *all* the workforce, male and female?

The impression I got, as I researched this book, is that the companies which are most successful in generating real equality do not simply say, 'Our current working practices are OK. It is the women who need help'. They start from scratch – thinking out what work needs to be done and how it must be done, and then asking the most important question: how to tap the talents of whatever workforce is available to get it done well.

I reflected that I should think about this myself. The work of an MP is never-ending; it can be a twenty-four-hour job. Most of the 650 MPs, with seats far from Westminster, need help both in the constituency and in expensive, crowded, dirty London, traffic jams and all. The local party organisation is helpful and will deal with phone calls for me in my South Derbyshire Constituency. An MP's salary allowance for secretarial and research assistance, however, would cover only one and a half full-time staff; some London MPs are obliged to pay the whole lot to one overworked person. Accommodation at Westminster is strictly limited – one desk per MP, in a room shared with another, and one desk per secretary, shared with as many as six others in scruffy, airless rooms which would almost certainly break the health and safety laws were it not for Crown immunity. With one of the busiest constituencies in the country, now over 83,000 electors (and no extra allowance), I could have been faced with a serious problem.

The answer for me, at least in part – found by trial and considerable error – was to recruit people who were happy not to work in an office at all, and who were content to operate without constant supervision. For some time I have been looked after in my work by three clever women, who cope with the torrent of correspondence, deal kindly and effectively with constituency inquiries, type my books, articles and speeches and generally make my life relatively easy. They all have children and one is a single parent. Two work exclusively from their homes, the third comes into the House of Commons office daily (officially part-time, except that she works even harder than I do) to deal with the phone and the paper which lands on her desk, the first point of entry to our system for most of it.

I take the view that I don't mind when and where they work so long as it all gets done and I can get something attended to very quickly when there's an emergency. Everything else is their business, not mine. If a child has to go to the dentist or be collected from school, why should that be a problem? The typing will wait till later. They can and do swap work around among themselves if one is ill or on holiday. The system only really grinds to a halt if they all decide to go on holiday at once – and then it's a good signal that I should do the same.

We are all working women, all working mothers, part of a team serving South Derbyshire. There are others in the constituency, mainly volunteers. Only once in seven years have I heard the comment there that a woman with children couldn't do the job and that came from a dyed-in-the-wool old Socialist. Yet in the 1983–7 parliament I was the *only* woman member with young children and a seat outside London, which made me feel like a freak, and in the current parliament there are only two others.

At least some attitudes are shifting, some things would no longer be said. More than ten years ago, newly appointed to chair Birmingham City Council's Social Services Committee, I was sitting in a first-class compartment on the train to London with the distinguished Director of Social Services, Ronald Liddiard. We were heading for a national meeting with ministers, the kind I was to attend later on the other side of the table. I had been the city's youngest councillor not long before, and was its youngest chairholder by a streak. The budget under my control was over £50 million even then, with 8,000 staff including 800 social workers, with 4,000 children in our care and so on.

The Director and I were deeply into our briefing folders when the train stopped at Coventry. Another Director of Social Services got on and put his nose around the door.

'Who's this, then, Ron?' he asked cheekily, smiling at me. 'The new secretary?'

I crossed my legs and idly twitched my skirt. Secretaries don't answer back.

Liddiard went scarlet and shook his head, motioning the man out: 'No, no. Oh, go away. She's the new boss!'

The day will come when such a mistake will be unthinkable. When that happens, this book will be redundant. But not yet.

Wouldn't it be nice if one of the effects of all this economic pressure were to remove the age barrier that consigns women over forty to the scrap heap? Anita Higginson of Brook Street, the agency which places over half a million people in jobs each year, told me that an informal check recently showed over 60 per cent of job requests to them have an upper age limit, usually forty or thereabouts. It is seldom clear what the younger woman can do that the older woman cannot, unless perhaps – the suspicion emerges like a nasty serpent – she is employed to soothe the ego of jaded middle-aged male managers, or worse. Surely they can't all be after 'dolly birds' in short skirts, can they? Recently a Derbyshire secretary, middle-aged and comfortable, was surprised to see her job advertised on the company noticeboard. She was told by her boss, one Mr Coveyduck, that the company needed a revamp and he didn't mind if the replacement could type as long as she had good legs. The outraged lady sued for constructive dismissal – and won.

Anita took to asking some clients insisting on an age limit if they felt she herself would be suitable for the job. She is a tall, elegant, articulate and very good-looking brunette. 'Oh yes,' they would reply, 'you're just what we are looking for!' She would then point out that she is forty-four and so excluded from applying.

The would-be employer in that case might be abashed and think again. Already in many parts of the country he has no choice: the 'dolly birds' are all taken. If he wants his letters done, he may have to accept grey hair, extra girth and sensible shoes, and put up with stories about grandchildren instead of boyfriends in the office. He may also find himself with a more committed employee whose work record is better than that of many younger people in the firm, and with fewer typing and spelling mistakes.

Diana Balsdon's thought-provoking chapter is about women re-turners at the National Westminster Bank. They are getting more

ambitious and are planning a career to take into account the break
for children. They do not accept a return to a lower job. Both
Marks and Spencer and the Civil Service have made it clear
that the career break should not hinder prospects of promotion.
According to a delightful article in the *Sunday Correspondent* on
New Year's Eve 1989, Catherine Worley, a personnel official at
the Department of Trade and Industry, was promoted while pregnant and will soon return to work after her second maternity leave.
Her job as a 'fast lane' career civil servant is to develop part-time
working. Another DTI colleague, Anna Walker, has three children
and has worked part-time since 1985, none of which has hindered
her promotion to head of the DTI branch which advises Whitehall
on competition policy. The two women are working on a scheme
for their department that will allow DTI staff up to five years off to
care for children or elderly relatives before returning to work at
the same grade. A parliamentary answer from Gillian Shepherd,
junior minister at The Department of Social Security, in February
1990 indicated that a scheme for civil service paternity leave is also
under consideration. Wonders will never cease. All this, while
yet the Government is officially bitterly opposing the European
Social Charter proposals which advocate just such changes. Odd,
that.

I make no apology for childcare issues forming a substantial part
of this book – surveys show that women who stay at home would
be only too keen to start work if there were someone to look after
the children. Gallup Poll carried out a survey in late 1989 for
the CBI and the Manpower employment agency (published as
Workforce 2000: an agenda for action) which threw up some
significant statistics. Among those with childcare responsibilities
who were questioned, Gallup found that 28 per cent of all women
with children would be interested in an *immediate* return to work
provided satisfactory childcare arrangements could be made, and
that 21 per cent of women with pre-school children would be
similarly interested. That's a lot of women.

Among single parents no less than 41 per cent would be interested
in a job immediately if the problem of childcare could be resolved.
Two thirds of those single parents are surviving on benefit. It must
be in the national interest, therefore, for government to encourage
some of these women to move from the expenditure to the contribution side of the economy by overcoming the childcare difficulty.
If childcare is being provided by the employer, the Exchequer

benefits considerably. In the 1990 Budget the Chancellor thought so too, making workplace nurseries tax free as they were before 1984. Not nannies, not childminders. He clearly wanted to encourage the creation of new, good quality childcare, led by the employers.

There is also considerable scope for up-skilling the existing female workforce and improving their productivity. They tend, for example, to be an undereducated group; when I went to college, over 400,000 men compared to barely 150,000 women were in full-time higher education. The women weren't dimmer, I would aver. At my university there were only five women's colleges to around thirty men's. It wasn't just harder to get in; for many women, it wasn't done even to think of trying. It was regarded as downright unattractive for a girl to be clever – remember all those bimbos in the Ealing comedies? Far fewer girls than boys, even now, stay on at school to do 'A' levels, and their corresponding paper achievements are weaker. So here we are employing lots of able women who, with the right training and encouragement, could hold down much more productive jobs. Provided, of course, that the training is done in the hours that suit them; that their own lack of confidence, hammered into them all these years, is properly addressed; and that the promotion they will then thirst after really is available. Otherwise they'll leave in high dudgeon, set up their own company and pinch your business: it has been known.

As the example of Ms Worley shows, the Civil Service has been trying much harder recently to spot talent among its female workforce. They are working in London, where it is fiendishly hard to get staff, and advising ministers about demographic trends long before anyone else had heard of the problem; it is more surprising that they have made still so little progress. Some efforts are a little ham-fisted.

One of my office staff was a very able and amiable young man, who attended the same university some fifteen years after I did. We got on well (he imitated me very effectively, I am told, at the Christmas party, wearing a dark curly wig and God knows what else). However, he was possibly less qualified for the most important job of all on outside engagements, holding the Minister's handbag.

When he was due to move on I asked if I could replace him with a woman; I did not mind someone who was not a high flier, perhaps a woman to whom they wanted to give a special chance. It might help her future career – I reasoned that if she could cope with me,

she could cope with anything (and, in fact, most of the staff in my
private office at the Department of Health were duly rescued by
promotion).

The official in charge of such arrangements was an understanding
young man. He came to see me.

'Minister, we have just the right person for you,' he enthused. 'I
hope she will suit; however, she is one of our *older* ladies.'

Fearing a dragon, I inquired how old she was. He glanced
discreetly at the folder in his lap.

'Oh, yes,' he said as he found the right page, 'she's about
thirty-five. Do you mind?'

I paused a moment, then: 'I'm forty,' I said sweetly . . .

My own attitudes have shifted and been sharpened recently.
During the summer of 1989, thanks to the United States government, I was able to spend several weeks touring their country from
coast to coast. Asked to nominate several subjects for study, I chose
'The position of women in American society' as one. Expecting to
find the place crawling with liberated, elegant ladies in the Jane
Fonda/Barbara Walters mode, I was surprised and disappointed.
Even though, according to official figures, about the same proportion of American women work as do here, I found that many
very able women seem to fill their time drinking coffee, going
shopping, doing handicrafts and good works, even long after their
children have grown and flown. Most of my friends and acquaintances were graduates; nevertheless, they did their own housework,
explaining to me as they parked the family's second or third car that
it cost too much to employ help.

Women should not, of course, feel *pressurised* to go out to work.
They shouldn't, in a free and prosperous society, feel pressurised
either way. They work for all sorts of reasons. Don't deride them
for wanting to improve their family's standard of living: that is
not greedy but simply normal, and we all do it – men most of
all.

The women who feel their choices are restricted are on both
sides. There are some who work because they must; there are some
who stay home because they can do no other. If there were more
childcare, more professional care for sick husbands and elderly
relatives, there would be easier choices for those at home. If their
menfolk earned more money, there would be more choices for the
women at work. Only we and our families can or should decide

where we take our stand on these issues as far as we ourselves are concerned.

Liberated women should, nevertheless, take account of the views of men: hence John Whelan's piece, as the working husband of a working mother. The objection may also be raised that *What Women Want* does not give much attention to the needs of the children. Most of the contributors are, however, committed mothers – and fathers – who care very much about their offspring, and who would disagree with the assertions of Bowlby, writing half a century ago, that mother and only mother can care for the kids. It does children good too, both boys and girls, not to get the idea that mothers are there solely to look after their physical well-being, but that they must all pull their weight around the house; they might just have less selfish and more even-handed relationships themselves in future.

The point is that the widening of women's choice must go only one way for some time, if we are to fill those jobs in business. It will cost money. But it will cost more, in vacancies unfilled and customers dissatisfied, if the effort isn't made. It will also cost money if the effort is made but misapplied. Hence the practical side of this book – Stewart and Jean Pickering's hilarious and expert advice on running a nursery; Hunada Nouss on how to ensure that the reductions in tax liability end up paying for much of the expense. It would give me the greatest pleasure to hear that Hunada's examples of how to save money on the cost of childcare had been taken up by employees and employers. Even before the 1990 Budget changes, there were some tax concessions for childcare. They were not used. The government is helping users of workplace nurseries from April 1990, but there are other tax concessions available.

Meanwhile, Sue Harvey from Luncheon Vouchers gives some details of one scheme already on the market; there are others, and will no doubt be more if hers is successful. The main problem appears to be the sex equality legislation. It has been pointed out by the Equal Opportunities Commission, perfectly fairly, that such 'perks' may be illegal if offered only to female employees; equality laws mean men too. How entertaining – how irritating – if this well-meaning legislation emerges as the main barrier to employer-subsidised childcare in this country.

We are left with one more problem. Can we women cope with all the demands being pushed on to us? It's all very well asking employers to employ more women. From the woman's point of view, how do I make a day stretch into thirty hours or so, to get everything done – house, children, husband, job – without becoming totally exhausted? That requires organisation and delegation, and willing helpers (or more reasonable demands) at home. That the majority of mothers are working suggests that other family members these days are a lot more helpful than they will sometimes admit.

Many women give up work. Others give up in a different way. Trying to juggle the competing demands of job, household, husband, children and everything else, it is often the marriage which cracks. We have the highest activity rate amongst women in Europe. We have the poorest level of childcare provision in Europe, whether publicly or privately funded. We have the highest divorce rate in Europe, with one marriage in three coming to a premature end, and 70 per cent of the divorce petitions presented by the wife. I don't believe these figures are a coincidence.

We are looking at fundamental changes in the nature of the British household, and in what British women want and expect from their relationships. The traditional family of male breadwinner with dependent wife and children now accounts for less than one household in ten. They are outnumbered by families in which both partners work. (A million households, in addition, are headed by single parents, 90 per cent of them women.) The two earner household may have come up with a solution for the extra demands on a woman's time when taking on a job as well as domestic responsibilities – or they may not have done. The men (and the children) may be much more helpful than their fathers used to be. The women are certainly much busier, and under more pressure, than their mothers could ever have imagined.

What about the emotional pressures – won't we all go crazy? For women like Clare Baggott, Joanna Foster and myself, that would be more likely if we were obliged to stay home. I find it psychologically quite easy to delegate the housework to much more capable hands than my own. My family do not require that I shop daily or indeed provide meals for them very often; they would all eat better if they accepted that omission and learned how to cook, but it is their choice to join the rest of the nation and head for McDonalds or the (excellent) table at the local pub.

I stopped feeling guilty years ago, after one weekend when I had been persuaded to go as a keen young councillor to a high-powered political conference on the future of welfare. My conscience aching,

I slaved for a week putting meals into the fridge and freezer, carefully wrapped and colour-coded, with precise instructions on which to cook for a string of nutritious and wholesome dinners. When I came back, duly fired with political enthusiasm, I found the sink full of dirty plates, the waste bin overflowing with newspaper and the fridge still crammed to bursting with my offerings. Susie, aged nearly three, was summoned.

'Did you manage all right while I was away?'

'Oh, yes, Mummy, it was lovely,' the mite answered with a disarming smile. 'We had fish and chips and 'mato ketchup four times! When are you going away again?'

This book is not intended to be a polemic or a tirade. I have never regarded myself as a traditional feminist. Being totally honest, I might admit now that I was never that interested in equality — quality, to me, has always been more important. Some of those writing here, including Joanna Foster of the Equal Opportunities Commission, are, however, in the vanguard of the fight for equality; I feel I have learned a great deal from their contributions to the book and from the conversations we have held as the work progressed. I am grateful to them all.

I would be sad, also, if *What Women Want* were seen as one long whinge. The prospects for women in the western world have never been better. The positive choices opening up in the Nineties are wider than ever; the temptation, indeed, may be to take on too much. I believe women have a lot more fun than men. Traditionally men have been obliged to plan a career with the necessity of providing financially for a house and family firmly in mind. Often they have been obliged to cling to work they disliked because their family responsibilities were too great to leave. Many women, on the other hand, have had much more freedom of choice; since their work was often not regarded as 'important', they could do what they wanted. Women are also permitted by tradition to feel deep emotions for in the end we bear and care for the children, a joy so incredible, so denied to men, that I for one have never wished to swap places. No work fulfilment will ever beat that.

All the writers here hope to assist both men and women in Britain today to make a contribution to our success, our prosperity and our general well-being. If we are to meet the challenges of the last years of the twentieth century, it will help, I believe, to know what women want.

SECTION ONE

The World is Changing

In the 1970s, when I first started out in politics in Birmingham, I received a lot of encouragement. It came, frequently, from other women in the Conservative Party, often much older than myself. 'Good for you,' they would say, as I explained why I believed that a young woman with two little children should be active in the political world. 'Wish I'd had the chance when I was young.'

Other women, closer to my own age, were not so helpful. I was puzzled about the age gap. The clue came from a distinguished blue-rinsed senior committee woman, pearls gleaming under a good suit, as we waited for guests to arrive for a ladies' fund-raising lunch.

'The world is changing,' she said. 'Each generation has its own problems and its own solutions; they are simply not aware of what has gone before. Your husband is an accountant, isn't he?'

'Yes,' I answered; 'he has worked for the same firm since 1967.'

'And you have help – paid help, I mean – with the children, and with your home?'

'Yes, indeed,' was the answer; 'it puts me seriously out of pocket, but I must have help or I couldn't work at all.'

'Precisely,' she continued. 'My husband is also an accountant. Remember this: when I was young in the 1930s, the wife of such a professional man would have been expected to work. Not doing paid work, of course; but work nevertheless, pretty well full-time outside the house, running the local Red Cross or doing church or other good works, serving on endless committees and the like. If you didn't – and some spent their time gossiping, of course – it was felt you were letting the side down. It would have been thought quite eccentric for such a woman to look after her own children. It was unthinkable that she should do her own housework or even answer her own front door; we had maids to do all that.'

The world of Richmal Crompton and the 'Just William' books swam before my eyes. Sunny lawns and big houses, husband off on the 7.26 to something in the city, Mrs Bott impressing her friends with a tea she had not made herself, the maid in frilly cap shooing the Outlaws away with a broomstick.

The cups tinkled; the guests were arriving.

'The war put paid to all that,' continued my companion. 'The generation of women who had to bring up their families during the war had a very hard time of it: husbands away, often for years on end, their whereabouts often unknown; dangers and shortages, having to make do and mend – that feeling of everyone being in the same boat, of sharing all the hardships, was a good thing in many ways, but it destroyed the old life forever. Most of all, women no longer had staff. Even wealthy women had to start doing everything for themselves – cooking and cleaning, and of course the endless grind of looking after the children. . . . It just wasn't so easy to combine outside activities with that lot any more. It was a pattern which continued long after the war was over. People's attitudes are often set for life early on, you know. These women just can't see how you manage to do it at all, but I do.'

By the time I was at university the women's libbers were very active. Germaine Greer was my bête noire. 'We burned our bras, and we burned our dinners, and we burned our candles at both ends,' sings K T Oslin about those days. I didn't; I faintly disapproved, disliking the negative tone of the movement of the day.

The legal and administrative barriers came down. Sexual equality was enshrined in the 1975 law; for fifteen years it has been illegal to pay women less or to discriminate on the grounds of sex, though it is still legal on grounds of age, which rules out a lot of women returners (the complexities of the law on marital status will be found in Section 5).

For a long time I had little patience with those who cried 'sexism' whenever they couldn't get on. It was at least plausible that these women were either not seizing the opportunities which had been opened up for us, or that they had, but just weren't good enough. When Margaret Thatcher came to power there were only eighteen other women MPs in the House of Commons, with vastly more male than female candidates putting themselves forward, a situation hardly changed throughout this century. I used to say (and still do, but less aggressively) that the reason why there were so few women in Parliament was that the good ones weren't interested and the interested ones weren't any good. In that case they would be better advised not to spend their time wittering on about liberation and *demanding that other people make them equal, but instead acquiring the skills, talents and experience necessary to compete and do well in a man's world.*

It was for reasons like these that I have never been involved with the 300 Group, which has campaigned to get more women into parliament (300 women would still not fill half the 650 seats, but would be many more than now!). I don't disagree with the aim; not only would the Commons be a more sensible and kindlier place, but it is wrong to miss out on half the talent in the land. However, the 300 Group's methods would be unlikely in my experience to produce large numbers of competent women politicians who would survive the rigours of the parliamentary scene and prosper. It isn't enough to form networks with other women: they are often too nice, for a start. The skills necessary must come from standing up in a roomful of horribly hostile men, or before an uncommitted mixed audience, being confident and competent to answer all their questions, complete with the digs and asides of a normal society – and win them over. There's no quarter in politics. Stand up to speak in the House of Commons and both sides will be waiting for the first slip. Tories will imitate a high squeaky voice, Labour men – chauvinists all – will utter ribald comments about hormones. The trick is to remember that you have the camera, you have the mike, you have the engrossed attention of the Hansard shorthand writer – and take no notice.

A lot of men aren't very good at politics either, but they tend to try and we tend to give up. The world is changing here too. As I write there are now forty-three women MPs. We were photographed for the 1989 Guinness Book of Records, Prime Minister and all. After the next election I shouldn't be surprised if there are fifty; by the turn of the century, perhaps a hundred. That would still put us behind many other Western countries, but it would be a decisive break with the history of the seventy years since Nancy Astor first took her seat.

So what has changed recently to bring women coming forward in much greater numbers? They don't argue about equality now – they just get on with being equal, or better. We see it in business, in the professions. Half of all medical students are women and have been for some time. Female students account for 44 per cent of all the higher education grant awards and the proportion is rising. How come they are doing it now, when my generation didn't and the previous generation wouldn't?

The chapters in this section of What Women Want *take a look at what is happening. The first is by Gordon Heald, Managing Director of Gallup Polls. In between advising the newly emergent democratic nations of eastern Europe on opinion polls, he dug out for me what is known about the changing position of women in British society. Women are taking charge of their lives as never before. Independence seems to be the order of the day for many; they have looked at the traditional roles of doting, dutiful wife and mother and have found them wanting. Patricia Mann, already a very senior figure in the advertising world, shows how images have changed. Advertising isn't politics; this is not the 'ought' but the 'is'. If attitudes there have changed so much, there is something fundamental going on. Marks and Spencer were very helpful in providing me with material showing how shopping patterns are changing. Sue Dicks originally wrote a short piece in the* Guardian *in April 1989 which caught my eye. Think about how you talk and write, for language influences our assumptions as well as vice versa.*

Voting patterns were always assumed to be homogeneous between men and women; we canvassers used to despair, standing on the doorstep, as yet another ground-down housewife would answer our polite inquiries with a drab: 'Oh, I don't know; the same as my husband, I expect. You'll have to ask him.' That was until pollsters like Gallup and MORI came along. The latter regularly publish their results split for men and women. In the seventies, it appears, women were more Tory than men. Left to their devices, women would have elected Ted Heath as the victor in 1974. By the 1980s the picture is different again. The 1983 and '87 figures are for the General Elections, won by the Conservatives, while the late 1989 figure was taken at a low point in the Conservative fortunes.

What is very striking is the substantial support enjoyed by Mrs Thatcher amongst the middle-aged and older women, which stayed rock solid between the two successful election results. Younger women, however, showed a dramatic swing. Although in 1983 young women were more likely to be Tory, by 1987 there had been a dramatic falling off, with the Tory majority over Labour of 11 per cent of young women voters (under 25s) turning into a deficit of 11 per cent, and a majority of 17 per cent for the next age group dwindling to 4 per cent. These very big changes were concealed by the hefty turnout of the older groups, where women outnumbered men in their support for the first woman Prime Minister.

Since then, the support for the Conservative Party amongst women voters has stayed much the same. The decline in her party's fortunes

VOTING PREFERENCES BY SEX AND AGE GROUP PER CENT

AGE GROUP	June 1983		June 1987		4th Q 1989	
	Men	Women	Men	Women	Men	Women
18–34						
Conservative	42	42	42	31	34	32
Labour	35	31	37	42	51	54
Alliance	20	25	19	24	5	4
Conservative lead:	+7	+11	+5	−11	−17	−22
25–34						
Conservative	37	42	41	37	32	38
Labour	34	25	33	33	56	46
Alliance	28	30	24	27	4	9
Conservative lead:	+3	+17	+9	+4	−24	−8
34–54						
Conservative	42	46	42	47	38	46
Labour	29	24	32	27	49	40
Alliance	27	28	24	25	7	8
Conservative lead:	+13	+22	+10	+20	−11	+6
55+						
Conservative	45	49	45	46	39	48
Labour	28	26	31	32	52	42
Alliance	25	24	23	20	6	7
Conservative lead:	+17	+23	+14	+18	−13	+6

comes from the shift in the male vote, now favouring Labour more
than their womenfolk in all age groups except the youngest. The
Prime Minister is still ahead among older women. Going from the
youngest women voters to the oldest, Tory support in late 1989 went
from 32 per cent of respondents to 38 per cent to 46 per cent to 48
per cent, with nearly half the older women in Britain saying they
would vote Tory, and less than one third of the youngest. Amongst
Thatcher's children – the young women voters who have never known
any other than a woman leader – the Prime Minister is weaker than
among women in any other age group; they are more likely to vote
for a male Labour Prime Minister, at least as the polls have stood
recently, then their less liberated grandmothers.

The voting changes are not news to the political parties, but they
must be giving our first woman Prime Minister pause for thought in
the run-up to the next election. It has been suggested that men have
responded to strong themes and strong leadership which might be
putting women off. We know that women are 'softer' than men; according to MORI, women are more likely to chat to someone who is lonely
than men (53 per cent compared to 38 per cent) or to have recently
visited someone who is elderly or disabled to see if they are all right (40
per cent to 33 per cent). On the other hand, we women have an
authoritarian streak: women are more likely to want drunk drivers sent
to jail (50 per cent to 42 per cent men), are much keener on random
breath testing (91 per cent compared to 78 per cent of men) and far
more likely to believe in God (81 per cent to 67 per cent of men).

Perhaps younger women would respond more warmly had Margaret Thatcher appeared to encourage more women, taken more interest
in women's issues? In eleven years she has appointed only one woman
to her cabinet. I sigh, for I think the world of her; and I don't know.

Joanna Foster, another contributor to this section, is Chair of the
Equal Opportunities Commission. Since her appointment at the
end of 1987, she has been our official guardian of equality by Act
of Parliament. She initiated a major review of the EOC's work,
published in January 1989, which stated:

> We have thirteen years of experience behind us; thirteen years
> in which we have persuaded employers of the importance of
> equal opportunities while at the same time underpinning this
> with successful law enforcement. We are now in a phase when
> the question 'Why bother with equality?' is being replaced with
> 'How do we make equal opportunities a reality?'

The emphasis has shifted from rights to practice. Fewer cases are being taken to court, even though far more requests for such help are being made to the Commission. Bad employers will have to be reminded, as ever, that they may be breaking the law, but good employers might respond better to a little advice and encouragement.

What, then, is bringing about these changes?

Perhaps the efforts of the campaigners of the seventies are indeed bearing fruit – not for the unliberated women of those days, but for their daughters. Teach them in school, girls and boys together, that they are equal; treat them as if they are equal, demand from all of them an equal response, and we might just find we are getting somewhere. Even the attitudes of the boys, as they learn in the home economics department how to sew on a button or bake a cake, are also much more positive. Drip away steadily with equal rights laws, train up the personnel department, win a few cases and the message of what's legal and what isn't will begin to penetrate – and more, be taken on board, incorporated into company policy, be regarded no longer as a confounded nuisance but as a good thing.

Today's young revolutionaries do not look upon themselves as such. There is nothing odd to them in wanting to use all their talents, in having a bank account, a driving licence and a credit card or two, in 'going halves' on a meal out, in planning a home and a family and a job and helping to pay the mortgage, for that is how all their friends are doing it. To my generation it is a true revolution, and I'm delighted about it; the youngsters don't even notice. If my blue-rinsed friend is right, they may carry these attitudes with them throughout their lives – in which case, the world has changed for a long time to come.

1
The Changing Background: the View from Gallup

by Gordon Heald,
Managing Director, Gallup Poll

Polls reveal, and official statistics confirm, that there has been a significant change in women's attitudes and behaviour since the early sixties.

If we look at patterns of voting, attitudes to marriage, having a family and divorce, the growing demand by women for a career rather than a job and their increasing financial independence, we realise that there has been a dramatic change. Furthermore, this social revolution is predicted to continue because the drop in the birth rate in the early 1970s is already producing a shortage of skilled manpower (or womenpower) and more and more employers, because of their need for new talent, are promoting women to senior management positions.

The scenario is one with which we are all familiar. But what do women really want? Why do so many feel guilty about neglecting their children when they try to balance a responsible job with looking after their family? Why, if they still believe that marriage is a lifelong commitment, are they are the ones in today's society who are mainly responsible for filing divorce petitions? Why do so many high-flying female executives in their mid-thirties want to give up their well-paid and exciting careers and retreat to their homes and raise a family?

Attitudes to Marriage and Divorce

One of the greatest dichotomies between expressed attitudes and actual behaviour lies in the area of marriage and divorce.

Repeatedly over the last decade, polls reveal that 85 per cent of women believe in marriage as an institution and regard it as a lifelong commitment. This is confirmed by the statistic that 92 per cent of women today are married by the age of thirty. Yet statistics show that 37 per cent of recent marriages end in divorce and most divorces take place within the first five years of marriage. Furthermore, three out of four petitions for divorce in 1987 were being filed by women – a trend started a decade earlier.

Britain now has the highest divorce rate in Europe, followed by Denmark, and, as a consequence, the greatest proportion of one-parent households in the whole of the European Community. Yet ironically, a survey of European values conducted by Gallup showed that Britain had the highest rating of satisfaction with home life, exceeded only by Denmark! The survey revealed that 75 per cent of women and 83 per cent of men in Great Britain rate their home life as satisfactory, compared to only 65 per cent on average throughout the whole of Europe. When we asked the British more detailed questions about different aspects of their home life, they scored significantly higher than the rest of Europe (see Table 1).

TABLE 1

Proportion of people who claim that they often feel this way at home

	Britain (%)	Europe (%)
Secure, safe, sound	77	65
Happy	74	55
Relaxed	74	64
Anxious	16	14
Aggressive	6	9

How do we explain this paradox? Do British men and women have hopelessly too high an ideal of marriage? Are our divorce laws too easy? Do too many women try to pursue a career at the expense of the more traditional home life? Are men unable to cope with women's changing attitudes? How much has education changed women's attitudes towards marriage and divorce? How much has the recent high level of unemployment caused an increase in marriage breakdown? Or are we simply deluding ourselves?

There are no simple answers to these questions, but they cover an area to which attention is increasingly turning, including that of governments. The cost of marriage breakdown is enormous in terms both of personal suffering and family breakdowns; and it is also vast in terms of social security payments. Marriage breakdown was estimated to cost the government £2 billion a year in 1988 – a 100 per cent increase over the preceding decade.

How Women View Marriage and their Partners

In a recent Gallup Poll women were asked why they stay with their partners. The overwhelming reason given by nine out of ten was 'I love him', followed by 'He's my companion and friend'. Very few mentioned financial reasons, although a few truthfully admitted that it was 'hard to find someone else'. A significant proportion (nearly one in three) admitted that they stayed with their partner for their children's sake (see Table 2). It would seem from these answers that most women still view marriage in terms of love and companionship and not from a mercenary point of view.

The survey also revealed that 84 per cent of women claim never or rarely to think about the possibility of separation, though 16 per cent did admit to this and 3 per cent claimed that it was *often* on their mind. It was the more highly educated women, or those who argued with their partner about money, who were more likely to fall into this last category.

While only 6 per cent of women admitted that they stayed with their partners only for financial reasons, when we asked them about other women in general, eight out of ten (81 per cent) agreed that 'there are women who stay with their husbands only for finanical reasons'.

When they were asked if their financial circumstances would get better or worse if they split from their partners, seven out of ten (70 per cent) admitted that it would get worse. Hence, financial and economic pressures do keep some couples together, but ultimately most women will divorce their partners if they no longer love them, irrespective of the financial pressures.

TABLE 2

Reasons why women stay with their partner

	%
I love him	89
He's my companion	65
He's my husband	32
The children	30
Security	19
Habit	6
Financial reasons	6
Religious values	5
Hard to find someone else	3
Nowhere else to go	1

What do women think are the main causes of divorce these days? Not surprisingly, partners being unfaithful is still rated the main cause of divorce, closely followed by financial difficulties. These are the two key factors cited by women. 'Growing apart' was mentioned by 38 per cent of women and among more highly educated women this rose to 48 per cent, compared to only 18 per cent among older women who had left school at the age of fourteen. Incompatibility and 'not suited' was mentioned by 33 per cent of women, rising to 45 per cent among more highly educated women (see Table 3). Similarly, more highly educated women were less likely to tolerate unemployment compared with their less well educated sisters. The reverse was true in the case of violence and drinking. This perhaps suggests that one of the factors influencing the increasing divorce rate is that as women become more educated they are unwilling to put up with the sort of marriages that their mothers and grandmothers tolerated. Increasingly they look for interests and tastes in common with their partners and if they start to 'grow apart' or become 'unsuited', this becomes a factor for considering a divorce.

TABLE 3

What women think is the cause of divorce these days

	%
Being unfaithful	63
Financial difficulties	57
Growing apart	38
Violence	36
Unemployment	35
Incompatibility, not suited	33
Drinking	32
Children grown up	7
Social class differences	4
In-law problems	2

It is not surprising, then, that many women are quite keen on the concept of a 'marriage contract', given the high divorce rate and the fact that many women earn good salaries and see a career path ahead of them. More than four out of ten (43 per cent) are in favour of a marriage contract which lays down how their possessions should be divided up if they ever divorce. They see this as 'saving problems later' and giving them a 'sense of security'. An almost equal number of women are opposed to the concept of a marriage contract (44 per cent), mainly because they think it is a 'wrong way to start' a marriage and 'it implies that divisions are possible'.

Women and Work

In 1976, 58 per cent of married women had a job; by 1988 this had increased to 68 per cent. Why are more and more women working, particularly those who are married and have dependent children? In 1988 for example, 60 per cent of married women with dependent children worked and of those with children under five years of age, 11 per cent are now in full-time work compared with 6 per cent in 1981.

Are women today working out of economic necessity or is it because they enjoy the personal and financial freedom associated with a job? In seeking an answer to this question we should distinguish between what a job offers them financially and what it offers in much wider terms such as self-esteem and companionship. Our surveys reveal that only a minority of women work out of economic necessity, but for divorced and separated women it is absolutely essential financially (see Table 4). Hence women's marital status is an important factor influencing their motivation to work. Another important factor is their level of education. In spite of all the emphasis on women and careers today, less than one in ten claim that they work because of career advancement, but this rises to one in five among women who have been educated to a high level.

Most women work, our surveys reveal, because it gives them independence and the luxuries of life that they could not otherwise afford; but again there is a tremendous contrast between married and divorced women as illustrated in Table 4.

TABLE 4

What having a job means to women solely in financial terms

	All Women	Married	Divorced/ Separated	More highly educated
	(%)	(%)	(%)	(%)
Essential for household finances	37	34	67	32
Financial independence	27	17	26	35
To pay for extra luxuries	21	31	0	17
Pocket money/pin money	6	8	4	1
To save for the future/retirement	3	2	0	2
To pay education bills	2	3	0	5

Apart from the financial implications of working, the more general motivations are much more determined by the level of education received. Getting out of the home and having extra money is a very important reason for working to a woman who left school at the age of fifteen or sixteen, whereas a woman with degree-level education is much more concerned about opportunities for advancing her career and a job which stimulates her mind as illustrated by Table 5.

TABLE 5

What having a job means to women generally

	All Women	Age of finishing education	
		15/16 years	21 or over years
	(%)	(%)	(%)
Having extra money	19	18	11
Like to get out of the house	14	21	2
Independence/freedom to be myself	12	11	12
Self-confidence/self-esteem	9	7	10
Stimulate my mind	8	6	16
Advancement in career	8	5	19
Enjoy it/fulfilment/satisfaction	8	9	7
Companionship	4	5	1
Just a job	4	4	5
Expected to work	3	3	2

Most surveys reveal that the majority of working women get satisfaction from their jobs and it is perhaps not surprising, then, to find that just over half (56 per cent) of women who are not currently employed would like to have a job but are not able to work. This is mainly because they claim to be constrained by young children at home or they cannot get the job they want.

However, about one in eight (13 per cent) of all women under the age of sixty are quite content not to work at all. In particular, women over the age of fifty and widows fall into this category. Very strong class differences also emerge: women from working-class households tend to shun the concept of not working, whereas half the women living in professional and managerial households who currently are not working are happy to accept this state.

In summary, work motivation is very affected by marital status and level of education. The reasons behind it are mainly financial, whether to provide necessities or luxuries, and the need for companionship rather than the desire to pursue a career.

Women and Household Financial Management

The days are over when the male breadwinner came home to his wife on pay day and she had to ask for the money she needed. Only 3 per cent of households now claim to arrange their finances in this manner.

With nearly seven out of ten couples (68 per cent) having a joint account, the commonest form of household financial management is that where the earner's wages are paid into such an account and the wife who deals with the daily running of the household draws money as required – about 36 per cent of households have this system. The second most popular system is where both partners put their wages into a joint account from which all household expenses are paid. This accounts for another 26 per cent of households.

Hence in many households there is mutual dependence in the way that the finances are arranged and survey results indicate that nearly three out of five couples claim that their partner completely agrees about the way the finances are handled in their household.

And when women are asked who is the more careful with money in their relationship, there is an even divide between those women who claim to be the more careful and those who admit it is their partner. Again, our surveys reveal that among nearly half of all married couples nowadays it is the wife who pays the bills and controls the finances.

In spite of all this new-found equality, however, most wives say that they are more the culprits than their husbands when it comes to spending on the little 'extras' and luxuries in life. Women do admit that they like to buy extra clothes for their family or little presents for their children and grandchildren, items for the house and cosmetics and perfumes. But three out of five claim that they sacrifice spending on themselves in order to buy something for their family. And when it comes to receiving gifts, the majority of women still like their husbands to give them presents instead of money, although one in five women prefer the latter.

Finally, when it comes to choosing a marriage partner, many women still take into account the man's financial prospects. Nearly one in three claim that they thought their partner-to-be had good financial prospects and another one in five admit that they married him in spite of the fact that they thought he didn't have good prospects. Nearly half of all women claim that the thought of money did not cross their mind but that they had married just for love!

Attitudes to Tax Relief for Childcare

Most recently, Gallup surveyed views for the *Daily Telegraph* on what people wanted from the 1990 Budget. Most people thought it would be a good idea to increase the tax on tobacco products and company cars (69 per cent in both cases), with increasing the tax on alcohol (60 per cent in favour) coming close. Just under 60 per cent wanted to see the ceiling for tax relief on mortgages increased from £30,000, with one in five wanting no ceiling at all and 58 per cent quoting a figure between £50,000 and £100,000! The average outstanding mortgage in Britain is still less than £30,000 though new mortgages in late 1989 were running at over £50,000.

In most of these, women did not show striking differences to men. Ask people how they feel about tax relief for help with childcare, and the generation gap opens wide. What is also notable is the very small gap between the opinions of supporters of the two main parties. But men are slightly more in favour than women, with nearly a quarter of women hostile to the idea: see Table 6. Perhaps predictably, support was greatest among younger generations, but more than half in every age group would like to see working mothers aided, including over half of pensioners.

The 21 per cent opposed to childcare assistance were asked to explain their opposition. The largest proportion, 38 per cent (divided equally amongst men and women) said such tax relief 'would encourage women to go out to work when they should stay at home'. Fifteen per cent said it would be 'unfair to families where the woman does not work' – the reason the Prime Minister has given against such tax relief in the past.

TABLE 6

Attitudes to tax relief for help with childcare

	Favour help	Don't favour help	Don't know
All interviewed	71	21	7
Conservative voters	67	28	5
Labour voters	72	20	8
Other voters	78	15	7
Men	73	19	8
Women	70	23	7
Aged:			
18–34	88	8	4
35–44	78	18	3
45–64	58	34	8
65+	54	31	15

Attitudes in Europe

It was in 1975, the International Women's Year, that the Commission of the European Communities initiated a research programme with the aim of finding out more about the attitudes of men and women to the position of women in society. The first opinion poll, organized in 1975, was followed by other similar inquiries in 1977, 1983 and 1987. Each of the inquiries polled a representative sample of the adult population of all the Community's member countries, i.e. nine countries in 1975 and 1977, ten countries in 1983, and twelve countries in 1987.

What has happened during this period to the opinions and attitudes of the European public? The purpose of the inquiry was to gauge the evolution of opinions and attitudes over the years, and to examine Spain and Portugal, where the inquiry was being held for the first time in 1987.

The awareness of the problem of woman's place in society, first measured in 1975, was then at a relatively high level, probably stimulated by the interest generated by the International Women's Year. Seven years later, in 1983, interest had decreased in all the countries. In 1987, however, there was a general resurgence of interest among the public of almost all the countries. It is in Italy, Spain and Portugal that the public is at present most aware of the question of this issue.

Women are traditionally more aware of the problem of woman's place in society than men, and over the twelve-year period under review, the gap between the sexes has not narrowed. It is at its widest today in Ireland, Greece, Spain and Portugal.

The concept of complete equality of husband's and wife's roles (Table 7) is still a minority view, held by 41 per cent, but it has gained ground since 1983. Four out of ten Europeans now believe that the ideal family is one in which the husband and wife have equally absorbing jobs, and in which the housework and looking after the children are equally shared between them. The model of the woman in the home is still strong (25 per cent), but is slowly fading. Between these two positions, there is the family in which the wife has a less absorbing job, and takes on more of the housework and childcare than her husband. Twenty-nine per cent prefer this picture.

The most advanced country on this issue is the United Kingdom at nearly 50 per cent, while as in 1983, Germany and Luxembourg are the least egalitarian, under 30 per cent agreeing. Spain and Portugal are more in favour of equal roles within the family than the European average.

To be still more precise, what do married (or cohabiting) men think of their wives working for pay? Here the evolution since 1975 is very noticeable: one third in 1975, a half in 1987, say that they prefer or would prefer their wife to work; the younger and better educated the men, and the higher the family income, the more widespread is this attitude. In nine of the twelve Community countries, the majority of married men are in favour of their wives working; Spain and Portugal are included. In the remaining three countries, Germany, Luxembourg and Ireland, the majority of men are opposed to this situation.

Let us now take a look at the stereotypes regarding women at

TABLE 7

Comparison of Attitudes on Equality in 12 European Community countries

Per cent agreeing/in favour.

Question: (see key below)	A (family)	B (driver)	C (surgeon)	D (obstet)	E (MP)	F (Parl)
Belgium	34	67	66	64	68	76
Denmark	44	87	85	83	87	84
Germany	26	57	56	60	64	76
France	45	77	70	66	68	82
Ireland	34	38	51	49	62	76
Italy	42	54	56	49	59	74
Luxembourg	20	48	58	60	63	77
Netherlands	43	76	82	67	79	78
United Kingdom	49	61	70	66	75	79
Greece	44	53	56	59	58	68
Spain	47	56	65	68	67	78
Portugal	43	84	67	69	64	69
Europe	41	62	64	62	67	76

Thus the UK is close to, or above, the European average on all question shown, i.e., is more supportive of equality and a more equal vote for women.

Key: Question A: Are you in favour of equality within the family

B: Equal confidence in women as train/bus drivers

C: Equal confidence in women as surgeons

D: Equal confidence in women as obstetricians

E: Equal confidence in a man or woman as MP

F: 'Things would be just as good or better, if there were more women in Parliament."

work: are there jobs for which people have more confidence in a man than a woman? Several examples were quoted during the inquiry: train or bus driver, surgeon, obstetrician, Member of Parliament (Questions B, C, D, E). In all cases, opinion has evolved since 1983: those who claim that they have equal confidence in both sexes to do this work are now in the majority (at least 60 per cent, irrespective of profession) and it is the men who have changed most.

Denmark stands out as the country where the idea of discrimination has almost completely disappeared. More than 80 per cent of Danes claim that they have as much confidence in a woman as a man for any of the professions mentioned: men and women give identical answers. The Danes are twice as confident about women bus and train drivers as the Luxembourgeois or the Irish. In the other countries, the men are still more reluctant than the women. It is in Ireland, Spain and Portugal that the difference of opinion between men and women is greatest.

The idea that 'politics is men's business' was already outdated in 1975, and is increasingly being rejected by public opinion. Only a small minority (European average 22 per cent) continue to support this prejudice, particularly in Germany and Luxembourg. As we were able to see during previous inquiries, men's answers differ little from those of women.

Most Europeans, (67 per cent) theoretically have as much confidence in a woman as a man as a Member of Parliament (Question E). Yet the number of women who stand for or are elected to Parliament is not great. What would happen, we asked, if more women were elected? One woman in three, and one man in five, think that things would be better; these percentages have barely changed in recent years. But this minority that is convinced of the potential effectiveness of women if there were more of them in Parliament is a substantial one: it is no longer a simple question of equal competence (which was what people were saying in their replies to the previous questions), but of a new input. In all countries, considerably more women than men found the idea of more women in Parliament desirable. This tendency is particularly strong among women in Ireland (50 per cent), the United Kingdom (42 per cent), and Denmark (41 per cent).

The following scored higher than the European average on all questions to do with equality and women's role: Denmark, well in front, followed by the Netherlands, the United Kingdom and France.

The following scored well below the European average on all parameters: Germany, Luxembourg and Ireland; in Ireland, however, women responders are often well in advance of men, particularly regarding the role of women in politics.

In the middle, i.e. close to the European average, sometimes a little above, sometimes a little below, the remaining five countries: Italy, Belgium, Greece, Spain and Portugal.

Polls reveal what people think and feel. There can be no doubt now, that while traditional opinions are still widely held, the life of many women has changed quite dramatically. Much of the tension and argument today about women's role comes from that divergence.

2
Image Makers and Image Takers: Women and Advertising

by Patricia Mann
Vice-President International,
J Walter Thompson Co Ltd

Any future historian examining advertisements as a mirror of contemporary society would easily be able to draw a number of
conclusions about the women who appear in them. The difficulty
would be in establishing which, if any, were a true mirror of the
society of the time: of its ambitions, if not its actuality.

In the 1950s and early 1960s a woman's greatest pleasure appeared
to lie in cooking and cleaning for a well-mannered family of two
adults and two children who always ate together. Her rewards came
from a sparkling home, spotless clothes and nursing her family
through endless minor ailments. Perhaps in those far-off days there
was at least some justification for taking the domestic role very
seriously. There was a much greater separation between domestic
life and its skills and the world of work. Home was a closed world
where the advice of elders was respected and the risk of any criticism
caused real concern.

Barbara Buss, then Editor of *Woman*, explained in 1965 how
her 8,500,000 women readers had changed:

> The young woman of today has a self-assurance born of the
> blurring of pre-war class divisions. She may also face an
> independence, and a loneliness, that was unknown to her
> mother. The magazine's editorial policy has broadened with
> the interests and opportunities of the readers. Its fashion,
> beauty, home-making and cookery features place more empha-
> sis on shopping, guiding newly affluent readers through a

plethora of consumer goods that were once considered luxuries. The 'how it's done' section gives less space to formal etiquette and more to explaining the important aspects of a bureaucratic age, like pensions, legal aid, family allowances. The basic tenets of the magazine are still two-fold: escapism and glamour, balanced with practical help and inspiration now extending beyond the home to every aspect of a woman's self-realisation and self-improvement.

For most readers, *Woman* claimed, the advertisements were an essential complement to the editorial matter, occupying about the same number of pages. Food, beauty, household products and fashion accounted for 92 per cent of the advertising revenue.

The woman who appeared in many of those advertisements did not seem to have made much progress. She could often be characterised as riddled with social anxieties about germs, dirt and other people's censure, with little intellectual grasp and absolutely no sense of humour, and permanently grateful to someone – her husband, her children or salesmen. But this was the decade when the pace of change in public attitudes accelerated and a much larger proportion of advertisements began to respond.

Advertisements have to communicate quickly. The vast majority have very limited space or airtime: hence the use of shorthand to convey a situation or background with speed. Shorthand often means stereotypes, however. To be meaningful to their target audience, the advertisements must relate to their existing preconceptions and prejudices – which are often unconscious and unchallenged. Communication requires a response, and that means knowing how the target group thinks, feels and acts.

At the beginning of the 1970s market researchers found that many otherwise intelligent women not only fiercely rejected women's lib activities but were also still disinclined to support *any* notion of equality between the sexes. The explanation proved to be the mistaken equation of 'equality' with 'sameness'; of interpreting the desire for equality as a wish for conformity with men, instead of independence and individualism.

Nevertheless, both the roles and perceptions of women were changing dramatically within a framework of anti-discrimination legislation which encouraged them to re-examine their potential, their aspirations and their ambitions. Feminist voices were raised on a variety of platforms in the media: in the editorial and on the programmes which provided the context for advertisements. A deliberate effort started, to change the stereotypes and, in so doing, to change women's view of themselves.

The United Nation's Commission on the Status of Women examined the way that women were shown not only in advertising but also in the media generally. Its report published in 1974 concluded: 'Women are offered, basically, two roles: that of the beautiful, but passive, glamour girl, and that of the housewife caring for the home and children. Both are shown as dependent on men and receiving their social identity not as themselves but through men.' A year later, a consultative panel of the US National Advertising Review Board drew parallel conclusions. It concluded that changing these stereotypes would accomplish two important goals: first, it would achieve 'a greater measure of fair treatment for women'; and, second, it would be 'an intelligent marketing decision'.

For many years the advertising agency J Walter Thompson (JWT) had been monitoring the changes in women's roles, aspirations and values, through research for specific advertisers and through its own studies of broader areas of behaviour. This regular research gave a range of insights into women's changing attitudes and ambitions. It showed how their self-perceptions were developing, that their need for self-identity was growing and that their expectations of marriage and family relationships were changing, as were indeed these institutions in reality.

A particularly rich field to explore, which has been studied in a number of JWT offices around the world, was the differences between working women with a deep commitment to their job and those to whom their job was of a lower priority. This led to the identification of four 'New Demographic' groups: the stay-at-home housewife, the plan-to-work housewife, the just-a-job working woman and the career-orientated working woman. Despite the differences, there was a good deal in common between these groups. The most successful advertisements communicated to them with relevance, with respect, with recognition of their changing roles and changing attitudes and, very importantly, with a light touch.

Some advertisements of the 1970s which tried to acknowledge the importance of the working woman appeared to be using a sledgehammer. In the United States a new cliché was rife: the decisive-looking woman with the executive briefcase. To demonstrate their sympathy with feminist objectives, many advertisers featured women in the roles of company presidents, chief executives, airline pilots and the like which were considered exaggerated and irrelevant by the women to whom they were speaking even in that aggressively upwardly mobile society.

Charles of the Ritz launched Enjoli as a fragrance specifically for the working woman ('the 8-hour fragrance for the 24-hour woman') and presented her as an unattainable omniopotent American superwoman. The television commercial sang:

> You can bring home the bacon, fry it in a pan
> And never, never let him forget he is a man
> Because you are a woman . . .

Magazine advertisements added: 'You can feed the kids and the gerbils, pass out the kisses and get to work by five to nine. You can work all day in the old rat race and even put a smile on sour puss face.'

Some independent young women featured in British perfume advertisements met with mixed success. Too often their style of 'independence' was more likely to be interpreted as selfishness, discourtesy or callous disregard for others. Although at first their roles tended to be conventional (air hostesses and television assistants seemed particularly popular), a wider range of advertisements soon began to reflect young working women sympathetically and success-fully.

By the end of the 1970s, women were clearly receptive to notions of equality of opportunity and individuality rather than sameness of character, temperament or behaviour. This was a big change from Barbara Buss's day. They did not care for the briefcase cliché, but they did respond to women with character and personality. Nor did they object to advertisements which showed them looking after the home or their children, provided they met important criteria. They should never be shown as stupid, gullible, mindless drudges, but as competent managers with skills and talents, and with at least a hint of life and interests beyond their home-making role.

There was considerable pressure from feminists for men to be shown taking a larger part in domestic tasks, but researchers were repeatedly told that total role swapping was not what women wanted. Their ideals of marriage had much more to do with sharing what had traditionally been designated male and female tasks, and rep-resentations of the change had to be approached with care.

Home decorating was a case in point. Conventional wisdom said that women were largely in charge of home improvement to the extent of deciding what needed doing and choosing the wallpaper and paint colours. The respective responsibilities were seen as the woman foreman supervising the job and the male painter and paperhanger actually doing it, even though many women were themselves extremely competent decorators. Because of these widely held perceptions, paints advertised as chosen by women on any dimensions other than colour, such as ease of application or durability, tended to be seen as 'non-professional' or 'amateur'. The understanding of product quality suffered. So it took a brave advertiser, Crown Paints, to show a pregnant woman decorating the nursery. The response from women was excellent, and because the advertisement appeared in women's magazines any negative effects on the male ego were minimised. Today the TV ads for an electric wall paper stripper show a woman, beating a man using traditional methods.

The editors of women's magazines had to keep closely in touch with the 'new woman'. A decade ago they were either trying to keep the familiar recipe of a publication in tune with the changing tastes, ambitions and environment of its readers, or taking a dramatically new approach to women's magazine publishing.

Jane Reed, then Editor of the long-established *Woman's Own*, said in 1979:

Readers feel guilty – half go out to work and the other half don't. There are so many choices for the reader that she has never had it so good, but it does bring problems with it. Although family-based, she has a choice – but she still searches for security more than anything else. With children off her hands, the older woman gets new energy and has more opportunities to broaden her life. Work is the biggest word in her life, but regretfully few advertisers tend to realise it and few advertisements confirm a purely work situation.

It was the magazines specifically for independent young women, marked by the launch of *Cosmopolitan* at the beginning of the 1970s and *Company* towards the end, that really broke new ground. Designed for women who were highly motivated towards their careers and who enjoyed their jobs even if they were not on the top executive track, they attracted a wide readership of married and unmarried women in their twenties. Dierdre McSharry, former Editor of *Cosmopolitan*, explained:

> The magazine is fortunate because its philosophy has been beaten out by its readers. We have the brightest, youngest and best-educated readers in the country. The *Cosmopolitan* woman keeps her identity while wanting a loving relationship and a career worth working for.

Maggie Goodman, Editor, stated shortly after *Company's* launch:

> This is the generation that takes nothing for granted, that believes *everything* is possible, that refuses to be tied down by convention. The 1980s will bring great changes in our life-style: our readers are not the ones who will be moaning about the past. They will be facing up to new challenges and cashing in on them.

Elspeth Howe, then Deputy Chairman of the Equal Opportunities Commission, declared in 1979:

> Marketeers, on both sides of the Atlantic, are still harbouring outmoded assumptions about the fairer sex. In many markets, manufacturers and suppliers of services are underestimating the number of working women, overestimating the number of full-time housewives and failing to take account of the changes in lifestyle that have occurred among both.

A UK conference on marketing to 'new women', held the same week, agreed with Lady Howe. Advertisers and agencies stressed the importance of distinguishing and understanding women's changing and varied roles and of recognising their aspirations; and the overriding importance of more precise targeting. The biggest difficulty was how to portray the 'new woman' in her many guises.

Most of the advice boiled down to 'be ambiguous'. With the emphasis on individualism and diversity, there were no widely acceptable role models to replace the traditional stereotypes. Looking back at advertising of the time, it is noticeable that many food advertisers in particular ducked the issue altogether by excluding people and concentrating on the product.

The beginning of the 1980s, therefore, showed a big effort being made by many involved in image making and in advertising. These changes took place long before the demographic timebomb started ticking. They were in response to the deeply held views of relatively few people, who through their efforts gradually commended themselves to the majority of women in Britain over the following decade.

The number of complaints to the Independent Broadcasting Authority (IBA) and to the Advertising Standards Authority (ASA) about the way women were portrayed in advertisements increased in intensity and in numbers. During the 1980s, the level of complaints on the subject to the ASA remained constant at around 4 per cent of all complaints a year, representing some 325 complaints annually (but relating to a substantially smaller number of individual advertisements). There have been two main categories of objections.

(a) Women as Sex Objects

Irrelevant nudity and the use of women in provocative poses, particularly when accompanied by innuendo, gave and continue to give offence. The vast body of research suggests that there is very little spontaneous objection to women being shown as attractive and making the most of their looks, or even to various degrees of undress, provided two conditions are fulfilled: that the presentation is relevant and that the execution is 'tasteful'. For example, women have objected to the ad for Bel Ami aftershave, complete with a Gustave Klimt drawing of a naked woman splayed-out on a bed looking exhausted, with the line 'To his fragrance, she surrenders'. Some complainants said she looked as if she had been raped.

An elegant model in underwear appearing in a woman's magazine, where it is unlikely she will be leered at by men, is unobjectionable to the majority. Equally, a 'tasteful' nude in a bath oil advertisement is felt appropriate: 'After all,' a reader remarked, 'we don't take a bath with our clothes on.'

Hackles rose when scantily clad women were shown draped over cars, at petrol pumps or simply to draw attention to quite unconnected products. The advertisement which recently attracted opprorium was headed 'Free Sex' above a line-drawing of a woman in a bikini. For Pete Jones Motorcycles of Shrewsbury, it continued: 'Now that we have got your attention, lads, please read on . . .' The ineffectiveness of such advertising was rarely in doubt: readers

attracted by a page-3 model are unlikely to give their full attention
to the virtues of the advertised product.

(b) Women as Mindless Drudges

Many complaints related to the stereotype of 'passive, domesticated,
stay-at-home people with no interests other than their children
and families'. The family-centred woman seemed automatically
identified by these critics as a mindless drudge, regardless of her
skills and competence. They wanted advertisements to feature only
liberated, independent, successful women with interesting jobs.

These were admirable objectives for the media generally, but less
appropriate to advertisements. The majority of products advertised
on television at the beginning of the 1980s were not primarily being
sold to women in their working role. Therefore there was rarely a
case for explaining or showing what their job was.

Ambiguity triumphed. As woman was shown away from her
home, there was no need to specifiy whether she was married or
single, with or without children, even whether she was working or
not – provided she appeared to be leading a fulfilling and satisfying
life. Where household or grocery products were concerned, advertisements talked to women in the context of their domestic lives.
To quote the Advertising Association: 'Food advertisements often
show women in the kitchen because it is mainly women who cook
and because they cook in their kitchens, not in their offices or
factories.'

There were also problems of perception. A man shown in front
of a keyboard was using a computer; a woman in front of the same
machine was instantly identified as a typist. A washing-up liquid
was kind to hands when a woman was shown using it. A man using
the same product communicated that it was strong and efficient,
but the very opposite of kind to hands.

One of the problems in assessing the opinion of groups of critics
was the difficulties they had in reaching consensus among themselves. The same advertisements would appear as examples of
approaches to be encouraged and to be stopped at all costs. Nevertheless, several groups took positive steps to encourage a reappraisal of
the way women were portrayed in advertisements.

Women in Media, whose members worked in journalism, television, theatre and advertising, held a Television Advertising Awards evening at London Zoo in 1979. Their 'Ad Nauseam' award went to a Fiesta Paper Towels advertisement. The citation stated: 'It represents the adman's cheap idea of a stereotype woman's liberationist. It shows a young, nagging, shrewish, bossy wife, shouting at and humiliating her husband. It was particularly disliked because it degrades both men and women.' The 'Ad Lib' Award went to a Skyline Kitchen Tools commercial. It 'shows an unglamorous middle-aged couple preparing a meal together. The man is doing his share in a natural and undeliberate way and both are apparently enjoying themselves.'

Under the title *Adman and Eve*, the Equal Opportunities Commission published in 1982 the results of research into specially commissioned print advertisements featuring women in contrasting traditional and modern ways. Although hedged with qualifications about the very tentative nature of the generalisations and the basis of the findings, it reported: 'In three of the four cases, the treatment which incorporated a less restricted, modern, female role-portrayal was consistently found to enhance the marketing effectiveness of the brand's advertising.'

The Trades Union Congress in 1984 published a pamplet, *Images of Inequality: The Portrayal of Women in the Media and Advertising*, with the declared intention of 'continuing to pressurise the ASA to alter its Code of Practice to provide some guidance on the depiction of women in advertising to take into account social change'. The ASA responded that guidance on where the boundaries lie was (and still is) regularly given through the published adjudications of its council:

It is no part of the function of the Authority to use the enforcement of the Code as a means of promoting social change, however desirable; though commonsense suggests, and observation confirms, that advertisers, no doubt moved by an awareness of where their commercial interest lies, will always be ready to adjust their appeals as the sensitivities of their audiences change.

The ASA itself had undertaken a major piece of research into advertisements in women's magazines, published in 1982 under the title *Herself Appraised*, as a contribution to the debate. In a detailed foreword to the study, the ASA's Chairman, Lord

McGregor, discussed demographic, occupational and social changes from the mid-nineteenth century as background, and concluded:

> One main question in the debate . . . has been whether little girls play with dolls because nature made them that way or because they are given dolls to play with. The balance of present-day answers inclines strongly towards a stress upon the importance of social influences. Nevertheless, the findings of our inquiry do not suggest wide support among the sample of women for the assertions about the effects of advertising on the status of women which have become part of the stock-in-trade of some leaders of the campaign for women's liberation . . .
>
> Changes in social attitudes, behaviour and politics mostly originate in the passion and dedication of small groups; and sometimes these are very small indeed. Even so, the Authority must have a care in its day-to-day work for the views of the generality of people and notes that an examination of the altered treatment of women and the family in advertisements over the last decade or so demonstrates that prudent advertisers have already made, and are acting upon, their own assessments of the directions of change. We trust that the evidence will serve to persuade other advertisers to follow, and thus to widen sensitivity and responsiveness to the developments which we have been discussing.

In 1988 about a third of the 929 complaints relating to taste and decency received by the ASA (out of a total of 7747 complaints on all topics) concerned the portrayal of women. (In 1989 the total was 296, including 194 duplicates.) It was therefore timely for the Authority to make a further study to provide information not only about current attitudes to women in advertisements but also to try to establish their prevalence and intensity among men and women in general was increasing.

The follow-up study, *Herself Reappraised*, published in spring 1990, provides a wider view, including attitudes of men to the portrayal of women in advertisements. There are major differences between the 1982 survey and the latest one. The latter uses over 2200 interviews to compare the views of the general public, men as well as women, with those of complainants to the ASA, whereas for the earlier survey only women were questioned.

There is a consistency in the themes arising from both surveys. They include:
- the need to reflect the equality of the sexes in advertising;
- disapproval of the portrayal of women in subservient or inferior roles; and
- disapproval of the blatant use of sex and sexual innuendo to attract attention.

The latest survey shows that the majority of people do not consider that women are stereotyped and thus degraded by advertising. Differences between complainant's attitudes and those of the general public are primarily a question of intensity. Although no more than 6 per cent of the general public considered that any particular advertisement should be stopped, where this view was held it tended to concern the same advertisements to which complainants objected.

Complainants tend to take advertising in general and specific advertisements in particular more seriously than do most members of the general public, according to the findings. Who are these people, complaining so strongly about sexism in advertising? They presented a remarkably coherent profile. The ASA reports:

> With regard to the objective characteristics of the complainants, it should be noted that they are more likely to be women, to be members of the upper/middle classes, to have had the benefit of higher education, to be readers of one of the quality newspapers (especially the *Guardian* or the *Independent*), to spend less time watching commercial television, to be a vegetarian and to be a member of some voluntary organisation or pressure group.

Despite these differences, the study confirms agreement in 1988 between all groups that there should be equality between the sexes and that this equality should be reflected in advertising. Portrayals of women as subservient or inferior to men do not meet these requirements. Nor does the use of sexual innuendo purely to attract attention, although relevant use of beautiful women, for example in a perfume advertisement, seems acceptable to all groups.

Today few marketing departments adopt the monolithic view of society which assumes that everyone was cut out from the same few basic patterns. It has been suggested that one factor which has accelerated the change is the marked increase in women graduates employed in marketing over the last decade.

There are no accurate statistics about the number of women working for companies which use advertising, although it is evident from observation that their number and influence has grown dramatically. There are, however, reliable data about women working in advertising agencies which are taken from the Institute of Practitioners in Advertising's (IPA's) annual census. The categories relate exclusively to advertising professionals: they exclude the numbers of people who work in agencies but do not necessarily have specialist advertising skills, such as those in finance and data processing departments and secretaries. The categories changed in 1985 to reflect the growing importance of account planning, so three points of comparison are given here.

TABLE 8

Full-time women professionals in IPA agencies

	1971 (%)	1985 (%)	1988 (%)
Executives	6	26	32
Copywriting	20	18	19
Art	10	14	20
Media	37	39	42
Production	11	25	29
Film production	27	62	59
Account planning and research	n/a	53	55

The trend reflects in part a very deliberate policy on the part of many agencies over the last decade to recruit women. It has also been true that many agencies have found more 'very good' female graduates coming forward than 'very good' male graduates, although the small group classed as 'excellent' candidates has tended to be evenly divided between the sexes.

There are few women at the very top of advertising agencies. February 1990 saw the publication of a study to find out why: *Women in Advertising: Findings and recommendations of a study commissioned by the Institute of Practitioners in Advertising* by Marilyn Baxter. Its terms of reference were 'to identify the reasons why there are so few women at the top of IPA agencies and to make recommendations to improve the proportion of senior women in advertising'.

The genesis of the report was a series of IPA seminars for graduate trainees and other agency newcomers. Although the audience consisted of equal numbers of men and women, the eight speakers chosen were all male. The IPA's President, Winston Fletcher, records in the report's preface:

> The young women made their disapproval of my apparent chauvinism abundantly clear. Why had I chosen no women, they asked? Because there are almost no women at the very top in advertising, I replied. Their faces dropped. Why not? Don't women ever get to the top? Many of them were so angry, and so depressed, I feared they might quit their newly started advertising careers even before the series ended.

The report observes that, despite the lack of women at the top, the advertising industry compares extremely favourably with most others. 'Only publishing and market research offer better opportunities to women.' One explanation for the under-representation of women at the top is the fact that there were very few female recruits fifteen to twenty years ago when today's top managers were entering the business. Twenty years ago only 19 per cent of the graduate entrants into professional jobs in advertising agencies were women. Fifteen years ago the number had risen to 23 per cent. By 1989 it was 45 per cent, or nearly one in two.

If present recruitment trends continue, women professionals will achieve equality of numbers but they will continue to be under-represented in top management, the report suggests.

Marilyn Baxter identifies a number of advertising characteristics, perceived equally by men and women, which are likely to favour men. The advertising agency world is a demanding client service business where 100 per cent commitment is required and late and weekend working is the norm at all levels. It is a creative business, 'full of volatile, awkward, unco-operative, unreasonable people with large egos who seem to respond better to bullying than to reasoned logical argument'. Communication, persuasion, motivation, analytical, strategic and management skills are vital. It is an ambitious environment, and can be highly political. It's a man's world – big on entertaining, often with a strong pub culture, with bad language and sexual innuendo commonplace.

The study found that men and women in advertising recognise that they exhibit different behaviour and talents. With the necessary caveats about sweeping generalisations, 'men are preoccupied with things, theories and power; women are preoccupied with people, morality and relationships'. Younger women, however, are significantly more self-assured and confident and are more determined to succeed through their differences rather than despite them.

For women the nature of the job and their own judgement of their competence are more important than formal or financial success. Men do better in competitive situations; women perform better when social acceptance is the goal. Men will work with anybody who is useful to them; women are more concerned with the quality of work relationships and want to be liked. Men tend to seek power in a single-minded way; women are ambitious in a wider sense that covers the quality of their whole lives.

The report analyses gender characteristics in relation to each of the major agency functions. Women have had greatest success in planning and research (to the extent that many department heads admitted to positive discrimination in favour of male candidates to redress the balance) and are most under-represented in creative departments.

Two main reasons are suggested for the predominance of women in planning: that most planners come from a market research background where women are strongly represented, and that planning makes most use of women's particular strengths and qualities. Perhaps more importantly, it is a relatively new discipline with few historical male traditions. Planning demands women's strengths of intuition, insight and understanding of other people. It is a support role, giving guidance and advice rather than taking charge. Planning is, however, rarely a route to top management.

The under-representation of women in creative departments was the most puzzling area of the study. Women have successful careers

as writers or artists in other walks of life and there is no apparent
reason why they should not be equally creatively talented in an
advertising context, especially when creative success is invariably
based on conspicuous talent; and when managing a creative department is seen to be more about creative talent than management
talent.

The nature of agency creative departments may be largely responsible, suggests Marilyn Baxter. Creative people have to be very
self-confident, determined to fight for what they feel is right. They
have to care for their ideas over and above their working relationships
and be prepared to be unpleasant, unreasonable and uncompromis-
ing in order to protect them. These tend to be male, not female,
characteristics. Creative departments are typically highly competitive and tend to be short on support, encouragement and praise. In
the words of the report: 'Environmentally, it seems that a less
female-friendly environment than a creative department would be
hard to find.'

In account management there are also difficulties for women.
The report stresses the need for authority. 'It is not difficult [to be
authoritative] if you are male, 6ft 2ins and built like a second-row
forward but quite hard for a young woman, 5ft 2ins and wearing a
skirt.' Taking young women for secretaries when they answer the
telephone or pour coffee, or patronising older women, robs them of
any authority. Women have to work harder to exert their authority,
whether dealing with (still predominantly male) clients or telling
other people what to do.

Account management is identified as the function that is most
demanding of time and least flexible, and therefore the most
difficult to combine with domestic responsibilities. As most
chairmen and chief executives come from an account management background, the paucity of women in top management
positions is not surprising.

Although all the agency heads interviewed – male and female –
rejected any suggestion of active discrimination against women,
many women interviewed felt they had been victims of varying
degrees of discrimination, prejudice, sexism and chauvinism. The
report says that discrimination is largely subtle and rarely overt, and
cites a number of examples, few of which are exclusive to advertising:
● language (being referred to as 'girls');
● unnecessary comments about dress or being advised to exploit
dress or appearance;

• being put on 'women's accounts' (cosmetics and toiletries) rather than 'men's' (alcohol, cars, technical products);
• overconcern with gender balance, such as putting a man in charge of a predominantly female department but never vice versa, or avoiding an all-female account team but not an all-male one;
• making assumptions about women's career or family motivations or asking what are seen as impertinent questions about plans to marry, start a family or husbands' attitudes which men are not asked; and
• tarring all women with the same brush ('we tried promoting a woman but it didn't work').

Agencies are now seeking the brightest and best people, regardless of gender. Agency managers are highly sensitive to casting, matching the agency team to the client, a process which filters out both women and men: gender is very rarely the issue, according to the report. Agency heads and some senior women said that asking women candidates about their husbands and children was not sexist but simply a practical way of testing commitment: men are asked different questions with the same objective.

'Where real discrimination exists is at the very top,' states the report. 'Agencies appear to be wholly relaxed, even enthusiastic, about promoting women to senior positions, but are much more reluctant to see a woman as *the* media director, *the* client services director, *the* creative director or *the* managing director.' One reason given is risk. Anyone being promoted has no track record as a department head, and is therefore a risk. 'Because there are very few female role models, agency managements who decide to promote women to a real management position put themselves out on a limb. It adds to the perceived risk, and thus it is generally avoided.' Another reason is simple prejudice: a belief that women are not suitable for top management jobs or that senior men will refuse to work with or for a woman.

A key question is whether women really *want* to get to the top of advertising agencies. In answer to the question 'Why aren't there more women at the top of agencies?' one reply – echoed by the great majority of the women interviewed – was: 'It's obvious: women are far too sensible to want to run advertising agencies.' To reach the top demands single-mindedness, determination and real ambition. According to the report:

In the process [those who have reached the top] were observed to have made enormous sacrifices, perhaps to have wrecked their personal lives, to have a narrow perspective on life, and to live, eat and sleep their work. Women's wider perspectives make them conclude that this is not a trade-off that they are prepared to make.

It is not that women in advertising agencies are unambitious; rather, they are ambitious for different things. In Marilyn Baxter's words:

They want to be as successful as they can be, want to be taken seriously, do not want to be discriminated against, want to be promoted to senior positions, want to be well paid, and want to be valued and considered important by their agencies and clients. But not all of them want to sacrifice everything else in their lives to achieve these things.

In particular, many do not want to give up their chances of motherhood and a family life. This is particularly front of mind with senior, older women but it is also an issue with the younger ones. However, the younger women are more determined to 'have it all' and do not assume that they will inevitably have to make sacrifices in order to get on.

On the whole, women in advertising confirm the generalisation that women regard job satisfaction, enjoyment and the intrinsic value of their work as more important than power or position. In this connection, the report says that women have a choice between succeeding at work or succeeding in motherhood. 'Many men are not motivated to get to the top either, but they are rarely in a position to opt out. Men generally have only their work in which to succeed; women have other possibilities.'

One section of the report, called 'Recipes for Success', draws on the experience of senior advertising women in developing the right attitude, dealing with men, coping with domestic responsibilities, maternity, appearance, role models and mentors, and career planning. In the last case, several successful women felt that women often do not plan their careers as well as men, nor do they think about 'positioning' themselves for promotion. Successful women take training seriously, for example. They may also take on outside responsibilities, leading to recognition in a wider business context and enhanced status within the agency.

A point which does not emerge from the IPA study concerns women's attitudes to change. Advertising is a world of constant change. An advertising strategy is under constant review, developing and changing in response to new research and information, competitive action or other changes in the market place. For creative people the prime requirement is innovation: to produce new, original, outstanding ideas which are relevant to the product's target group and consonant with its characteristics.

With all the necessary caveats about making invidious generalisations, older career women have not always demonstrated a total willingness or facility for coping with change. This is a thread through many women's careers in a variety of walks of life. Seeking out, creating and accelerating change has not come naturally. Instead, what one might call a nesting instinct has operated: settling down into a job, liking the work and the people, and regarding those satisfactions more highly than financial reward, overt status and the fierce competition to the top of the career ladder. The security of exercising proven skills and expertise may have seemed preferable to the risk of the unknown in general management or in running a specialist department.

That said, there is a substantial difference between such women and the younger generation in agencies who are brimming with confidence, organising their work and planning their careers with none of the self-doubts or wariness of their older colleagues. They are well-educated, competent and comfortable in their own skins and the differences in style and job satisfaction compared with men of their own age may well be minimal.

The growing number of women involved in the commissioning, planning and execution of advertising has coincided with the biggest advance of the last decade. It is the real respect accorded to consumers. Gone is the little wife whose identity depended on her family, and who was grateful to the reassuring men who told her how to earn their approval.

Readers, and particularly viewers, are very much brighter than that. Not only can they work things out for themselves but they enjoy doing so. The tone of voice of advertising changed markedly during the 1980s. The patronising and dictatorial approach of earlier years was quite clearly out of tune with consumers who thought for themselves and who made their own informed choices. Advertisements invited participation and allowed women to complete the message for themselves, relating the product of their own lives or dismissing it as irrelevant.

Perhaps the most significant evidence of women taking a proper place in television advertisements in what were traditionally regarded as male provinces is their unobtrusiveness. It requires a conscious effort to note that many presenters of financial services happen to be female, that the manager with a computer is no longer identified as a typist, that a woman's voice-over explains the benefits of power tools.

For home-based products, other lessons have been learned, not least that it is not only possible but very effective to reflect the realities of family life. Oxo's Linda broke new ground. She gets cross, tired, exasperated. Her children are not plaster saints. She has a sense of humour, a sex life and a husband who is perfectly capable of cooking when she is out. As one research group put it: 'That's what family life is like – war and peace – and she's got them all sussed out.'

When an advertisement shows a credible, humorous, competent woman who thinks for herself and clearly has a life beyond the kitchen, no one bothers any longer to suggest that she should really be identified as having an important job in a substantially male world.

Significantly, Britain seems to have escaped the incompetent wimpish male equivalent of the dumb blonde. Simply because more women are winning does not mean that more men must be shown as losers. Men and women are comparably capable, resourceful, self-confident, intelligent, imaginative and independent. Advertisers and their agencies must continue to develop their reflection of the new equalities, and to ensure that their communications research is sufficiently open-minded to identify and respond to continuous change.

3
Watch Your Language!

by Sue Dicks

'Glory to Man in the highest! for Man is the master of things.'
Swinburne (1837–1909), *Hymn of Man*.

'In the Act and in every Act passed after the year 1850 . . . words importing the masculine gender shall include females.'
Interpretation Act, 1889.

'Women are particularly good at discounting and not recognising their abilities.'
MSC Training Manual, 1983.

When I gave up a secure teaching job, I thought I had done my homework thoroughly. Indeed, there has been only one unforeseen shock to my system: I had not realised that in giving up professional status I would stop being a woman. What follows, and the conclusions I draw from it, form a cautionary tale for employers.

In my mid-forties, and with what I take to be a reasonable degree of maturity and intelligence, it seemed I had become a girl again. Occasionally I was elevated to the equally dubious status of 'lady'.

It happened like this. After twenty years in a profession, I got myself a secretarial qualification. (I aimed to combine the work with freelance journalism.) At the interview for my first part-time office job, I remember the male executive saying anxiously, 'There is one thing we do ask.' What was in store? 'We do ask the girls to make our tea.'

I wasn't going to let a little thing like that worry me; I wouldn't brew yet another storm in the teacup of humourless feminism.

I had, of course, missed the point. The source of the trouble lay in the term this man used to describe his female employees. How different would it have been if he'd said, 'We ask the secretaries to make our tea'? I think it would have been difficult to the point of revolutionary – and it would never have been said. Let no one pretend that the term 'girl' is not derogatory: it suggests young, decorative, useful, available – the ideal of every old-fashioned male chauvinist, in fact!

Nowadays I no longer work with old-fashioned chauvinists. I am employed by a university department where everyone is as intelligent, enlightened and generally as nice as a woman could wish. This makes it all the more depressing that old linguistic habits survive here too, as they do in many generally well-meaning sectors of society.

The staff meeting provided a good example. Secretaries, administrative and academic staff sat down together in truly democratic and egalitarian spirit. An academic matter was raised. 'Do the girls have a vote on this?' asked a senior member of staff. It was clear that she was referring to the less senior female staff present, several of whom were older than she: so much for equality! I may have been in a less important job, but I didn't think I'd become a less important person.

I agree that I had a different perspective from that of many women doing similar work. I had spent years in the relatively egalitarian cosiness of school staff rooms. In that environment I acquired my sense of identity and now I can afford the luxury of amused detachment.

I'm only too aware that it is a luxury. My concern is for those with different experience for whom the options may be narrowed. You are less likely to metamorphose into a career woman if you're not identified as a woman – as a mature person – in the first place. Worse, you may even stop wanting to. The self image is a powerful thing and to be devalued linguistically is to be devalued by society.

To understand how this devaluation takes place, it is necessary to think about the way language works. There is a tendency to regard language as handed down to us as if by some divine decree, complete with instructions as to the correct usage thereof, and resistance to innovation is frequently expressed in emotive terms. Yet our language has constantly adapted to reflect cultural change.

More important, there is a two-way process: language both structures and reflects our reality. As new words and usages evolve in language to express social change, our attitudes are in turn formed or modified by them. Why do parents take such care in choosing children's names? They know the 'labels' their daughters and sons take through life will help form, however erroneously, certain expectations about them.

It is hardly surprising that many women have their own expectations modified by the ways in which society refers to them. There is now legislation to prevent the more obvious uses of sexist language, such as in job advertisements, but the problem goes far beyond compliance with the law.

It begins with names. A boy, when he reaches adulthood, seems to become a man by a fairly painless, automatic process. He acquires the only title most men ever have, 'Mr', and keeps his surname. If he marries, his name will always precede his wife's on anything addressed to them both.

A girl, as we have seen, does not automatically become a woman. She has to choose between 'Ms' or 'Miss', with the latter still widely assumed to be appropriate to make it clear she is not legally married. On marriage she usually forfeits her surname and chooses between 'Mrs' or 'Ms'. All the titles define her in terms of her relationship with a man. Although the practice is declining, she sometimes loses her first name too, as in 'Mrs John Smith'.

On forms to be filled in, a woman will find that 'Mr' is always the first of a list of titles from which to choose, followed by all the alternatives that could describe her status. If 'Ms' is included, it generally comes in as yet a third choice, instead of replacing 'Mrs/Miss'.

The use of titles to denote a woman's marital status is not enshrined in the language. At the beginning of the nineteenth century, for example, 'Mrs' was used for any woman over a certain age. It seems it was when women first worked outside the home in considerable numbers, after industrialisation, that 'Miss' was used for the unmarried older woman. Perhaps men needed to know their 'availability' or otherwise, once they were away from the defining circle of the home? Whatever the reason, it is certainly necessary to ask who today needs the information and why.

Employers should look carefully at how they present information about their staff. Consider these two lists – which could be of those attending a meeting, or of the partners in a firm as listed on the official letterhead:

J. Brown	Mr John Brown
E. Wright	Mr Edward Wright
Miss S. Jones	Ms Sue Jones
A. Smith	Mr Alan Smith
W. Evans	Mr Will Evans
Mrs J. Cooper	Ms Jane Cooper
D. Stevens	Mr David Stevens

The left-hand list could have been even worse if the first names of the women only had been added. I have seen such lists very recently. As it stands, what does the left-hand list tell you about attitudes to women?

The very layout presents women as exceptions to the norm. It draws attention to their numerical minority, and in using more than one title it further suggests they are not, like the men, a homogeneous group. A fragmented group, of course, always has less power. There are many examples in print of women's names having more names and titles prefixed to them than the men's in the same context; there seems to be some compulsion to qualify the references.

A great deal of this process is probably not conscious at all, but it is no the less powerful as a result. Feminist linguists who have exposed the male bias of the Queen's English have sometimes stressed that it is the unconscious, even well-intentioned outcome of the language inevitably developed over several centuries of cultural patriarchy. Others see it as a sinister male plot!

Some women express considerable outrage at even a single usage they see as discriminatory. Others claim to be content with their lot and dissociate themselves from the whole silly business. Their attitudes towards themselves and their work may well, however, betray a vision of their own worth (or lack of it) that some of us would attribute at least in part to the messages they receive from the language and images all around them.

To insist on calling a manhole cover an access point may justifiably seem like paranoia. It argues a departure from any sense of proportion. In reality, whatever the inherent absurdity of that example, it has to be seen in the context of the whole language. When you have heard about man-hours, manpower, man's work, man management, man-made, the man in the street, the layman, mankind, man-to-man discussion and manning the desk, then indeed you may manfully argue for a sense of proportion.

Besides the probable inaccuracy of many of these terms nowadays, what matters is the cumulative effect of exposure to them over a period of time. The effect is to suggest that power is the prerogative of 'man'. The effect is gradually to erode a woman's sense of her power or even her presence.

The use of 'man' alone as a supposedly generic term is hardest to eradicate or modify. If we read that 'man has gradually abused his environment', we are not of course supposed to think that woman has stood self-righteously aside during this process. As the old adage – and law – has it, 'man embraces woman'.

Most women would do without the grammatical embrace and settle for a little flesh and blood respect, to say nothing of realism, because of course the argument is nonsense. 'Man' has been used so long and so widely as the specific term that it cannot function convincingly as a generic one. We all know man is male. Who reads a phrase like 'man is the summit of creation' and instantly pictures a woman – or, still less, a couple – on that sought-after peak?

Many experiments have been carried out in schools and colleges where students or pupils have been made thoroughly familiar with the generic use of 'man' and then been asked to illustrate such phrases as 'man at work' or 'social man'. Not surprisingly, the drawings and writings have portrayed males predominately or, more often, exclusively.

Do we seriously expect a child to learn that Mummy is woman and Daddy is man and then later to have a ready understanding of how man can also mean Mummy? Would not the most grammatically informed of speakers see absurdity in statements like 'man breastfeeds his young' or 'the postman is pregnant'? Of course they would, because it is the specific meaning that always wins the day. There are plenty of more precise words to use, like 'humanity' and 'people'.

In November 1989 I was watching the moving television news pictures of the opening up of the Berlin Wall. A particularly memorable image was of a mother re-united with her daughter after some years' separation. The commentary was economic and eloquent and I was caught up in the moment. Then the commentator came to the climax of it all: 'And soon every man will tell his son this was the Berlin Wall.'

The world seemed to shrink again. I am sure what he meant to convey was the idea that all children of the future will be told about the Wall by their parents as just another part of human history. 'Every man' has a generic, a global ring to it, but the picture then conveyed to us was specific: a father and a son. History has so often been the chronicle of 'mankind's' achievements and man has so long dominated the public sphere that the choice of such images is not surprising.

Writing as long ago as 1933, the grammarian Otto Jesperson explained the difficulty: 'The word *man* requires special mention on account of its ambiguity . . . in most combinations it will be understood of a male human being.' He quotes from a 'feminist poem' by a Miss Hutchinson, apparently writing in the nineteenth century: 'All, all are men – women and all!'

He goes on to the heart of the problem: 'It is a natural linguistic consequence of the social preponderance during many centuries of men that when a word for one sex is derived from a word for the other, it is nearly always a male word that is taken as base.' Hence women's dislike of terms like 'authoress', 'stewardess' or 'usherette' which are linguistically derivatives, or even diminutives, and therefore suggest the female roles are similarly secondary to or deviations from the male norm. 'Author', 'usher' and 'steward' are perfectly adequate, gender-neutral terms that describe the work and not the sex of the worker. Disraeli got it correct. 'We authors, ma'am,' he said to the Queen, who rightly took it as a bit of deliberate flattery.

The real danger of such linguistic habits is that they both reflect and create the impression of 'male' as the universal norm. This patriarchal assumption is one that is all too easily made – and perpetuated. Keeping to the letter of the law is one thing, and certainly the Sex Discrimination Act has helped outlaw much thoughtless sexism in behaviour, but it is only a start.

Language has the power to hurt. The main aim should be not only to avoid breaking the law but to avoid using that power offensively. It seems to me that the mark of a civilised person is to use words with care and with consideration for the feelings of others.

Randolph Quirk (*A University Grammar of English*, 1973) is an astute observer of the systems and idiosyncrasies of our language. This is what he says about those 'dual gender' terms like teacher, criminal, servant and butcher: 'The dual class is on the increase, but the expectation that a given activity is largely male or female dictates the frequent use of sex markers: thus a *nurse* but a *male nurse*; an *engineer* but a *woman engineer*.'

True, such phrases reflect the welcome news that there are some male nurses and some women engineers, but they do nothing to encourage more of them! One might add 'woman doctor' or 'woman MP'; it is their rarity value which is thereby endorsed. Expectation certainly dictates the use of sex markers but, conversely, their use dictates the expectations: that nurses and engineers remain, respectively, female and male unless proved otherwise.

An even more blatant statement of this expectation is any word ending in 'man', though this tends to be one of the more difficult areas. Professor Quirk lists 'chairman' as one of the proven 'dual gender' terms and I am tempted to agree. It would seem that the element of 'man' here has for once either become truly generic or just lost its force.

However, there is the danger that the prolonged use of '-man' terms for common jobs will reinforce the notion of an exclusively 'man's world'. Ideas like these, when they become part of a woman's conscious or unconscious interpretation of the way society operates, may do as much as any explicit discrimination to put her off and thus exclude her from such jobs. Lord Justice Butler-Sloss is a very distinguished *woman*. Invisibility is a contagious habit.

So there's no escaping the tedium of the chair. 'Chairperson' is a linguistic outrage to some and 'Madam Chairman' a hermaphrodite joke to others. The essential thing is to have the debate in the first place. It shows that a value is placed on some people's feelings and their desire for equality more highly than other people's pedantic quibbles.

The success of some existing neutral terms is encouraging. When I first started teaching, there were a lot of masters and mistresses about, which caused several problems. If you wanted to refer to both of them, you either had an explosive mouthful or used one term for all. Things being what they are, you used 'master'. Apart from anything else, 'mistress' has much less favourable connotations than its virtually incorruptible companion. (This was the fate of many female names – like dame, lady, bitch and vixen!) Luckily we had acceptable alternatives to hand and soon we all became teachers and tutors, with 'headteachers' slowly becoming acceptable and widely used, at least in the state sector.

At the time of writing this chapter, there was an ambulance dispute. The BBC and ITN were fairly scrupulous about referring to 'ambulence crew', drivers' or 'staff'. However, journalists and interviewees said 'ambulancemen' so often it came as quite a surprise to see on the screen that some of them were women. Alistair Burnett (ITN News at Ten, 22 January 1990) introduced the bulletin with a comment on developments in the 'ambulancemen's talks' – against a background photograph clearly showing a good proportion of women among them! Wasn't this at the very least a discourtesy?

Feminists are often accused of wanting to make women 'masculine' and blur the cherished difference. Nothing could be further from the truth. They would like difference emphasised; they would like jobs and positions of authority described in terms which neither exclude them nor suggest they are temporary exceptions. 'Few women are asking to be called men, but more women than anybody has bothered to count are asking that they *not* be called men.' (Kate Swift and Casey Miller, *Words and Women*, 1976.)

There are plenty of guidelines, usually lists of alternative words, to help people avoid offence. Like the laws, these need to be understood in the full context of how women feel and how language works. The trouble with wordlists alone is that we can find ourselves playing a potentially absurd game of superficial word-swapping in which nobody wins.

A delightful hoax article in *The Times Educational Supplement* on 1 April 1988 described a computer program designed to eradicate the most innocent little sexism (if there is such a thing) from our screens. If you typed in 'policeman', it would rightly alter it to 'police officer', and it had ways of dealing with longer input too. In response to 'The average first division footballer pays great attention to his boots', it flashed this reminder on the screen: 'Footballers can be female too!'

Admittedly first division football isn't yet a female stronghold, but the sentence is a good illustration of a common problem. 'Footballer', technically, is one of those common gender names that should be safe. Yet when we want to follow it up with a singular pronoun, we have no similarly neutral one. 'He' and 'his' are the ones used and, while there may be some case for their suitability here, the male pronoun is resorted to in numerous contexts where it is far less welcome.

'Barrister' is a similarly neutral term – in theory. I recently heard one (a man) give a talk about legal careers to an audience of undergraduates, at least half of whom were women intending to enter the profession. He made no attempt to avoid using 'he' throughout, as in: 'When a student qualifies, he . . .' This was a discourtesy to half his audience, an inaccurate picture of the situation described and a reinforcement of the notion of male exclusiveness.

Perhaps the speaker would have agreed with Philip Howard (*New Words for Old*, 1980) that only the 'lunatic fringe' of women 'strain at such semantic gnats as neuter pronouns' and that 'in most cases "he" or "him" can be understood to include "she" or "her".' I really cannot share his faith that people constantly say one thing when they really mean another, nor that their listeners always understand or accept the implicit as well as the obvious. There is nothing neuter, common or genetic about 'he'. Not to me, there isn't. Like man, he is *male*.

Mr Howard virtually admits this when he concedes that it may be necessary to emphasise (by adding 'and she') in job advertisements that both sexes are referred to. He can think of no other likely context in which it would ever be 'important to emphasise that both sexes are included in the pronoun'.

So how do you sensibly emphasise that you mean both halves of the human race? You can of course go on adding 'and/or she/her', but it can get clumsy or tedious. There's no law against varying it, incidentally. Why not say 'she or he' sometimes? The same goes for all those happily married linguistic couples: husband and wife, boy and girl, brother and sister, son and daughter. Reverse the order occasionally. It might even jolt your listener's attention: she or he would realise you were talking about real people, not just clichés. Alternatively, you can often change the structure of a sentence by making it plural ('When students qualify, they . . .') or transposing clauses ('A student who qualifies may . . .'). It just needs a little skill with our very resourceful language.

A further option is to use 'they' even though you mean the singular. It will of course antagonise the grammatical purists who will insist that it is violating ancient and immutable laws. It was as late as the eighteenth and nineteenth centuries that most such 'rules' were drawn up, largely by grammarians who were classical scholars and transferred to English their observations of the literary forms of Latin and Greek. They were not so much describing the way our language was used as indefatigably prescribing *how* we should use it. If two alternative constructions were possible, one was right and the other a 'vulgar error'.

Many of their strictures seem like common sense and appeal to our sense of 'logic' and order. However, they were totally inflexible, denied the essential process of linguistic change and rarely recognised *usage* as a criterion. Academic considerations overrode human issues, leaving split infinitives to loom larger than hurt feelings.

To this era belongs the belief that, in the interests of grammatical concord, the singular pronoun 'he' must be used to 'embrace she'. It was even enshrined in an 1850 Act of Parliament! More recent writers record where this is observed in the breach. David Crystal (*Who Cares about English Usage?*, 1984) describes the sentence 'Anyone can have a drink *if they want*' as the usual 'informal way out' of having a 'really awkward construction' like '*if he or she wants*'. Quirk too explains how '*they* is often used informally, in defiance of number concord'. 'They' has been used in the singular for centuries.

This century's apostles of the traditional grammarians have been the writers of popular usage manuals, like the late H. W. Fowler (*A Dictionary of Modern English Usage*, 1926). To him 'As anyone can see for themselves' is a structure that 'sets the literary man's teeth on edge'. Speaking as a literary woman, I'm interested in the tooth-gnashing properties of: 'God send every one their harts desire' (Shakespeare); 'Nobody prevents you, do they?' (Thackeray); and 'Nobody likes a mind quicker than their own' (Scott Fitzgerald). It's all 'enough to drive anyone out of their senses' (Bernard Shaw).

Since our attitudes are formed in and by words, we need to use language not underpinned by patriarchal assumptions. As the last decade closed, women's magazines concerned themselves less with mechanisms by which women could gain equality in the workplace and more with exploring the attitudes, including their own, that prevented them from using the existing ones.

Anne Caborn writes in *Options* magazine (March 1989) on 'Why Women Must Ask for More'. She cites a firm which advertised a job at £19,000 per annum, for which 90 per cent of applicants were men. They re-advertised the same job at £14,000 and 90 per cent of applicants were then women. One explanation for this suggested by Irene Harris, the founder of Network, is that 'men are brought up to know their own worth'.

Ros Miles concludes (*Cosmopolitan*, June 1989, 'News Report: Sex Discrimination') that equality 'means ridding ourselves and men of the notions that lead both sexes to expect less of women'.

Some women try to educate themselves out of these notions by attending courses in assertiveness or personal effectiveness. These are nothing to do with being selfish, aggressive or antagonistic, but simply with gaining the confidence to have some control over their own lives. A potentially capable woman who spends all day in a job saying 'yes,' and then goes home to find her husband and teenage son (who work similar or shorter hours, usually for more money) with their feet up waiting for the shopping/cooking/laundry service to begin, needs help. She needs help in developing a sense of her own worth and then expressing that in practical terms.

Her inability to do this without support is not surprising 'given that society's expectation is that woman will be passive and dependent while men will be active and independent'. (Nancy Paul, *MSC Training Manual*, 1983.)

But times are changing again. Seventy per cent of women now work outside the home at some stage in their lives. Yet many of them still do long hours of housework as well and are expected to be the parent solely responsible for most aspects of childcare. Not surprisingly, women often take their domestic roles into the workplace. The role of secretary, originally male, later became a natural one for women, whose 'desire at all times [was] to support effectively the work of others'. (*Secretarial Work* Association of Graduate Careers Advisory Services, 1989.)

We are still often told that motherhood is the most fulfilling role a woman can ever have and the most important contribution anyone can make to society. In which case it is particularly sad that, after several years doing it, so many women feel totally lacking in confidence and self-esteem when they come to 'go back to work', as we so ironically word it.

A Christmas 1989 toy brochure had a centre spread divided for boys and girls. For boys there featured prominently a gun, a car and a toy computer. For girls there were a tea set, a vacuum cleaner and a toy typewriter. It isn't wrong for a girl to play with tea sets but it is wrong for children of both sexes to have their choices influenced and limited by such images. Stereotypes are always crude because they limit options. What was worse in this case what that all the boy's options were those traditionally associated with power and status and all the girl's were those of subservience and menial roles. Will that help build her confidence as a member of the future workforce?

When she goes out to work as an adult, how will she be treated? I recently met a young woman lawyer who found, at a weekly meeting with her all male partners, that she was expected to make and pour the coffee. She and they were technically equal in status.

After a while she gently suggested that someone else should take a turn, especially as it meant she missed a little of the meeting. The 'partners' smilingly agreed – and asked the female canteen assistant to come up and do it.

The images and words women would like to see now are those which show the caring and supportive roles as positive and desirable, and therefore as genuine options for both sexes rather than the automatic burden of one. We need to get away from the equation: female = supportive role = low status. Service need not be subservience (or female) any more than power need be tyranny (or male); both stereotypes need to become redundant, along with all the assumptions that support them.

We do not have a truly egalitarian language as long as we, unconsciously or otherwise, continue to belittle the efforts of one sex. Which brings me back to where I began and to my anger at not being treated as a grown-up. 'Girl' is defined in dictionaries as meaning, or having meant, a child, a female child, a servant, a sweetheart, a young unmarried person. Only in the most recent is it accorded the meaning 'a woman of any age': that usage seems to be a product of twentieth-century attitudes.

I was recently in an electricity showroom near an elderly couple waiting to be served. Two uniformed assistants were in view. One was a young man in his early twenties wearing a badge saying 'Sales Assistant'; the other was a woman in her mid-thirties whose badge said 'Sales Manager'. 'Shall we ask that *man*?' said the wife. 'No,' replied her husband, 'let's ask that *girl*.'

Four Britons, one a woman, were shortlisted in November 1989 to be the first cosmonauts. Helen Sharman, an attractive twenty-six-year-old, is a scientist and football player – hardly a feminine stereotype! She was one of two chosen to go into the last round. On the hoarding by the news-stand I saw: 'Man and girl go into space.' It made it seem less the giant leap forward for woman-kind than it might have been.

Perhaps when attitudes have changed even further, our words will change to reflect them. Meanwhile, the two processes are concurrent. When we see unconscious discrimination operating, we need to make a conscious effort to prevent it.

Dale Spender, a woman writer and activist of unflagging energy, was once reputedly asked how she coped with her punishing schedule. 'Nobody ever told me I can't,' was her answer. Writer Alison Baines (*Success and Satisfaction*, 1988) asks: 'How is the message that individuals "can't" constructed and delivered? Not overtly.'

Not overtly, but by implication – constantly. As long as women are treated as dependent, secondary or invisible in our daily language, the struggle for them to be otherwise will not be eased even in the next century.

Parts of this chapter were published in a different form in the Guardian, *15 April 1989.*

4

Equality and the Future

by Joanna Foster,
Chair, Equal Opportunities Commission

For all of us the pace of change in modern life is breathtaking, driven by the astounding scientific and technological developments which shrink the world and underline our global interdependence and the fierce international competition for markets and resources. This pace of change challenges us in every aspect of our lives. For women this is especially true – as most of our lives are already very different from those lived by our grandmothers and mothers.

Trying to contemplate what our children's and their children's lives will be like requires another quantum leap of imagination. The main differences for them seem to be in aspiration, expectation and opportunity: aspiration about what they would like to do with their lives, expectation about what they think they can achieve and opportunity that gives them choice.

The vote and the Pill are of course clear contenders when it comes to calculating the predominant influences on women's emancipation in the past. I suspect that we will look back in ten years' time and add 'skills shortage', 'demographic timebomb', 'the legislation', and the Single European Market to this list. The first two, I hope, will turn out to be positive factors for women and not just the illusion of opportunity flickering in the employment soothsayer's crystal ball. The third – the legislation – is no illusion, for British and European Community legislation will continue to be a major influence on the way people and organisations behave. The fourth, the Single European Market, has the potential to be both a positive and a negative influence on our lives.

To manage the future we must weigh up where we are now as women, where we want to get to, at what price and in what way.

The Battle is Over?

'The battle is over,' an Oxford undergraduate said to me not so long ago. 'We have no need for the Equal Opportunities Commission as these days women can become Prime Minister, a judge, a mining engineer, a manager or a merchant banker, and can have children too. Combining career and family these days is easy,' she added. My remonstrations, pointing out that it was certainly possible but not yet easy, seemed to fall on deaf ears as she disappeared in a self-confident aura to discuss with her boyfriend his job offer in Newcastle and hers in Bristol – a discussion she might not find quite so easy after all!

At the beginning of the 1990s the battle is far from over; equal opportunities are, alas, not yet a reality in Britain, despite great progress in some areas and despite the famous demographic trends, the increasing shortage of scarce skills and the highly significant upward trend of women with family responsibilities entering the workforce.

Since 1980 a further one and a half million women have become economically active and it is predicted that another quarter of a million will do so in the next two years. It is also predicted that 90 per cent of the new jobs in the UK over the next five years will be taken by women, the majority of whom will have major family responsibilities. All these factors have influenced the situation. An increasing number of employers, faced with these new challenges and the fierce competition to attract, train, and retain 'the best', to capitalise on their most precious investment – their people – are making efforts to change. They are now *looking* more 'women- and family-friendly'. However, it is still the minority of employers and service providers who have actually changed; only the few so far who have listened to what we as women want and need if we are to contribute fully and effectively to paid work *and* our community and family lives in the way we would like to.

We know for certain that the future is about knowledge, the technology and management of complex information; about working in increasingly diverse groups; about working flexibly and trans-nationally. It is about being multi-skilled and open to continuous learning, relearning and unlearning. It is about managing the stresses of change. It is also about relationships and the changing nature of our family lives – it is about the enormous pressure to be super-achievers and to balance, with no apparent effort, the often conflicting pulls of our different roles.

Balancing our Lives

What women want, and I believe what men want too, is to find a way of achieving this balance, to build into our working and family lives a quality which includes time to stay healthy and sane, time to listen, discuss, share and enjoy, time to recharge our creative batteries.

What is stopping us doing this? What do we need to do to ensure we fashion the future in a way that will make more of a reality of that young Oxford undergraduate's expectations that having a career and a family is easy as well as possible?

On the work front, what we want are jobs which give us the satisfaction of making a worthwhile contribution and offer us the opportunity to develop our skills, to build a career and to participate fully in the decisions that effect our lives; we also want our contribution recognised and rewarded fairly. These are qualities that men too want in their work, and they also encounter barriers to achieving them. The statistics, however, still show that the barriers for them are different, and easier to overcome. Only 26 per cent of managers in the UK are women, a pattern echoed in all kinds of organisations, as was underlined in the Hansard Society Report *Women at the Top*, published in early 1990.

Equal Opportunities for the 1990s

At the Equal Opportunities Commission we stood back last year to think through the barriers and challenges ahead and identify some of the key issues. We developed a strategy and some specific objectives for the equal opportunity agenda for the 1990s.

There are still plenty of barriers. The important thing to hang on to is that we know *how* to overcome and manage them; some barriers and issues, however, are much easier to tackle than others. The barriers centre round traditional attitudes about equality of opportunity as well as the concrete and logistical outcome of these attitudes – practices which take as the norm the traditional roles of

men and women and assumptions about who does what at work
and at home.

The Myth of the 'Cornflake Packet' Family

Man as breadwinner and leader, woman as homemaker and supporter are of course, the most commonplace assumptions and ones
which are still deeply embedded as the stereotypes on which so
many decisions about terms, conditions and work promotions are
based. Those who make these decisions discount the fact that fewer
and fewer women have the choice of whether to stay at home or to
work outside; that fewer and fewer families (5 per cent) conform to
the myth of the 'cornflake packet' family consisting of Dad out at
work, Mum based at home, working but not earning, and two
children; that a rising number of women (930,000) are the heads
of lone-parent families and that 50.4 per cent of all households
contain a married woman who is working and therefore contributing
to overall household income. The view is still amazingly prevalent
that we women still work for pin money or to have something
interesting to do while our children are at school and our houses
are whirring with new domestic technology.

These attitudes result in widespread prejudice and discrimination.
At the Commission we continue to receive hundreds of enquiries,
complaints and cases from women of all ages, in all sectors of work
and at all levels of jobs; and from those women in the community
or home-based, hoping or needing to get back into education or
the job market. These women experience at first hand the challenge
of being different, and none more so than black women and those
from other minority ethnic groups. These women have talent,
energy and ideas which are in short supply – it is a real waste that
prejudice and traditional attitudes and practices hold them back. It
also exemplifies inequality of opportunity.

Equal Opportunity in Spirit but not in Practice

Attitudes are changing, however, if slowly. I believe that in general
the concept of equal opportunities is now much more widely
accepted in Britain: accepted in theory, at any rate; and accepted
when it comes to women who have followed a career pattern and

managed their lives along male lines – that is, by behaving in so
many ways like men, and not being thrown off course by childbirth
or having to take the major responsibility for the household. We
have seen this so clearly in the USA, where women have climbed
the career ladder so much faster than women here. Many of those
women have become 'clone' men, except that they are different in
one major way – a way which makes them socially suspect, which
hinders them when it comes to trying to break through to the most
senior level, through the 'glass ceiling' which separates them, from
their male colleagues. These women do not have children. It is this
issue – the family issue – that is undoubtedly the major barrier to
making equal opportunities a reality.

New Roles: New Attitudes

We are all faced with the major challenge of adapting to the new
roles we as women are increasingly playing in the community and
the workplace. We are trying to adjust to the impact this revolution
is having on us all. The ambivalence being experienced by both
men and women regarding this change is also considerable. As
women we know that for us to succeed (and sometimes, we feel,
just to survive) there have to be some fundamental changes. One
of these is more sharing of responsibilities at home. Here our
ambivalence as women seems to be a stumbling block as well as
men's deep-seated nostalgia to return to the 'slippers ready' regime!
We don't seem to be ready to give up or delegate some of our
traditional role as managers on the home front, yet we take on more
and more outside and then wonder why we get exhausted. Many
believe it is because the home is the one area in our lives where we
feel we have control.

Susan McRae's report for the Policy Studies Institute, *Flexible
Working Time and Family Life* (published in 1989), revealed to no
one's surprise that the 'new sharing man' is still more a myth than
a reality, although many men felt that they were helping more (and
they are – *slightly*). The figures, alas, did not back up this feeling,
nor do the high divorce figures. Although we have the highest
divorce rate in Europe, it is also interesting to note that we have a
great yearning for marriage, with 39 per cent of women remarrying
within three years. There are though, clearly still many marriages
and families where listening, discussing, negotiating and respecting

each other's hopes, expectations and aspirations are not part of the relationship or the family norm.

Not only do men and women have a lot of work to do in coming to terms with each other's emerging new roles, but also important is the attitude men have towards other men who play non-traditional roles and make unconventional choices. 'I hope very much I will see more of my children than I saw of my workaholic father,' one young man remarked to me. I believe that this is a view widely shared. When, for family reasons, Norman Fowler resigned his Cabinet post early in 1990, both men and women paused and pondered the observation he made: 'We cannot just put our children on a shelf and expect to take them off and dust them down when we feel like it.'

When I worked at INSEAD, the international business school in France, two of my colleagues, Paul Evans and Fernando Bartolemé, published a book based on research into the attitudes of European middle managers and their wives. Called *Must Success Cost So Much?* and published in 1981, the book revealed poignantly the regrets that this group of managers had about their international careers; they had missed out on great chunks of their family experience – 'My daughter will never have another third or fourth or fifth birthday,' said one. The wives at INSEAD too clearly found that the glamour of this international style of life had worn thin: mobility, relocation and their effect on the family will increasingly be an issue for all of us in Britain as the Single European Market gathers speed. In their book *The Reluctant Manager*, published in 1989, Robert Goffee and Richard Scase of the London Business School, point out the similar concerns expressed by the group of women and men managers they studied. These sorts of conflicting pulls on families will become more and more commonplace as our population ages and the demands of the growing number of very elderly fall on the middle-aged, particularly women. The carers issue is also going to be a very major one for us all in the coming years with 'elder care' as well as childcare an item for the boardroom agenda.

The 'Queen Bee' and 'I'm not Sure if I Can' Barriers

A further barrier against our progress towards equality is, sad to say, the attitude some of us have to other women. This can take the

form of the 'queen bee' syndrome, the term used to describe the
approach of a woman who has climbed up the career ladder and
then pulled the ladder up after her – signalling to other women
following her that if she could do it without help so can they. Those
of us who have managed the ascent must leave the ladders in place
and very actively encourage other women up as well as use our
position to see how we can change the culture and systems to make
it easier, not more difficult, for women to develop their skills. The
Prime Minister has, of course, a leading role to play here.

Our attitudes to ourselves as women can also pose a problem.
This is the 'I am only . . .' and 'I'm not sure if I can . . .' barrier.
The doubts we have about our own abilities stop us applying for
that promotion or a place on an education course. I meet countless
women who have enormous talent but who lack confidence to 'go
for it'. I emphasise to them that their experience is important and
their skills transferable – especially the women who have been based
at home for some time and feel they are surrounded by superwomen
who appear to manage their glittering careers and their family lives
so competently. Bury the superwoman idea! I see, and have often
referred to, my life as being 'a patchwork' of different experiences
with every 'patch adding colour texture to the whole'. I now see
one of my 'I'm only' phases as being very useful to my understanding
of the needs of other women and other women returners.

One of my personal 'I'm only' phases has helped me to understand
the needs of other women and other women returners. I went
through this stage when I lived for some years in the USA and every
woman I met seemed to have a PhD, baked her own bread before
breakfast and looked good in a tracksuit. It was then with trepidation
that I embarked on my first degree and, to my great surprise and
pride, discovered that 'I could'! The 'could' bit never expanded to
bread, tracksuits or a PhD, but it did prove to me that my grey cells
were not yet totally used up. The skills we women acquire in
managing households and families make those of many managers
look simple. What we need is to learn to sell and transfer these
skills more assertively to a different environment. We also need to
learn not to be defensive about our role as homemakers and mothers
if that is the choice we have made. Equal opportunities is about
choice.

Recipe for Success

How do we handle these challenges and what are the key issues that need addressing – urgently – if we are to make the most of what is clearly the most favourable period for women's advancement since the war? How can we help our concerns find a significant place on the national agenda – politically, in the community and in the workplace? Here are the priority issues as we see them at the EOC:

Work and the Family

● Get the work/family balance better for *both* men and women; support working parents and carers of elderly or dependent parents.
● Get much more childcare provision without sacrificing quantity for quality. Give parents a choice of what sort of care they prefer. Encourage government, employers, local authorities, educationalists and parents to form partnerships to ensure that care is accessible and affordable and covers pre-school and after-school hours and holidays. Improve the standing and training of childcare workers and look after the needs of carers.
● Push employers for more flexible working conditions for men and women and more 'family-friendly' policies and practices, including enhanced maternity, paternity and parental leave; career breaks and, of course, decent, non-dead-end part-time work which carries the same equivalent pay, benefits, training and opportunities as full-time work; job sharing at senior levels; and attitudes that don't marginalise or berate part-timers.
● Get family issues onto trade union and collective bargaining agendas.

Education and Training

● Break down the barriers in education that still too often discourage girls – and boys – from making non-traditional subject choices and perpetuate the stereotypical pattern of who goes on to study or work in what area. Here, of course, parents, careers advisors, teachers and governors all have a major role to play.
● Invest in training for women – for those already in work to enable them to develop new skills, particularly new technology and

management skills. Training should include personal effective skills and good career/life-planning counselling. Invest also in training those women wanting or needing to return to work and whose technical skills and self-confidence both need a booster. Focus too on the needs of black women and those from other minority ethnic groups who, so often, have particular challenges to meet and discrimination to counter. We need to address the education and training issues with boys and men as well as with women. That means giving boys 'life skills' and introducing far more widely, equal opportunities awareness training for teachers, managers and trade unionists. Assuming that it is just women who need the training and need to change is one of the problems.

• Encourage equal opportunities awareness training for men as well as women in organisations. Through training, help organisations to realise that equal opportunities are about good management practice and use of human resources. Focus too on changing the traditional 'cultures' in so many organisations.

The role of the Training Enterprise Councils (TECs) and Local Enterprise Companies (LECs) in Scotland is crucially important in ensuring that equality of training opportunity really comes about in the UK during the 1990s.

Closing the Pay Gap

• Work towards closing the large gap that still exists between what women earn and the benefits they receive and what men get (women earn 25 per cent less on an average hourly basis than men). Tackle the 'job segregation' issue where women do 'pink collar' jobs – work traditionally done by them and rewarded with 'pin money'.

• Get rid of sex as the determinant of earnings by looking at job evaluation schemes, payment structures in general and collective bargaining.

Equalising Pensions and Removing Other Fiscal Disincentives

• Make sure that women can be economically independent in old age and not disadvantaged by their 'patchwork' lives; remove the fiscal disincentives that still, for instance, make it not worthwhile for some women, in particular lone parents, to get back to work.

Bringing Equal Opportunities out of the Margins and into the Mainstream

How we tackle the above issues is of course vital. How we integrate equal opportunities into the mainstream of thinking, strategy planning, resource allocation and decision making is one of our major tasks in the coming years.

I hope that by the end of the 1990s equal opportunities will no longer be seen as a marginal topic just to do with being a woman, or being black, or being disabled, but will be recognised for what it is: an issue that affects all aspects of both men's and women's lives. At the Equal Opportunities Commission we will continue to work for this goal with the government, Parliament, the Civil Service, professional and trade union organisations, employers through our Equality Exchange Network, educationalists through our Education Network, women's organisations and the voluntary organisations in general, and with the media.

We shall also continue to work with the overall European dimension strongly in mind. Whether we are developing our legal and law enforcement role or our development and educational one, what is happening and will happen in Europe is of the greatest significance to all of us, and to the practical realisation of equal opportunities.

What We Want as Women in Europe

As a member of the European Commission's Advisory Committee on Equal Opportunities for Men and Women, I find it immensely interesting and useful making contact with my counterparts from the other eleven member states. As well as meeting regularly in Brussels we also get together several times a year at conferences on equal opportunities held in one of our countries.

For instance, when Spain held the presidency of the Commission in 1989, we all met in Toledo, to review the progress achieved by the equal opportunities drive in our respective countries. Our findings formed the basis for the Third European Commission Equal Opportunities Action Programme now being developed. This programme highlights the fact that very similar concerns are being expressed by women all over Europe; it focuses on the action now needed to tackle the key equal opportunity issues facing women, men and their families. The action programme points out that a Single European Market with the economic barriers removed can only become effective if the social barriers are removed as well – barriers such as those in the UK that stop women developing and contributing their skills and creative energies. We see both opportunities and threats in the way the Single European Market is developing. As in the UK, the employment opportunities have probably never been greater for women who are well qualified, mobile and who have good family support, but the situation looks very different and threatening for the majority of women who currently work all over Europe in the 'pink collar' jobs referred to earlier in this chapter.

Of the twelve member states the UK has the second highest proportion of the labour market who are women (44 per cent), a rate that is well above the EC average of 38 per cent. Women's employment throughout the EC, however, has grown much faster than men's, and our work as women has contributed enormously to the overall improvement in the European Community's economic performance. Yet, as we see from the pattern of employment here in the UK, so many of the jobs being done by women are tenuous or 'atypical' (Eurospeak for part-time or on a fixed-term contract, seasonal or home work). These are jobs that offer little employment protection, access to training, promotion or occupational pensions. And they are in sectors of employment which the Commission has identified as likely to be adversely affected by the growth of the Single Market – clothing, pharmaceuticals, confectionery, woollen and cotton goods, jewellery, photographic equipment, toys, textiles and footwear.

The work of the European Commission has always been extremely important and relevant to our work at the EOC and to the development of equal opportunities in the UK. The principle of equal treatment of men and women at work is enshrined in Article 19 of the Treaty of Rome, to which all member states are signatories. This relevance is well illustrated by the European Commission's Equal Pay Directive, which led the UK to alter its Equal Pay Act in 1986 to bring it into line with the European definition: that equal pay should apply not only when men and women were doing exactly the same job, but also when the work was of equal value. This was very important because in the five years before the UK Equal Pay

Act was implemented in the early seventies, many employers had simply altered job titles or shifted women around so that they would have no basis for an equality claim. Since the 1986 amendment we at the EOC have supported some key equal value cases through the courts and we shall continue to fight for this recognition that women's work is of equal value to that of men. Marks and Spencer, Tesco's and Sainsbury's are responding.

The work of the European Commission's equal opportunities networks has also been influential, publishing the findings of research by, for example, the Child Care Network, and the IRIS Network which is so successfully developing examples of good practice in innovative vocational training for women.

For equal opportunities to become a reality in Europe and for the issues to be securely on the European agenda, we must now push for the equal opportunities dimension to be integrated into all aspects of Community policy. The Social Charter clearly has a major role to play in doing this. It covers issues which are of great relevance to us as women, and in particular to our employment. It deals with mobility, equal treatment for men and women, equitable pay, working time, conditions of employments and part-time and 'atypical' workers, social security and social protection, the development of vocational training, and health and safety at work which will include the protection of pregnancy and maternity provision, as well as addressing the important issue of fathers having more time to share parental and family responsibilities.

These are all issues close to our hearts as women. We have to make sure that our voices and the voices of all women in East and West Europe are heard and that our needs are addressed. We want to be able to make choices and to help build the Europe we all want for ourselves and our children.

5
Purchasing Power:
The View from Marks and Spencer
by Edwina Currie MP

To the women of Britain Marks and Spencer is vitally important. With its five billion pound turnover, it is our biggest and most profitable retailer. Its contracts with thousands of firms – overwhelmingly, most of the goods sold are still made in the UK – give it an enormous influence on the quality of British manufacturing too. Fourteen million customers a week go through the shop doors, with women accounting for 86 per cent of all M&S spending. Some 70 per cent of all the women in this country and 54 per cent of all the men shop at M&S. One in five of the shirts in Britain and a third of our underwear bear the St Michael label. Even the Prime Minister admits to wearing their stuff (and so do I).

Marks and Spencer and their competitors have been overseeing a revolution, especially in the humdrum world of bras. It appears that these days we don't burn them, we wear them, gather collections of them and will even let you peek a little at the latest lace, just to tell everyone we are still women.

A fascinating article, 'The A to Z of the Bra' appeared in the *Today* newspaper on 29 September 1988. Maureen Barnes, then Marks and Spencer's senior buyer for bras and body shapers, said 'Six years ago 75 per cent of the range was plain or embroidered. Suddenly the reverse has happened, and everything has lace on it . . . Women want a bit of femininity in everything. They feel confident and they are happy for their underwear to be seen.' And sure enough, according to the (female) reporters, she was showing a glimpse of her own lace trimmed camisole . . .

These days, it appears, women are buying a wardrobe of bras: an everyday one, a sporty one, a glamorous version for evenings. Yes, I thought to myself, reading this hard-edged marketing dressed up

with a little titillation. That's me. I need four sets of underwear –
one lot clean and one dirty, in the flat in London and in the
constituency. If the evening dress plunge bra has found its way into
the wash in Derby while the gown is languishing on an hanger in
Westminster, I'm in deep trouble. According to Ms Barnes, however, women are still conventional in their choice of colours. White
accounts for two thirds of the bra market, followed by black and
natural jointly. Red, it seems, is only sold in the months before
Christmas, when the purchasers are – men. Ah, so now we know
what *they* want.

Bras alone are a business in this country worth over £300 million
a year. Market research shows that most women cannot remember
the brand name of the advertising campaigns for most of the bras
they buy. The advertising question was particularly vexing for
Playtex, who were strongly associated with older women and less
than perfect figures.

Playtex managing director John Usher, introducing a £2 million
advertising campaign at the end of 1988, said: 'The name Playtex
conjured up an image of rubberised girdles and stays that would
hold your tired, miserable old body together . . .' So they used a
gorgeous young woman, husky voiced and sophisticated, who wraps
a slinky dress around herself and intones, 'I wouldn't wear anything
without Cross Your Heart'.

The typical St Michael woman customer is better off and older
than the national average. This business is not a supermarket; the
policy of another well-known name, 'Pile it high, sell it cheap'
would produce a *frisson* of disapproval here. Good value and
customer service cost money. Don't expect cheap stuff, and don't
expect that it will fall apart at the seams after the first wash. If it
does, or if you simply change your mind – this is the most amazing
bit – just take it back and change it, or get your money refunded.
Some of these rules have been company policy for donkeys' years.
How are M&S adapting to the needs of the 1990s woman, more
likely to be working, more likely to be full-time, with more money
and less time to spend shopping? A key 1985 speech by the chairman, Lord Rayner, revealed an awareness of the route to take:

A consumer's need for basic commodities is not unlimited.
The providers of those commodities, if they wish to stay in
those markets, have to trade either on price or on convenience
of access, or else transform the commodities into specialities

by ungrading them . . . In the case of food, education and travel have widened people's tastes. Many supermarkets are now selling products which a few years ago were almost unknown to the general public. Changing life styles, less time to prepare food, women with careers, mean there is a greater demand for prepared or convenience food. In particular, there is a rapidly rising demand for high quality foods – Chicken Kiev, Duck à l'Orange . . .

On homeware the firm decided to put in more service: every lampshade has a plug and a bulb. Is that because women are the most likely purchasers? I asked Clara Freeman, one of M&S's divisional directors. 'With our first range of lighting four or five years ago, which co-ordinated with our very popular bedding and curtain designs, we thought, it is the woman who is going in to buy that, and the last thing she wants when she gets home is to find she hasn't got a plug; she wants just to take it out of the carton and plug it in. Like all revolutionary ideas, it's so simple,' she said.

Was it based on market research? 'No, we didn't really go in for that kind of research,' Barry Hyman, head of press and public relations told me. 'It just came up in the kind of constant self-criticism that goes on in this place, criticising ourselves and trying to do better.' Clara continued: 'Then of course we got terrific feedback, and now it's established as a principle: with any goods of that nature, they must be ready to use. It just seemed so obvious.' Obvious to her, and to me, but perhaps not to male manufacturers, at least till now.

The main changes in M&S policy came along with Lord Rayner's 'Chicken Kiev' speech. Many more goods on the shelves now are ready to use, with a far wider range of lines: not just towels but soap dishes and pot plants; not just bedspreads but complete matching ranges of just about everything you could find in a bedroom, including wallpaper, and ditto for the kitchen. I was told firmly that these developments had nothing to do with chasing a new kind of customer. 'One-stop shopping' was certainly a good marketing idea; but the old M&S used to sell everything, including wet fish and biscuits loose from tins. Only in the difficult years of austerity after the war had they concentrated on clothing, with the intention of returning to something closer to Marks' penny barrow diversity of everything for the home as soon as conditions permitted.

The real revolution is in the food departments which now contribute nearly 40 per cent of all M&S turnover. 'Right from the beginning,' said Clara, 'the foods were a very sophisticated, co-ordinated package which brought in a new clientele to M&S.' Some of the stores are food only now. Around 85 per cent of all the customers here are women; four out of ten tend to be in full time work compared with the national average of only one in four – to find the extra money for some items on sale, they'd have to be. In the Marble Arch flagship store I saw the most tempting (pink, not white) fresh veal escalopes at £9.99 per lb. Nearby, five shelves groaned under Scottish smoked salmon beautifully sliced and wrapped at £13.50 per lb. A dressed half lobster in its shell on a bed of potato salad looks wonderful for a mere £9.50. There are more racks of wine than you'll see in any French supermarket; the dozen different brands of champagne start at over a tenner a bottle, with the M&S own label at £15.

I *know* I'm not being fair: you can also enjoy the 7 oz of gently floured and seasoned whitebait, ready to fry, for £1.99; and now I recognize those impressive goujons of sole, immaculately bread-crumbed and also at £1.99 served by a friend at dinner the other night. Come to think of it, six rump steaks, glowing red in a plastic bag for £10.36 is fantastic value, and those two chicken korma pancake turnovers at £1.75 look very tempting for tea . . .

I dare you to find fault with M&S's food counters. Over 6 per cent of our food purchased for home consumption comes from those spotless shelves. Expensive? Not if you want everything ready, all the fiddly jobs done, the dirt removed, the fat cut off, the bones out, the waste already disposed of; not if you want to serve your guests gourmet food at high street prices, hiding the packet so they think it's home made from the Anton Mosimann cookbook. These days, serving the garlic dip in the M&S jar is smarter – everyone starts arguing about which is their favourite.

Women used to slave over a hot stove for menfolk who expected (and needed) three cooked meals a day. With virtually no means of storage, everything had to be made fresh and shopping was a several-times-daily activity. What women want is the work taken out of feeding the family, and a quality they could never hope to reach themselves. 'Put it on the shopping list, darling, M&S will have it on Saturday.'

Lord Rayner also forecast the growth of out-of-town and edge-of-town shopping.

Today's customer wants more convenient shopping, and since so much shopping now is done by car, this means better access and better parking. The problems of accessibility, and improvements in the motorway system favour the development of the free-standing complex and there are bound to be more out-of-town stores.

Is that still the plan, taking into account at the time of writing the disapproval of Chris Patten, Secretary of State for the Environment? It is, according to Barry Hyman, but they don't intend to go overboard. 'In the 1990s we see ourselves as developing three or four sites a year over three or four years – perhaps only a dozen to twenty new sites over the next decade on top of those we have already. We are not looking to dot them every 2 miles up the M1. We will not develop on green field sites. We are looking for land which would otherwise lie unused, on the edge of a motorway or a piece of ex-industrial land.'

What about late night shopping, extended hours, Sunday trading? 'That already happens', said Barry. 'Most of our stores are open for longer hours than they used to be; Bank Holidays are no longer closed days. We're not looking for Sunday trading, though we do it in Scotland where it is part of the tradition, for the three or four Sundays before Christmas.' The staff are asked to volunteer and there's no shortage. There is already late-night shopping in many stores, till 8pm, or later in the food only stores. 'We bus the staff from the West End stores home after late nights if necessary,' Clara added.

Market research tells companies such as Marks and Spencer that there will be much more home and remote shopping by the end of the country; they are sceptical. 'It depends a lot on traffic and parking in town centres,' said Clara. 'If women are going to spend the rest of their Saturdays in a traffic jam or trying to get into the car park, who knows what will happen?! Anything which adds to choice and flexibility and cuts the hassle has to be given serious consideration.'

Lord Rayner didn't think TV shopping would be an attractive idea, back in 1985, regarding shopping as an important social and leisure activity. He's right as far as the USA is concerned, where going shopping is a national obsession. From what I could see on my last visit there, the ever more elaborate malls in city after city are virtually indistinguishable from each other, all with identical chain stores, even the same cookie stalls and muzak; only the fountains look different.

However one form of distance shopping is really catching on at M&S – the catalogue, recently introduced for items such as cases of wine, hampers, bedding, furniture, luggage. You may not have to see your three-piece suite with matching side tables until it is delivered to your home two or three weeks later. Little touches appeal. The delivery van has a phone on board, on which the driver will contact a customer to make a firm appointment or warn of delay if there's a hold up in traffic. When they reach the customer's house, the men will put their white gloves on, deliver carefully and take all the rubbish away. Clara was very keen that I should get the point. 'That added element of service is really fundamental,' she explained. 'This is a personal view, but buying furniture in this country is one of the most difficult activities. That is why furniture was one of our most successful launches. We just said, what is it that people want?'

Clara was clearly exasperated (aren't we all?) at the casual attitudes of many other furniture stores which refuse to deliver for months, and then there's a scratch on the table top and they've knocked a chunk from the wall on their way. Not for the first time in the discussion I noticed how the woman executive kept referring back to her own experience, to the typical woman and her family, whereas the man did not. It was as if she could visualise them, had been there *herself*, whereas he was speaking on behalf of others. Perhaps there is something in the notion, which I have tended to resist – as reverse sexism, if you like – that women managers have something special and different to offer. If the women are customers, they understand them, having worn – wearing – the same shoes.

The in-house credit card helps, of course. Soon after the Store-card was introduced in 1984, two million customers took it. The number now stands at around 2.5 million and accounts for 'a regular 15 – 20 per cent of our business every week of the year, and more at Christmas,' according to Barry Hyman. 'Aren't you ashamed of charging people 30 per cent?' I asked severely. 'More than that!' grinned Barry. 'No, not at all. A lot of customers' (he didn't say how many) 'don't take the credit facility at all. They pay off their purchases every month so the credit is free.' Clara added, 'For the busy family on a Saturday, who can go in and maybe pick up something for the house, and do the weekly shop, and get a few bits of schoolwear for the kids – you sweep through the store with your card and it's a convenience.' You don't even need to write a cheque; the till will do it for you.

And no doubt it encourages them to buy more? 'No doubt.'

Marks and Spencer is one of the nation's biggest private employers of female labour, with the majority of the company's 60,000 employees nationwide being women. 'Most of our shop floor employees are part-timers,' said Barry. 'Lots, obviously, are long serving part-timers, who have been with us thirty years or more. It is usually possible, taking into account the needs of the company, to arrange rotas to suit them, whether it is to allow fetching children from school, looking after a sick husband or caring for an elderly relative.'

John Stanley, the Divisional Director responsible for corporate affairs said in a speech in Milan in 1987 that 'High staff morale is a prerequisite for friendly and courteous service. The key to high morale is the way staff are treated in the organisation.' He listed seven policies which contributed to happy staff. Number 4 was 'generous help to employees who suffer hardship' – and, by implication, being caring when an employee has a problem. Said Barry, 'We always do that, if at all possible. Of course, if they all want every Saturday off, that could be a bit difficult.'

Had the company been thinking about the demographic time-bomb? I was told that recently the board had completed a review on the subject. I was astonished. Here is one of the world's great firms, a major employer; hadn't they had problems with recruitment? No, not really; the review was a precaution, and done because they knew there might be problems in future. But they don't have any trouble at present getting the numbers they want.

It is clear why this is so. Marks and Spencer have for years, as long-standing company policy, been employing women as they would like to be employed, with flexibility and consideration. The working conditions are excellent and the training first-class – where else will you find a shop assistant who knows where the merchandise is and is helpful at the till? The opportunities for promotion are there too. In retailing, perhaps more than any other trade, women start work with no qualifications and can expect to rise, if they want to, through the business to management levels, including running a shop. If Marks and Spencer can do it, there's no excuse for anyone else.

This helps explain why they have no nurseries, and no plans for any at present. To make progress in the competitive world of high street trading, they now utilize every scrap of floor space to sell.

Even the old stock rooms have gone. Instead, stock is available at
a few hours notice from warehouses contactable using the latest
communication technology. It would take a very big need indeed,
which could not be satisfied in any other way, for the company to
turn over valuable and fiendishly expensive city-centre shopping
space to a crèche for employees. Good employer that M&S is, the
need simply isn't there. Add other aspects of the firm's employment
policies, such as profit sharing for all employees after only three
years, the staff then have both the funds to buy their own childcare,
and the incentive to stay with the business, to make the career break
as short as possible and to get back to work. 'As a business, we see
all this as the trend,' explained Clara.

The company only recently decided to give the matter more
thought. In a circular to staff dated January 1990, David Sieff,
Director of Personnel, announced new policies for the recruitment
and retention of staff. Management will identify management jobs
that could be undertaken by part-time staff; whenever a new vacancy
arises, part time alternatives will be considered. The firm intends
to set up a register of staff and ex-staff including recent maternity
leavers who would be interested in working part-time, with details
of dates available, days and hours willing to work. Managers are to
hold discussions with staff *prior* to maternity leave (their emphasis).
Vacancies will be circulated to people on leave and discussions held
with them prior to their return. There's retraining within three
months of return if appropriate.

A 'child break' is to be introduced for managers, to be agreed on
an individual basis, of up to five years maximum, but the employee
has to resign and the years will not count towards pension and other
benefits. Again, a surprise; I would have thought such a company,
conscious now of the need for women to provide for their own
pensions, would have offered restoration of full pension credits if
and when the employee returns. Keeping in touch is, however,
regarded as very important. Each year the employee works for pay
for the equivalent of a minimum of two full weeks. David Sieff's
paper states firmly, 'Normal contact will be maintained throughout
the child break: annual career discussions with the appropriate
personnel manager, a two day annual meeting for an update on the
company, house magazines to be sent.' For staff who take 'short'
maternity leave with a break of four months or less, the existing job
will be held open where operationally possible, with full pay for the
entire period, payable on return to work.

What tickled me most about this excellent, succinct policy note was that the word 'woman' does not appear once. Someone at M&S has been thinking hard about biased language. Sue Dicks (see Chapter 3) would be proud of them.

Interestingly, as well as being an example of a successful woman in a managerial position, Clara Freeman was herself taking advantage of the company's 'short' maternity leave to have her second child. On the day she had started her maternity leave she had been promoted to divisional director, in charge of childrens' clothing, reporting now straight to a board director. She is thus now one of the two most senior women employees in the entire business.

Had she always intended to become one of M&S's most senior executives? 'No,' she said. 'I came in as a graduate management trainee on the normal ladder. I just wanted to do the job I was doing that day as well as possible, and looked forward to the next step. Certainly, in 1975 when I started I did not plan to be where I am today, though I was always keen to get on.' Ah, what a politician's answer. The point is that the company was keen to help too. 'The company has done nothing in the last fifteen years but encourage me. In fact I got my first promotion within the first couple of years to a level of real responsibility, and since then I've had nothing but lots of opportunities, lots of challenges.'

We talked briefly of the changes Clara and her family had made to ensure that her career and her home life were compatible. 'I haven't really made any fresh arrangements,' she explained. 'I set out when I had my first child, Laura, to make sure all the domestic chores were taken care of, and in the two years since, that has proved satisfactory.' And she listed them: the full-time nanny who lives in during the week, the housework similarly attended to, a supportive husband who is good at doing the shopping at weekends. It helps too, I suppose, if you work over the shop.

Did she know when she made her childcare arrangements, about the concessions on National Insurance and tax relief for which both she and the company might qualify as set out in the chapter by Hunada Nouss – this discussion predated the Chancellor's welcome changes in the 1990 Budget? No, not originally; she had heard something about them since, but had not pursued them. I am left marvelling that a brilliant manager essential to her company and used to handling multi-million pound budgets, has nevertheless chosen the most expensive way possible of providing her own childcare.

Still pondering the problem of the demographic timebomb, I wondered whether M&S would try to retain or employ more older workers as well as women? 'The culture of the business has been moving steadily the other way, for people to retire younger rather than older,' said Barry Hyman. 'The retirement age for management generally is sixty, but it's a rare manager who stays that long these days. We have *no* plans to change that.'

In fact managers at M&S can opt to retire at fifty after thirty years' service, though the full pension takes a little longer. Many plan right from joining to take their retirement in their fifties and go off to do something quite different, perhaps part-time. (The Japanese often do that too – saying goodbye to a full-time career with a generous pension at fifty-five and then carrying on with something else, often a family business, till seventy.) Will M&S be able to continue this arrangement, I mused – or perhaps it is yet another aspect of being a good employer which enables them to pick and choose the senior people they want? Barry looked as if he hoped there would be no changes before his retirement, some way off . . .

I recalled a South Derbyshire constituent of mine in his mid-fifties, working locally for an international company, who had tried in 1987, when unemployment was still over two million, to take advantage of his firm's early retirement scheme. He was turned down as a few months too young and came to see me in high dudgeon; I advised him to reapply later. The firm got busier, there was a lot of overtime available, big customers to be seen to. My constituent was simply too busy till late in 1989 to reapply.

He was turned down again, this time on the grounds that he was too late. His firm had taken note of the patterns of demography and the increasing shortage of skilled men, and has scrapped its scheme in the meantime. Sitting across the table from me at my advice bureau, my constituent was most indignant.

'Look at it this way,' I offered. 'Isn't it nice to be wanted?'

'Huh!' he grunted. 'I wasn't actually planning to be wanted for an extra *nine years*. I've got other things to do. How'm I supposed to explain this to the wife?'

I bade Clara farewell and wished her luck as Barry showed me down the two flights of stairs to Baker Street.

Down the road the huge M&S shop was softly lit, silver escalators softly purring, shelves crammed with merchandise. Chattering foreigners argued noisily and tried to decipher 'nightwear'. Arab ladies puzzled over sizes and pulled their scarves closer over their faces at my glance. Clean-looking staff manned the check-out tills, a surprising number of them young men as well as older women.

A blue Chanel-style suit, trimmed with black velvet, gold buttons a-gleam, was sitting on the rack. Perfect for Tory party functions. My size. Everything matching. Blouse nearby would go perfectly, right size too.

'Buy me,' it said. 'Buy me; I'm here, and I'm convenient . . .'

So I did. And walked down Oxford Street, clutching the distinctive green bag, indistinguishable from two million other women that day all feeling that we had found precisely what we wanted.

SECTION TWO

Who's looking after the children?

Whenever women mention their need for childcare, the eyes of men start to glaze over. It isn't quite clear, they imply, as to why the women shouldn't make their own arrangements if they want to come back to work. If a woman makes that choice, what has it to do with the employer? Why should any employer start spending good money to help? With interest rates and the community charge and 1992, they argue, they have enough on their plate satisfying their customers who are screwing down their prices, without playing around with marginal issues like this.

Ah, but . . . it's a different response when the key employee of a fast-moving firm wants a new, bigger company car; if cost benefit analysis were ever done, many of those vehicles would be off the road tomorrow – or paid for out of the employees' own pockets. Not many employers would grumble, 'If he chooses to get here in a Ghia, let him pay for it himself'. Similarly, who would deny the canteen manageress when she complains that she needs a new oven? No one these days would say, 'If they choose to be here over the lunch break, they should make their own arrangements and bring their own food'.

Why not? Because the boss realises that without such arrangements these days, he (it is usually a he) wouldn't have a business. The key computer specialist or salesman would negotiate himself something posher down the road; the shop-floor chaps would pack away their snap tins and roll out, calling the boss a mean beggar. Benefits for the employees might look like company welfare, but in reality this is competition policy – competition for the better workers, or even for having a workforce at all.

I am constantly amazed at how many employers in my constituency, where unemployment stands at 3 per cent, complain bitterly *that they cannot get good-quality staff, skilled or otherwise, and then ask me what the government is going to do about it. It should dawn on some of these good people that part at least of the answer lies in their own control.*

The only available spare workforce in this country is women with small children, two thirds of whom are still at home. If their responses to opinion polls are to be believed, one fifth of those women should return to work at once if the sole problem of childcare could be addressed. There are a million single parents included in that group of women. Two thirds are living on benefit, which even for one child can work out at £85 per week or more. Four out of ten single parents would return to work immediately, if they could get help with childcare. If only 250,000 did so, the net turnaround to the Exchequer could run into over a billion pounds a year. Guess who is paying for that? So here we have a group of women who want to work, who feel their choices are currently being stifled, who are costing us all a great deal of money, who do not come across as the happiest or most successful people in British society today; and who can't get to work because there is no one available, or no one reliable, or no one they can afford, to look after the children.

Childcare is the one issue, more than any other, which affects the employment of women in their twenties and thirties. That's why we seem to go on about it. It is the issue above all others which agitates the mind of the working mother.

The answer to my querulous employer is therefore three-pronged. Why should you help women employees out with childcare? Because they are there, they want to work for you and they can't if you don't. Because it's costing you and the nation a fortune to keep lots of them in idleness, and many don't enjoy it much either. And because the strategies you are currently adopting with increasing desperation in some parts of the country to fill the jobs vacancies – the increased pay, the overtime, the agency payments – are probably costing you as much if not more as helping out with childcare might. You could even save yourself some money.

There's no rule of thumb; employers will have to do the sums for themselves. But they might just find that one of Sue Harvey's childcare vouchers costing £15 or £20 per week for an employee on the permanent payroll are cheaper than paying an agency or double time on Saturday to get the work all done for the weekend. It might just occur to them, if they read Chapter 8, that the company could save a lot of money in National Insurance contributions with an exempted benefit in kind, whether for all employees who need it, or just for that splendid woman in the buying department who is forking out so much of her own cash for a nanny.

There is a lot of material in this section of the book for employers. The best will take these ideas on board as a matter of principle, knowing that good employee policies attract the choosy employee – often the best. But I don't kid myself. Lots of others will do it only because they have to, during the 1990s.

So I make no apology about starting this section with the thoughts of a working mother. Clare Baggott is a PhD computer specialist, a woman like gold dust in Britain. In a more sensible society she would not have any of the problems with childcare she is obliged to face, more or less alone at present. For those employers fired with enthusiasm to set up a workplace nursery, Stewart and Jean Pickering, who are among the most experienced in the field, and are advisers to the Home Office, explain how they set about it and their experiences over the last seven years. If your question is 'Shall I do the same?', read this chapter first; it might succeed in putting the faint-hearted amateur off, as for the sake of the children it should. However, everyone should know about the careful arrangements suggested by tax adviser Ms Nouss, and the neat new voucher schemes endorsed by the government of which several are now coming on to the market. Make your accountants work for you; put these chapters under their noses and insist they tell you how to save money and keep your staff happy all at once.

Until recently, there was a hefty tax on all aspects of childcare provided by employers and regarded by the Inland Revenue as a perk. Suppose the good employer goes to the trouble and expense of providing a nursery; the charge is £30 per child and the employer's subsidy if £60. A low-paid worker on (say) £120 would, till April 1990, have to pay 25 per cent tax on the £60, as well as tax and national insurance. No wonder many found themselves better off at home.

The Chancellor has just made it easier for all of us in the 1990 Budget. Employers were complaining that they were setting up workplace nurseries but their workers could not use them. So now these facilities will no longer be taxed as a perk. The tax concession will also apply to holiday and out of school care for older children, and the nursery does not have to be on the employer's premises. A most welcome change, which is just what many women wanted.

6
The Working Mother

by Dr Clare Baggott
Digital Engineering Co. Ltd

My own case underlined to me the fact that many women work not just because of demographics, or population changes, but for financial reasons. The high cost of housing and living has to be met. There has been a rise in the number of single parents and non-traditional family structures. Indeed, only 5 per cent of families now conform to the model of husband at work, wife at home with the children. Eighty-four per cent of families with children have two parents in the home, compared to 94 per cent in 1971; the proportion of families headed by a lone female has now risen to 15 per cent, while households headed by a lone father have remained at 1 per cent for the past five years. Thus a growing number of women require an income to support their families. Women also want to ensure a degree of financial independence for themselves and their dependents.

In the early 1980s the average career break a woman took to raise children was seven years. In 1988 this had dropped to three years. What will it be ten years from now? Beyond the financial need, advances in equality of education and opportunity mean that a lot of women choose to follow their own independent career. Women, on the whole, no longer equate personal success with supporting the success of their husbands in their chosen professions.

The demographics mean our society needs women to work. They represent 52 per cent of the population in the United Kingdom and will make up 50 per cent of the workforce in the next decade.

I work for several of the reasons outlined above – to help support my family and for a degree of financial independence. And I also work because I want to! It's stimulating, exciting and fulfilling, and it allows me to use my education and training. Society has helped pay for my training (nine years more than if I had left school after 'O' levels): I'd feel guilty about not giving anything back, as well as unfulfilled, if I didn't work.

I am in my mid-thirties, married with two children aged six and seven. I have a first degree in French and history, and a PhD in history. I work full-time in the computer industry. My husband works full-time, also as a computer specialist. We have used a variety of different child-care 'solutions' over the past six years. Currently we have a French *au pair* who lives as part of the family, helps with the housework and looks after the children before and after school, and all day during the school holidays. Apart from that, he and I manage with very little other help.

Women: the Working Majority

The most recent information we have on working mothers at the time of writing dates from 1988. Currently 44 per cent of the work force are women, and it is predicted that by the year 2000 they will make up over half the UK workforce. Of the one million new people joining the workforce in the next ten years, almost 90 per cent of these will be women. Most of these workers will have major family responsibilities and many will be returning to work after a career break.

Most women in the UK today work, even with young children. And progressively more women work all the time. According to the General Household Survey, more than half (56 per cent) of women with dependents worked in 1988, against 47 per cent in 1973. Several thousand more are actively seeking work and appear on Department of Employment registers. Among women with no dependent children, three quarters work.

A quarter of mothers with young children (dependent children under five) now have a part-time job. Less than one fifth of them (19 per cent) worked in 1981. The proportion of working mothers with dependent children under five has doubled compared to a decade ago.

One in five mothers with children aged five to nine work full-time, and half work part-time.

There are more women who work than women who do not work. There are far more working mothers than mothers who do not work. But just as the nation still thinks of 'women' as a minority, and we aren't, so 'working women' are thought of as a minority, and we aren't that either. Women are the majority of the population; women will soon make up over half the country's workforce, and of those women, the majority of them will be working mothers. Working mothers are the norm, not the exception. It is about time attitudes towards us in Britain caught up with that fact.

Current Childcare Options: Theory *versus* Reality

For working mothers, the dominant – *overwhelming* – issue is childcare. Most working mothers could describe the types of child-care options theoretically available. However, they would be un-usual if they have ever had all these options open to them at any one time. For example, as I write, childcare options in my home town of Wokingham, Berkshire, are painfully limited.

Wokingham is an ordinary town. The population has grown rapidly over the past twenty years, in line with the expansion of the hi-tech industry and general economy of the area. It is also an established dormitory town for commuters into London. The econ-omy of the area is buoyant and prosperous. There is practically full employment. But it is by no means an extraordinary, special or different town. Many women live in similar towns throughout Britain. It is very much part of Britain in the 1990s. As most of the children here have working parents, it might be expected that there would be a plentiful supply of childcare help. Not a bit of it.

Childcare options open to working parents here in Wokingham are limited to child minders, private day care (nannies and so on), the occasional private day nursery and *ad hoc* arrangements. These options are expensive, scarce and under-regulated. There are no publicly funded nurseries, no workplace nurseries. No parent in Wokingham can feel that they have a real choice of childcare. This picture is repeated throughout the UK.

When I myself was first looking for an occasional, part-time child minder I rang the Social Services department responsible. They could not help me at all – so I advertised locally, found an unregistered minder and arranged for her to be registered. By the time the registration process was complete, I had had my second child!

Thereafter, it proved impossible to find a child minder with spaces for two children under school age. At one point, when I was still studying, I was able to get my two children into the crèche attached to the college only by pretending that my baby daughter was older than she really was. I managed to work and study part-time from 1983 to 1986, using whatever mixture of childcare solutions I could cobble together – my husband, friends and neighbours, other students. I started working full-time in 1986, when my daughter was two and my son three. I hired an unqualified mother's help/nanny, and used live-out nannies until the children started school, when I started to employ *au pairs*. It has felt as though we have lurched from crisis to crisis in our childcare – hiring and firing; pulling out all the stops to arrange temporary cover when the nanny was in hospital; wondering whom to call first when it was 8.45, the nanny hadn't arrived and I had a 9.00 meeting with my boss.

Until you are actually faced with the need to arrange childcare, you cannot begin to imagine how stressful and time-consuming it can be and how much of a lottery it is. Many of my friends, neighbours and colleagues face similar problems all the time. A colleague was due to return to work after six months' maternity leave. She had to return part-time, as she could only arrange childcare to allow for that. The realization soon hit her that she will deal with this problem for the next dozen years and more! This serious waste of talent should surely be recognized as a problem, not only for the mother, but for her potential or actual employer, and for the country as a whole.

For it is still usually the mother who takes responsibility for arranging, monitoring and paying for childcare, even where the father is supportive. The burden on the single parent is even greater, and when the stress of finding adequate childcare is added to the financial disincentives to many single mothers who work in traditionally female, low-paid jobs, it is not surprising that so many are caught in the poverty trap.

Who Holds the Baby?

We badly need a shift in attitudes to working mothers and their children. For this to happen, seeing children and childcare as a shared responsibility for men and women is essential. This includes the wonderful day when a child is born. It can drive you crazy, trying to arrange time off when a baby arrives. The UK has some of the least favourable maternity, paternity and family leave provision in the whole of Western Europe.

There is no statutory provision for paternity leave or family leave in the UK. Provision is for women only, and only covers maternity leave. And even for women, barely half – 54 per cent – of pregnant working women are eligible for statutory maternity leave because they have worked for their current employer for less than two years. In most European countries all women are eligible on production of a certificate of pregnancy, even if they have only been with their employer for a short time. At present only two or three women out of ten in the UK return to work after taking maternity leave – this compares with four out of ten in France, and eight out of ten in Sweden (and in both these countries, all, not just half of women, are eligible for leave).

While some employers give men formal paternity leave, it is not required by law in the UK. So although most fathers (90 per cent according to a survey in 1984) do take time off around the birth of their children, this usually comes out of annual holiday entitlement or as unpaid leave. As a father in France, you could take up to thirty-three weeks parental leave to care for a child or children while the mother returns to work. The European Commission is now proposing parental leave that will cover all parents, not just mothers. That will add to business costs, but might be a better option than paying to retrain a new worker – if you can get one.

When we compare childcare provision in the UK with that in the rest of Western Europe, we see that there are significant differences. The UK is almost the bottom of the list: only Ireland and Luxembourg have less publicly funded childcare services. In France there is provision in state-funded childcare services for a quarter of the country's youngsters up to two years of age and for 95 per cent of three-to-five-year-olds in pre-primary schooling, eight hours a day.

Workplace nurseries gain a lot of media attention, but in practice there are hardly any. By October 1989 there were still only a hundred workplace nurseries in the whole of the UK. Interestingly, considering the lack of money they provide for other people's children, the public sector as employers – local authorities, hospitals, colleges – provide the best nursery provision for the people who work for them. Since 1986 at least ten councils have opened nurseries for their staff.

The result of this appalling lack of public childcare facilities is that most children are looked after either in their own home or in someone else's. Registered child minders provide places for 4 per cent of children under four. In 1985 there were just under 145,000 registered child minders in the UK. The definition of a child minder is anyone who in his or her own home for reward looks after a child under compulsory school age for any period or aggregate of periods of more than two hours in any six days. The local authorities keep, by law, a register of child minders. The registration process will usually involve a doctor's and a Social Services reference, and a house inspection.

Many local authority day-care advisors feel that the correct place for childcare for the under-twos is in a home-based care environment. In addition, there are regulations which can limit the size of private nurseries to fifty children, and which restrict the proportion of places which can be made available to children up to two. Government opinion also favours home-based childcare. Yet there are not enough child minders in the UK to satisfy the demand for this type of care. There are often local waiting lists of three to six months and more before a prospective child minder can register with her local authority. Local authorities are simply not putting enough resources into support for childcare. If all child minders now on waiting lists were to be registered promptly, this would add a great many to the available pool and ease some of the childcare problems in many areas.

All other forms of home-based childcare are undertaken by relatives, *au pairs*, nannies, neighbours, friends. These are, of course, unregistered, unaccredited, unregulated. Unless you are registered, it is illegal to look after someone else's child on a regular basis in your home for payment. Yet there is only provision for a tiny 6 per cent of our children up to the age of four in regulated, registered, childcare environments. This contradiction has serious ramifications for the health and safety of our children and for the future of the UK economy.

If a close relative is not available to act as the primary care giver for the other 94 per cent of UK children under four, can we guarantee the quality of the care available to them? Is this equality of opportunity for parents and children? No: it means a scramble for what is available; it means a mad panic whenever the childcare arrangements look to be breaking down. It is so inadequate, casual, unsupported, verging on the illegal, that we as a nation should be ashamed.

The Older Child

Childcare for school-age children is no better. Schools in the UK are set up primarily as educational not childcare establishments. We need to differentiate between childcare and education. While childcare should be educationally and socially supportive, it fulfils a different need from education. This is not the place to argue the pros and cons of the national curriculum, though it is interesting, if you want to explore this avenue, to look at the national curriculum provision in Sweden, as well as at its publicly funded nursery schools, childcare provision and statutory support for working parents.

Schools in the UK are open on average for six and a half hours a day, five days a week, thirty nine weeks of the year. Most parents, even in the educational field, work longer hours than that. So what childcare options are available for school-age children when their schools are closed?

Boarding schools or private education, for those who can afford them, can alleviate the before-and-after-school-hours childcare problems, but frequently give shorter terms and longer school holidays.

In a few London boroughs, and some towns and cities in the UK, out-of-school clubs have been established. These will collect children from school (or use the school's facilities for the club), provide them with a snack and look after them until they are collected. But there are probably no more than 500 of these schemes run primarily with childcare in mind. Indeed, currently less than 1 per cent of publicly funded provision for day care for children in the UK is for out of school care. (This compares with 20 per cent provision in Denmark – a statistic that country is deeply concerned about, feeling it to be very much too low!)

Some day nurseries offer out-of-school hours care for school-age children. Other than this, childcare is once more the domain of child minders, relatives, neighbours, mother's helps, nannies and *au pairs*; or else the children have no organized childcare provision and take themselves home and look after themselves until their parents return from work.

Workplace nurseries are only a very small part of the childcare picture. The pressures on and the needs of both parents and their school-age or young adult children are very different from the needs of the pre-school child and its parents.

I discussed this subject with a group of working mothers at our local Working Mothers' Association meeting. We have a membership of around thirty working mothers in Wokingham. Some work full-time, others part-time; some are on maternity leave or are thinking about returning to work; some are established single parents, others are recently separated from their children's fathers. We don't all work in the computer industry; we have a nurse, a hospital teacher, a couple of research scientists and various other professionals amongst our membership. Sarah said that she now found it harder working full-time, since both her children had started school, than she had done when they were babies. She no longer had the broken nights, but was now worrying about finding enough time to read with them, do music practice, keep up to date with school projects. Ann, with a teenage daughter, had to be ready, usually at the most inopportune moments, to take the opportunity to talk, to communicate, to discuss the real feelings and emotional needs of adolescence. When we look at the time scales of childcare, a child will need various types of childcare arrangements and support for at least the first fifteen years of its life. Most new parents cooing over their newborn baby don't know what they're letting themselves in for!

Children frequently need a supportive adult available to them when they come home from school, to share the day or to help with reading or project work. In many ways, when a parent is organising childcare for pre-school and younger children, their needs are fairly easy to categorise and fill. But it is more difficult, as children get older, to provide an acceptable substitute parent figure.

For school-age children, parenting and childcare moves out of the domain of the mainly physical into provision of emotional stability and security. Older children have more diverse emotional and intellectual needs, which parents want to support and help fulfil as part of their parenting role. The role of the parent is not just to provide adequate actual or substitute childcare, clean nappies, regular feeds for their infant. It lasts a lot longer than that and entails much more.

Indeed, quite often, a working mother can feel more isolated when her children start school. Children who have been in any form of childcare before school age are usually there because their parents are working. Working parents are, in that environment, the norm, not the exception. However, once the child starts school, there can be a lot of pressure for a parent, especially the mother, to be involved in the school during school hours. Parents are frequently invited into school – for example, to read with their children. This can make the children of working parents feel set apart from their peers. It can also make the parents feel excluded from school and under pressure to conform to accepted norms.

Few of these attitudes are deliberately designed to 'show up' the working mother, but they do continue to reinforce the idea that a working mother is abandoning and not doing the best for her child. It is particularly galling when the teacher concerned is a working parent too, who might just be more considerate.

Public Support for Childcare

One of the major problems contributing to lack of quality childcare provision is that public funding for it is very low. In its past two terms of office the government has made it clear that though it supports the provision of quality childcare options in the UK, it would not put real money on them. The occasional word of encouragement has been offered, but little or no action or financial help.

The Working Mothers' Association (WMA) was formed in 1985 to provide a national framework for a local support network of working parents. It also serves an important national role in providing information, lobbying policy makers, and trying to influence and effect changes in the law, the tax system and the attitudes of employers, to help resolve the conflict between a parent's responsibility to children and to work. It is in part funded by the Department of Health, so someone in government understands that there is a problem. In 1988 the WMA published its charter, a mixture of long-term and short-term goals in the areas of childcare provision, employment rights and financial support that could be satisfied by the public sector, employers and individual initiatives. I have been a member of the WMA's committee since 1988 and have specific interest in the areas of corporate cultures and the role that employers can play to support the working parents on their staff. For more information on the WMA, or for specific information and help, please do contact the office on 071-700-5771.

Governments recently have said nice things about childcare, but they have not taken a clear stance on the issues. For example, the WMA received a letter from Roger Freeman, Junior Minister at the Department of Health, in July 1989. In it he stated that, in terms of childcare provision:

> We believe that there should be a range of services in each area and that this should be decided locally. Central Government thinks it would be inappropriate for it to be prescriptive from the centre about the level or type of provision. Our primary concern is the health and welfare of the child rather than the interface between the day care services and employment opportunities.

He continued by acknowledging the need for childcare provision:

> I know that in some areas working parents may have difficulty finding suitable provision for their children, but the number of registered private and voluntary day nurseries and registered child minders continue to increase.

I would contend that most working parents in most areas have to put in a lot of effort, and have great difficulty in making suitable childcare provision for their children. Increases in childcare provision are too little, and too slow.

Mr Freeman went on to explain the Department of Health's viewpoint:

> The Government's view is that publicly funded services should be targeted on children from families with particular health or social difficulties who are likely to derive the most benefit. If working patterns are to help people combine employment with their family responsibility, we believe employers should take the lead in the provision of childcare facilities for their staff.

This view directly contradicts the findings of the report of the Commission of the European Communities Childcare Network, published in 1988. The report, entitled *Caring for Children, Services and Policies for Childcare and Equal Opportunities in the United Kingdom*, was prepared by Bronwen Cohen. Some of its main conclusions were as follows:

• UK childcare provision is seriously underfunded and is failing to meet the needs of parents and children;

• A comprehensive national policy for childcare is urgently required with a 'lead' government department taking overall responsibility;

• Public funding is essential, whether it takes the form of direct funding of services, supporting other service providers such as voluntary agencies, or subsidising the purchase of childcare through the tax and benefit system.

Roger Freeman took the opportunity in his letter to remind us that in the Children's Bill, which was to come before Parliament in the autumn of 1989, regulations for independently provided day-care provision were being updated and modernized, and that the registration age limit was to be raised from under five to under eight. The Bill (now the Children's Act 1989) gives local authority Social Services departments the duty to review, in conjunction with local education authorities, their own day-care provision and the facilities they register, and to publish the results every three years. One problem which will result is that it will taken even longer to get child minders and nurseries registered than it does now. These measures would, Roger Freeman hoped, 'increase interest in and awareness of services for young children generally'. But nowhere was there any promise of public support or financial aid for the extension of the public provision of childcare for any age group.

What is Wrong with this Government's Stance?

There can be no real argument against public funding. It is not just that the public purse is deeper than everyone else's – after all, it's our money, and no one likes paying income tax or VAT or the poll tax, in Wokingham or anywhere. But, more importantly, the public interest is not being served by children being cared for in casual or unsafe conditions. The public interest *is*, surely, served by ensuring – not just urging – that a range of safe, affordable options is genuinely available.

There's an odd anomaly about government attitudes to childcare. The Department of Employment's policy differs from the Department of Health. A single parent who is on a government (ET) training scheme gets £50 per week per child towards childcare costs. The moment she starts work, that help stops – and most are then trying to find the £50 (or more, if there are several children) out of taxed income. They can't, very often, and stop at home. So who is wasting public money? While one government department is funding childcare, another takes an opposing view. This is a basic inconsistency on a vitally important issue.

Almost all extensions of childcare provision over the last decade have come from private enterprise. Some local authorities have taken an active role in providing childcare support within their area; others barely fulfil the minimum requirements. And many local authorities are very slow to register child minders or give planning permission and registration support for new day nurseries and workplace crèches.

Parenting is expensive. It gives no tax advantages, just costs. Tax relief is not available to most parents receiving average or above average earnings for the cost of childcare, so most directly paid costs have to come out of net income. If, as an employee, a parent receives any benefit whatsoever for childcare, including the payment of nanny or child minder's fees, the amount concerned may be treated as a taxable benefit. The new exception to this is the provision of subsidised places in workplace nurseries announced in the recent Budget. The only other exemption to tax liability on childcare benefits is for employees who have an annual income of less than £8,500, including the value of the benefit, which rules out a lot of people in Wokingham and everywhere else.

The Inland Revenue's arrangements are highly discriminatory. An employee earning less than £8,500 per year can have subsidised, non-taxable childcare from her employer, but a better-paid employee pays tax on her childcare benefit. Yet we need the qualified professional woman to work; indeed, the biggest threat to the continued growth of prosperity in this country, is the shortage of skilled recruits.

There are some tax concessions for childcare. But figuring out how to take advantage of them takes some skill, or an accountant, and the government certainly keeps quiet about the loopholes which do exist. Read Chapter 8 for more information.

It is seen as the responsibility of the parents to finance childcare, without state subsidies or incentives. This is not entirely an irrational argument, as we mostly choose to be parents, and presumably have some idea what we are taking on. But *most* people choose to be parents, most parents work, and most parents are taxpayers. If I can

have a subsidised canteen at work or a free parking place without it
bothering the taxman, why the fuss over subsidised childcare? Perhaps it is because governments and the Inland Revenue don't take
women's work seriously. Yet I too am a taxpayer! And more women
workers at all levels will be even more desperately needed as the
demographic time bomb takes its toll.

The Battle to Attract Women Returners

Policy makers are aware that the woman returner is essential to the
labour market. All the analyses show that the largest pool of
untapped labour in the 1990s will be the traditional 'housewife' –
or, in current jargon, women who have taken a career break to have
a family, but who have not yet gone back to work.

Employers know that women returning to work after a break have
usually had experience in a working environment. These women
can be retrained; their skills can be updated for today's working
environment. They will also bring to the workplace the organisational and management skills they have developed while raising a
family. They have the skills, the attitudes and the abilities that
employers need.

But if employers want to attract and retain women with family
responsibilities, there needs to be more flexibility to meet
their needs. With a dual role of mother and employee, restrictive
issues such as rigid work hours and lack of childcare need to be
addressed. Recruitment policies and practices need to be reviewed
to remove barriers. Employers need to adopt employment
practices which help employees reconcile their jobs with parent-
hood.

All employers will be trying to attract skilled staff. Yet few are
currently targeting their fringe benefits to the needs of women and
parents. In a survey of 1,000 personnel professionals in 1989
(*Personnel Management* magazine, October 1989), while 10 per
cent of companies surveyed provided mortgage subsidies, only 8 per
cent made better-than-average statutory provision for maternity/
paternity leave, and only 1 per cent offered childcare allowances.
Few employers are creating schemes to attract non-traditional
sources of labour. Only a quarter of this 1,000 had schemes for
part-time work or job sharing. Under a fifth offered flexible hours.
And only one in twenty offered opportunities for home-based work.

In general, employers are being short-sighted. No wonder they are still moaning that they can't get the staff.

Pressures on Working Mothers

I was at a conference in Oxford in October 1989 entitled 'Women – Workforce of the 90s'. Over lunch we were talking about childcare provision and working mothers. We touched on the feelings of guilt that many women feel as working mothers. I said that I was relieved that, personally, I had never felt guilty about being a working mother. Yet I did feel that it was my overall responsibility to ensure that the household functioned normally, according to traditional values. I also felt that I had 'chosen' to go out to work full-time, rather than stay at home with my children or follow part-time work opportunities that would allow me to be with them more.

One of the women leaned across the table and asked, 'Could you really afford not to work?' – and it suddenly dawned on me that I had been living with some fairly shaky base assumptions about my role over the past three years. Although my income is required as part of the family budget, I still felt that my expected role was to be a stay-at-home mum for my children. Because I had 'chosen' to go against my assumed role, I saw my return to work as my own individual problem to which I should find my own individual solution. I viewed my economic role as secondary to that of my husband and, probably arising from this, my husband's role in childcare and domestic responsibilities as supportive rather than equal. Yet the reality was that my income was (and is) absolutely necessary to pay our mortgage and bills. Without my money it would be a real struggle to live with any degree of comfort in a place like Wokingham.

There is still a lot of pressure on women to behave like the stereotyped roles of our mothers and their mothers, who in most cases stayed at home and nurtured their children when fathers were out at work earning the money to support the family. It is no good wishing back those days; most women now would not want to be like that, and if they do, the choice is there. It is a choice most women reject, and more would do so if the childcare options were available.

The Way Forward

When women stop feeling guilty about their role as working parents, and when employers start to count the cost of losing them; when policy makers put some money and action behind their words, childcare provision in the UK will improve. Legislation is needed to improve the current provision for maternity leave, paternity leave and dependent care. Taxation regulations should be clarified.

Childcare Now! is the national mass campaign which brings together parents, childcare workers and organisations to focus public attention on the issue of better childcare provision (the organisation can be contacted at Wesley House, 4 Wild Court, London WC2B 5AU). It campaigns for the implementation of the recommendations of the European Commission's Childcare Network, which pinpointed the UK as Europe's most inadequate provider of childcare for working parents. In particular, Childcare Now! campaigns for:
- Central government co-ordination of day-care policy, earmarked public funding and a clear commitment to improve both services and employment provision;
- A partnership between local authorities, employers and voluntary organisations to provide a choice of high-quality childcare, free or at low cost, for pre-school and school-age children, allowing those who care for them the opportunity to work, study or participate in public life and the children a positive play and social experience;
- Services which provide both for children's education and care within an environment which is anti-racist, anti-sexist and caters for children with special needs;
- An improvement in training, pay and conditions for workers which would include statutory maternity and paternity leave, parental leave, better conditions for part-time workers and time off when children are ill;
- Free or low-cost childcare.

Government can and should take the lead, and put resources into the provision of childcare. Apart from any other consideration, government, including the NHS, is the nation's largest employer. It could encourage more resources into the provision of childcare. It should make improvements in statutory maternity and paternity leave regulations. It could reduce the financial burdens on parents.

Many local authorities and Social Services departments see themselves as the guardians of the rights of children. Social Services
departments play a vital role in helping protect and develop children
at risk, and assisting children with special needs. But they also need
to develop and start to play a major role in supporting the provision
and choice of childcare available to parents and their children.

It is not that policy makers do not know the solutions to problems
in current childcare provision: they are just not implementing these
solutions. A clear policy is the framework that supports solutions.
Partnership solutions – between taxpayer, policy makers, employers,
parents and child-carers – cannot work without policies. Policies,
money and action are the way forward.

Partnership Solutions

Partnership solutions, with the involvement of public funding and
support, local authority leadership, employer support, all with a
community base which reflects the needs of parents and children,
do exist.

One interesting child-minding project is administered from a
converted council flat. Thirty-five registered child minders serve
the local housing estate. The office finds child minders, offers them
training and support and matches them to parents and children. It
will act as an information centre for parents and will provide
replacement minders where necessary. The scheme is paid for
through a pool of funds made up from local rates, government
finance and employers' contributions, as well as the parents' fees.
Subsidies to run the scheme come in part from employers' contributions, but they do not have direct control over who benefits from
the scheme. One of the key attractions of the project is that it offers
equality of opportunity to all working parents in the district.

Unfortunately for us in the UK, this project is based in a suburb
of Paris. There are many similar schemes in operation throughout
France, and a complete range of facilities which provide a choice
of care to cater for different children's needs. Let us hope that we
can start to develop such provision of childcare nationally on this
side of the Channel.

The Role of Employers

Employers are becoming increasingly aware of the need to understand the particular problems of working parents, and to assist them. The predicted skills shortage is adding impetus to changes in the workplace. Traditional work models and patterns need to change to support the preferred working patterns of today's employees.

Employers should, of course, target their resources as effectively as possible. But change is difficult. The owner of a company selling used cars, for example, is not an expert on childcare needs and provision. Yet the odds are that many of his staff have young children, and that his women staff – the secretary, the cleaner, the accountant – are juggling two roles at least and dashing off from work to collect the children from school or from the child minder or neighbour.

Employers do not always know how to effect change. It can be easy to feel that any solution must help, but this is not necessarily the case. The same amount of time, effort and resources can be invested in different ways, with different amounts of benefit. Employers need to consult the working parents among their employees to find out the best way forward. They should also try to look on childcare provision, population trends and skills shortages, working women and working parents, from the longer-term perspective. They should explore alternative solutions. The workplace nursery, for example, is not the only childcare possibility. Helping fund a community-based childcare effort (for example, a jointly funded nursery and after-school club, with the costs shared between employers, local authorities and parents) might be more appropriate and less expensive. It would also be supporting a childcare solution that identifies and addresses the childcare needs of all children, not just babies and pre-school children. If an employer helps provide a workplace nursery place for a baby today, what is there to respond to the childcare needs of that same child in five years' time, when it starts school? What of the parents, these skilled and valued employees, then?

There are three main areas in which employers can help:
- In making childcare provision and/or financial subsidies;
- In changing working patterns and corporate cultures;
- In working in partnership with local authorities, other employers, parents and childcare organisations.

Employers should not feel they have to go it alone. They can work with specialist agencies and organisations for support and advice and partnership schemes. Employers should look at ways of creating overall childcare and dependent-care policies that support all aspects of working parents' needs: from childcare provision to changes in working patterns. Employers will be able to expand these ideas to benefit other employees who, more and more, will find themselves having responsibility for aged dependent relatives, another side effect of the demographic changes.

Here are some improvements employers can consider. Some of the solutions will be more practical for large employers, but even those with just a few staff can give practical help, especially in terms of flexibility and human support. They can:

• Give positive support to employees with family responsibilities;
• Review maternity leave policy, provide paternity leave, provide family leave to cover sickness and childcare crises;
• Give practical assistance to employees by compiling an information pack on local childcare provision; supporting the formation of a workplace working parents' group; giving help and support to individuals at times of family or childcare crises;
• Pay for childcare provision – set up a workplace nursery if appropriate, or help pay for places in a community nursery; set up a childcare cheque or voucher scheme which will help employees' childcare costs; sponsor out-of-school schemes in the local community; sponsor summer-camp schemes for employees' children;
• Review work patterns – allow staff to work flexitime, consider part-time work or shift work; try job sharing – some of the work could be done by someone working from home; reduce hours during school holidays;
• Initiate changes of attitude and policy within the organisation to encourage and support working parents – review 'office norms' around working long hours, team meetings in the pub after work, meetings which overrun without advance notice; encourage line managers to support the family needs of their staff;
• Work with local employers and local authorities to finance and support childcare initiatives in the local community.

Employers can take heart by remembering that if you look after your staff, the odds are that they will look after you. It is not cost-effective or smart to push employees into working patterns that endanger family life. They'll burn out, or they'll leave. Long-term loyalty and effective working, in almost any business you can name, comes from staff feeling that they are looked after in an atmosphere which encourages them to give of their best.

Parents Can Help Themselves

I originally became involved with my local WMA group three years ago when my children were aged two and three and I was looking to return to full-time work. I received a lot of practical as well as emotional support from the group. Since then I have helped set up working parents' groups in my workplace. These are really helping many working parents to feel less isolated and more connected with others 'in the same boat', to share information and to talk over problems – problems of finding child minders, of managing a career as well as a baby, a home, a boss and the daily job. And fathers, as well as mothers, join the groups.

So, parents, until employers and policy makers start moving, you will have to help yourselves. You will find support in your local community, over and above official childcare schemes, in the following ways:
• Join – or start – a local working parent support group. This is a good way to get moral and practical support, to find a nanny share and develop contingency plans to tide you over the next (inevitable) childcare crisis;
• Develop good relations with neighbours and see if you can arrange mutual crisis cover, for example to collect the children from school if you are stuck in a meeting and cannot get away;
• Put effort into developing your personal network and your crisis help-list. Even if you never have a childcare emergency to face, you'll sleep better at night knowing you have some contingency plans.

Parents need to assert and communicate their needs within their community and in the working environment. Your children's school can be a source either of frustration or support. Here are some action plans for parents of school-age children:
• Develop good relations with your school. Get to know your parent governor, or become one yourself. Try to check that the needs of the children of working parents are being represented in the school environment and schedules;
• Talk to the school's head about your desire to be involved in school life, but your need to have advance notice of days off, special events, parents' evenings, sports days;

• Use the fact that both parents work as a positive opportunity for the child's father to become active in the school. Until recently it has usually been the mother who has been closely involved with school, especially at the primary level. If both parents work, they can take it in turns to attend special events;
• Keep the school notified of changes in your schedules, and make sure that you can be contacted in an emergency.

Schools can devise strategies to help support the children and their working parents by:
• Giving plenty of notice of in-service training days to help parents plan supplementary childcare or time off from their work;
• Giving long advance notice of school-based events to which parents are invited;
• Acknowledging in the day-to-day life of the school that many children have both parents who work, so that a child whose mother works, and who attends a school which depends heavily on parental help for classroom reading practice, is not penalised or made to feel neglected or excluded because hers is the only mum who does not come in to school;
• Helping support working mothers by not assuming that it is always the mother who will deal with a sudden emergency at school. Father can be phoned at work as well.

As a working parent in the 1990s, the social population trends and skills shortages are on our side. We do not have to apologise for being a working parent – most people are! Our employers need our skills. Get them to help share the childcare load:
• Talk with your employers and see if you can influence them to provide childcare or financial support for childcare;
• Talk to your employers about work patterns. One of the most significant advances for working mothers will be through flexible work patterns, part-time working, career breaks and job sharing;
• Set up a workplace action group or support group for working parents, or, if one already exists, join it and support it.

And, finally, try to influence policy makers to put real support behind childcare provision. Lobby your local authorities, your MPs, your Euro MPs for increased provision of and financial support for childcare and improved employment rights for all parents.

What Do Working Mothers Want?

We want to see dramatic improvements in the choice and range of quality, affordable, adaptable childcare open to us and our children. We want a dependable, quality childcare environment, whether we choose to be the major provider of that care or whether we delegate the care to others, either day-to-day or occasionally.

We want a steady, dependable income. We want to be able to afford to make choices, to work or to stay at home with our children.

We want to work within a supportive environment that acknowledges our various responsibilities to work and career, to family, to society. We want a working environment that supports the needs of working parents and values and rewards the contribution that all women, including working mothers, make to the success and financial viability of their employer's business and of society.

7

How to Set up a Nursery

by Stewart and Jean Pickering,
Kids Unlimited

Government policy has just changed for the better on workplace nurseries. From April 1990 they are no longer regarded as a taxable 'perk' for the user parent. The tax concessions do not apply however, to nannies and childminders. As a result there is likely to be considerable growth in the number of employer-based nurseries.

We greet with great delight the opportunity to expand a business which has so much potential for good, and has been needed for such a long time: the nursery business.

For those of you who wish to work with young children, to enhance their opportunities and scope for development, we give you our whole-hearted support.

For those of you who look purely at the financial gains, we say, find something else to do. The next generation are too important to be viewed purely as profit.

The driving forces behind the development of childcare are both economic and demographic. Unfortunate but true! We can, however, build on these forces to create something which is wholesome and dynamic for our children.

'We set the scene, the children are the players.'

In 1981, when Simon, our first child, was approaching the age of two years, Jeannie made the decision to return to work. This in itself did not seem to be an event of any great significance. A return to teaching on a part-time basis would bring a useful addition to our income and would represent a step towards a return to full-time teaching for Jeannie. We certainly did not feel that we had made any revolutionary decision.

We had both been teachers, Stewart in physics and maths and Jeannie, the creative one, in dance and physical education. Stewart had moved out of the profession, more by accident than by design, into the shark-infested waters of the music business, having built his own studio. We managed to make a living entertaining hordes of spiky-haired, studded-jacketed punks back in 1979 – perhaps not the best time to be involved in the aesthetic side of music, but every job has its challenge!

Jeannie's part-time job posed a major unexpected problem: who would look after Simon while she was at work? We gave the matter serious thought and decided that a nursery was the right environment for our son, giving him the chance to mix with other children, to relate to other adults, to experience, learn and develop. Having not been parents before, we were suddenly thrown into the misery of trekking down dingy rooms sparsely furnished with tired, battered equipment and staff of shabby appearance whose qualifications were questionable. In many cases, clutching a two-year-old, we found ourselves in school rooms with rows of desks, and were told primly that he had to be dry at all times.

The facilities we visited were in complete contrast to those we had enjoyed during our teaching experience and work on learning methods during our college courses. (Jeannie had done projects on child art aesthetics in education and learning through play.) We were left with a bleak choice: Jeannie's job or our child's well-being. As a compromise we opted to leave Simon with a neighbour while Jeannie worked: at least now we felt that he was well cared for. But we were troubled by the feeling that if we really wanted a nursery for our child, and if we were having problems with quality and availability, there must be other parents in the same boat.

Jeannie began to think again about the research she had done on play and development of the under-fives. In her despondent mood, worrying about Simon, she wondered what this country was offering its children of this age group. At college she had been educated to believe that the first seven years were vital ones. What were we doing to maximise opportunities in those early years? Through observing Simon and watching other children she realised that the potential of this age range was tremendous. Their eagerness to learn, lack of inhibitions and desperate need to explore and experiment were so attractive, such a challenge. Having taught other age groups, where a teacher has to work hard and motivate, she realised what a joy it would be to have such a willing and receptive audience.

The seed was sown. We pooled our expertise: Jeannie her experience of working with primary school children in a creative environment and Stewart his ability with figures and a desire to expand his business and financial knowledge. He wanted music in there too – and, revolutionary for a nursery – computers.

The challenge was to create a beneficial environment and style of working with children which appealed to the child and therefore to the parent also. We did our sums. The business plan looked tight in the early years – financing costs were high and the salary bill the main expense. But if we sold our house (for £23,000: this was 1983) and found a property with accommodation and nursery space, financed it partly by mortgage (£30,000) and partly by a business loan (£26,000). With Jeannie taking the manager's salary, then it looked achievable and secure, since the major investment was in property and in a rising market. We would lose some privacy since we would then be 'living over the shop', and in fact for nine months we inhabited two rooms in the attic. I would continue working as a freelance recording engineer and do some supply teaching to buffer us over the early years.

We had done our homework. But the task of finding suitable premises, the eighteen months of living, often rather miserably, with a small child in limited accommodation, the battles with the planners, estate agents and neighbourhood committees were to test our resilience to the core.

> Who will help me find a suitable location?
> Not I, said the little planner . . .
> Who will help me finance it?
> Not I, said the little bank manager . . .
> And where shall we locate our nursery?
> Not here, said the neighbours;
> Not here, said the local councillors.
> And who will help me fill this nursery?
> Oh, everybody. That was not the problem!

To cut a long and exasperating story short, we finally had the stroke of luck which was the breakthrough we had been looking for. When we say 'luck', we believe that if one makes waves, these trigger a response. The one we had was to a news article covering our planning application and associated wrath of the locals at the possibility of their peace and tranquillity being disturbed by our proposal to bring in hordes of (other people's) undisciplined, scream-ing brats. Nothing could have been further from the truth. A well-run nursery will scarcely be noticed once it is established – not like a school, where all the children are out at playtime, and all go home at the same time, many collected by parents (not from this neighbourhood, of course) blocking the roads with their cars.

The response came in the form of a phone call one evening. The manager of Clairmont Nursery School in Wilmslow, Cheshire, indicated to us that the owners of the premises were wanting to sell: would we be interested? The property was a Victorian double-fronted detached house, in need of some renovation and attention but basically sound. The school had been open for ten years and already had the precious planning permission for forty-eight children. It was open for five mornings per week, three afternoons (two-hour sessions) and a mother-and-toddler group. The then manager had been offered first refusal but had declined for a variety of reasons. The owners felt strongly that the nursery school they had inaugurated should continue to serve children. We respected that view and, with no time even to open a bottle of champagne, signed the papers and set about refurbishing the building ourselves and installing some new equipment during the summer holidays, a task which we only just finished before 'Kids Unlimited' opened for business on 12 September 1983. At 2am when the children are arriving at 7.45am on the same day, you don't feel much like champagne either – not that we could have afforded it.

It was obvious that the former school had been well managed, but on a shoestring. The reputation it had earned was good although its philosophies were not our own and we had some discussions with parents who were determined to have their children reading 'Peter and Jane' books at the age of three.

We endeavoured to keep everybody happy by taking on board the 'school' customers alongside the few full-day nursery children. The old staff and parents assured us that no one would require a full-day service, and certainly we would have no children staying for tea! Parents were convinced that the 'educational standards' would fall, that the presence of babies would limit the older children. The town had no previous experience of day nurseries, so all comments related to imagined concepts. We even heard that advice was being given to parents who asked about childcare facilities that 'Kids' was extremely expensive. In fact, hourly rates were very similar to those of playgroups at that time, only we were open ten hours a day. Somehow a number of the locals didn't seem to grasp the mathematics, or even attempt to understand the service we were offering to parents and children.

We made our mistakes, as absolute beginners will. The children going home at the end of the first day with red paint on their shoes caused some raised eyebrows. In our rush to open we had painted the floorboards in one area bright red, which looked stunning. The paint had been left to dry for four days, but had obviously been applied rather liberally. On the day of opening, under the impact of busy feet, the surface of the paint had cracked, exposing still-soft paint underneath, which then proceeded to spread on to shoes, socks and clothes. We offered to pay for any damaged clothing, but no one took us up on that. We had broken the ice in no uncertain way and had to answer the question 'What make of paint are the children working with?' for months afterwards.

Seven years on, the doubters have been proved wrong. By September 1984 we had forty-five children and were having to turn some away from the morning sessions. In response to demand we opened our second nursery in 1985.

This came about when the premises adjacent to Clairmont were put on the market – a 1950s bungalow built on land once part of the nursery grounds. It was against the advice of our accountant that we pursued the purchase of the bungalow. Our business had not really turned the corner and we really struggled this time to find the finance. The vendors, our neighbours with whom we were always on very good terms, were very supportive.

However, we couldn't bring ourselves to tell them, as from Clairmont's attic windows we watched their removal van park outside, that our finance had fallen through that morning. The supposed rubber stamp by the board of the financial institution who had promised to lend us the money had not happened.

Not ones to be deterred by small problems, we set about finding a replacement mortgage. This was far from simple as we had done the rounds already. On reflection, how we achieved it, we don't know. We think that our contacts and our perseverance paid off. Being wiser, more experienced and less desperate today, perhaps we wouldn't attempt such risky manoeuvres. We could easily have gone bankrupt; as a partnership we had put everything on the line.

There were now no neighbours next door, only the tennis club. Even so, the local population were against our planning application to change the use of the bungalow, citing increased traffic and loss of amenity. The local councillor added his weight to the opposition case. We knew we had a battle on our hands when a site visit was called for, and a group of neighbours stood on the pavement opposite verbalising their thoughts in no uncertain way.

We had already taken a considerable risk by buying the bungalow, and had moved in prior to planning permission being granted. Although the bungalow was ideally situated for nursery use, at that point it was still touch and go whether we would get planning approval. Thus we entered another period of upheaval, but at least the pressure was taken off our waiting list for a time.

Fortunately for us, in planning terms there were no legal sustainable grounds for refusal and with some sensitive lobbying of the other councillors and discussions with the neighbours, permission was granted subject to the provision of eleven parking spaces (for a thirty-place nursery).

Planners and local councils have a difficult task in assessing which is more beneficial – to encourage desperately needed nurseries to develop in locations where they appear likely to have detrimental effects on the neighbours, or where they may contravene Green Belt regulations or may not fit in with the local plan, or to uphold their planning policies. The UK is slowly waking up to the consequences of its historically low provision of nursery places and some areas are now relaxing strict parking and outdoor play requirements. As committed environmentalists we recognised all the issues and the dilemmas our application posed. We certainly are not in the business of making money at the expense of the environment.

We were now well on the way to achieving what we had set out to do. Our nurseries were developing in terms of organisation and curriculum. We 'had our finger on the pulse', Jeannie knowing all of the customers and understanding their needs and those of the children, and Stewart monitoring the administration and financial aspects. We could, perhaps should, have been content with what we had created: two thriving nurseries offering a total of seventy-five places full to capacity, with an after-school service for the older children, set up in a prestigious part of Cheshire. But knowing that what we were operating was beneficial for the children, and was capable of being further reproduced, and with our waiting list yet again increasing, luck beckoned once more. Banner headlines in the local press proclaimed: 'Refuge Assurance proposing to relocate in Wilmslow'; and 'Controversial planning application. Refuge Assurance propose to build on site in a Green Belt area'. After dominating the Manchester skyline for the best part of a century, Refuge Assurance required accommodation more suited to the computer age. Approval was granted for an ambitious design to be built on the chosen site, then owned by ICI.

The thought of 600-plus staff arriving in Wilmslow indicated only one thing: an increasing demand for nursery places! We couldn't afford to purchase more premises, even if we could have located anything suitable, with the Macclesfield area planners as cautious as they are, and with house and land prices rising, pushing suitable big houses even further out of our reach. Perhaps the Refuge had a corner of land available, or part of their office design or . . . ? We rang them.

The Deputy General Manager, David Moss, was co-ordinating the relocation. His wife was nursery trained and qualified and worked for Manchester Social Services. The union was pressing for a relocation package, nursery included. On the company's new site was an old house, Harefield, which was to be converted into staff facilities (gymnasium, snooker, bar, showers and so on), but there was some spare space available.

For the first time we were asked to explain our ideas and philosophies, and to show our nurseries to the managers and directors of a major insurance company. We put the phone down in amazement and looked at each other, hardly daring to breath. A dream was being realised – a dream of good childcare, well financed in good facilities, accessible to working families like us.

To our delight, the response was favourable, although there were some doubts at high level as to whether a nursery was needed or would be beneficial to the Refuge staff. We spent some time assessing contracts and operational factors. Then the bombshell dropped. Although we had already held several discussions, company policy at Refuge dictated that they needed to go to tender. They had visited another local nursery whose owner was invited, along with us, to submit costings and information about services.

We spent the next month writing and rewriting our first ever tender document, determined that we weren't going to lose this one, especially since we had done all of the running. It was a numbing exercise, waiting for an answer. It was good news in many ways for children that the company had decided, more or less, to go ahead with some kind of nursery. But by now we were keen it should be ours.

Our tenacity paid off and the contract was awarded to us. The

Refuge requested that we then visit the premises to advise on the design. They offered us the luxury of having space which, within the limitations of leaving support walls in the place, we could carve up as we wanted. So, with our still-evolving knowledge of nursery design, we set about the task with enthusiasm. Our architect had done a preliminary layout with which we could work.

Those of you who know something about nurseries (and primary schools) will have come to the conclusion that a major percentage of the problems revolve around toilets and washbasins. What is the ratio of children to toilets, of children to washbasins? Is there a need for separate nappy-changing areas, services? If disposable nappies are to be used (most nurseries do use these today), disposal could be a problem. How easy is it for children to gain access to the toilets? Do the children require privacy in the toilets, or should the design enable staff to give assistance easily? Doors or no doors? An early decision on the good location of the toilets/changing/ washbasins will be helpful towards the smooth running of the nursery: don't leave it till last.

We invited the local council's Social Services under-fives officer, Jean Walsh, to check through our designs and to pay a visit to Harefield. All private nurseries must be registered by the Social Services, who are entitled to make regular inspections. There is legislation in the form of the 1948 Nurseries and Childminder's Act, with amendments in 1968.

The Social Services generally decide on the required number of toilets. Usually the Environmental Health and Fire Departments work with them, but the Social Services dictate the policies to the innocent prospective nursery operator, be it private individual or company. We have met with disillusioned personnel and equal opportunity managers of significant experience in their own field who have been reduced to bewildered novices in the 'How to open a nursery' game.

The relative autonomy of local Social Services Departments has led to some strange anomalies. For example, we now have two nurseries in different parts of Yorkshire of a similar size (fifty children apiece). In one we must have five washbasins in the toilet area, in the other ten. In day-to-day operation rarely more than two or three basins are used at any one time. A large number of basins simply means more to clean.

Generally the ratio of toilets to children is one to ten. In some areas we have to have one to six, one to five or even one to four.

Do we have different eating and drinking habits in different parts of the UK or is it something in the water?

With the full support of our local Social Services, and working on the square footages laid down and bearing in mind the walls which had to stay where they were, we divided our allotted space in Harefield into a baby room, a large room for general activities and a more compact area for the computer and the pre-school activities. The nursery is fairly open-plan except for the baby room, and takes only twenty-six children.

The kitchen was easy to design – the contract caterers handled that. All the food is prepared by the caterers to our menus, which are carefully thought out. We avoid synthetic or controversial colourings, and foods containing other additives, such as preservatives, are used solely when necessary and only provided they are 'safe'. We don't add sugar or salt, and as much as possible we encourage fresh vegetables and other products. Vegetarian meals, fish, white meat and red meat are rotated for a balanced diet. Allergies, religious stipulations, medical problems must all be carefully monitored.

Most parents are more than happy with the meals we provide – 'better than at home', some have remarked – and the belief that children won't eat such 'different' meals is untrue. Once in a group, they respond quite differently from how they do at home. We feel we are cultivating nutritious tastes in the children, at least while they are with us. They can get their fill of beefburgers, chips, cans of Coke and so on at weekends!

However, the best of intentions can break down – literally – at times. At eleven o'clock one morning during the early days of our first nursery, our renovated antique cooker suddenly decided to give up on us with lunch half-cooked. The quantity of food was too great for any microwave to handle, so we dashed to the 'Strawberry Pig', our local chippy, for fish and chips all round. A careful check for bones was made (we only took over-twos at the time) and a feast was had by all.

We have a separate space in the kitchen where we prepare the baby foods and sterilise bottles and so on. We use only disposable nappies, towels and tissues, to minimise any risk of cross-infection. Our laundry requirements are therefore fairly minimal, consisting mainly of washing bedding, so we share the washer and dryer with the other Harefield facilities.

Outside we have a flagged area for riding bikes, partly covered to enable the children to go outside even if it is raining, and to enable the babies to sleep out in their prams in all but freezing or foggy weather. There is also a sandpit and a tree-barked area with climbing frame adjacent to the nursery. We are fortunate too in having access to a large grassed area, on part of which we have laid down tree bark and have installed fixed equipment and spring animals. For extra safety beyond our normal day-to-day staff equipment inspection, we have a regular maintenance check carried out by the supplier.

Access to the outside area is essential, especially for children who stay with us for the whole week (Monday to Friday). The play area does not need to be huge, since the children are taken out in small supervised groups. Some authorities, making comparisons with schools' play areas, are demanding 200 square feet per child. For a fifty-place nursery (including ten babies) this means 10,000 square feet. (Perhaps we shall see a nurseries' football league in the near future?!) In most parts of the country this amount of space is not achievable, except with great difficulty and at great expense. Our two areas at Harefield are together only 1,000 square feet and experience shows that is quite sufficient. Certainly we feel that in central London 10,000 square feet is not necessary.

There are still areas of the country without nurseries. Strange as it may seem, we have had calls from two local authorities asking us how they should go about registering nurseries. It makes you wonder how those living in the area have managed without professional day care for their children all this time. And it is worrying when the body that should be controlling standards is asking this sort of advice from those whom it is supposed be monitoring.

Councils in some areas of the country insist on strange arbitrary rules, such as 'No under-twos in the nurseries' or 'No babies under nine months'. Why should these rules be enforced if there is competent care for the children? Another example is 'No nursery larger than fifteen/twenty-four (or some other number) places'. The nationally recommended maximum is fifty places, which we observe. Some local authorities, however, permit up to seventy-five.

Surely the parent can decide if the child is suited to a nursery, and if so at what age. If the local authority's under-fives officer prefers registered child minders for the under-twos, she should be free to *give* that advice, but not to *impose* it. Would it not be sensible to have a basic national standard? Children cannot be so different in Cheshire from in, say, Surrey, Wales or Shropshire. Even staffing requirements differ from region to region, ranging from one adult per two children to one adult per eight.

The variety of local authority attitudes we have met encompasses the whole spectrum of human behaviour from sympathetic, reasonable and supportive to downright obstructive. The authority with the 'Catch 22' clause is alive and well.

But don't be put off by the Social Services if you meet up with the obstructive variety. Quite often they have the children's interests at heart, even if this is not apparent at first. They have a duty to perform in protecting children from the unscrupulous, and we must support them in that.

The 'softly, softly' approach usually works if councillors and childcare advisors are making unreasonable demands, beyond the requirements of the legislation. Usually, at the back of their mind, they know this. If you prove to them that you also care about the children and are not trying to get away with the absolute minimum standard, they are usually open to discussion and to reason. Often matters improve when one difficult person reaches retirement or moves on, to be replaced by a fresh face, who may well be a sympathetic working parent herself.

Obviously a good working relationship is to be desired. Once your nursery is up and running, all the required information, such as registers, contact numbers for parents and so on, should be available to the authorities. The organisation of the nursery must follow the patterns and standards laid down. Any changes, particularly where there has been some disagreement, should be notified to the authorities and discussed. Regular fire practices should be carried out and the children trained to respond to them sensibly. It can be difficult sometimes to get the right *gravitas* into such events, to show their importance, but it is essential that the nursery staff and any visitors take them seriously.

Back at Harefield, we had designed the nursery and checked through our equipment lists to be ready for ordering; and we had booked an artist to add some interest and character to the walls. Thus we eagerly awaited opening day. Our staff were excited to see our company, 'Kids', growing, with the corresponding opportunity for promotion. However, two months before the nursery was due to open, with the builders only one week behind schedule, we were taken aback by a call from the Refuge.

A good year or more previously a survey had been conducted among Refuge staff as to who would require a nursery place when the company relocated. A moderate number had answered positively.

Our views on surveys among staff as to their childcare requirements are by now well known. If a company is looking at a nursery as a way of defusing the demographic timebomb as far as recruitment is concerned, a survey misses entirely one key group of staff – those who do not yet work for the company: the potential new recruits. The staff who are already working for the company have, by definition, sorted out their childcare problems, or have no young children. In a survey starting 'If . . .' they may well express enthusiasm, but that is not the same thing as using a facility once it has been created. They may, of course, not be totally happy with their current arrangements, but if your children are three or four years old, you are unlikely to want to disturb them prior to going to school. Parents also prefer to see a nursery, to meet the staff and to feel confident that the facility is the right one for their child before they commit themselves to a place.

Moreover, the fact that nurseries have not been generally available in the UK for decades – at least since the end of the Second World War – means that most parents are only just beginning to get over the feelings of guilt they experience on leaving their child somewhere other than home and with other adults. Parents have only recently started to accept the concept that exposure to a wider range of activities than home can provide, in an environment purely designed for children, and with staff who are professionally trained in childcare and pre-school education, will be great for the child. These feelings, so mixed, so emotional, must have a profound affect on the questionnaire responses. The dilemma of continuing a career or staying at home with the children is still one faced primarily by women.

In the case of the Refuge questionnaire the responses had indicated that about twelve nursery places were required. We had twenty-six available. In the period between the questionnaire being circulated and the nursery almost opening, this number of acceptances had dwindled to a mere two.

The Refuge management were wonderful. Instead of saying they would pull out, they suggested that *they* would understand if *we* decided to pull out at that time. But we could not let our first journey into workplace nurseries disappear into oblivion before it had even begun. We were confident that, once the nursery was open and parents had had a chance to see its quality, the care and attention we devoted to it, and how well other children were settling, they would vote with their feet.

We therefore suggested to David Moss that we take external customers on board. We had the usual waiting list standing in the wings. The taking in of non-employee children effectively made the nursery immediately more interesting by making it busy. An empty nursery is not attractive to parents, staff or children.

A further advantage was financial. We agreed a commission to the Refuge on external users. This effectively offset some of their costs in the early stages. Thus we opened our first company-based nursery in November 1987.

On day one there were fifteen children. By March 1988 there were twenty-six. Gradually more Refuge employees took up places. Many of the parents were new recruits, but there were also some key personnel women returners. We ceased booking any non-employee children from about September 1988 and received notification from the company that all places would be required by spring 1990.

It is probably worth noting one factor we had all missed. During the first twelve months, many employees were being bussed from Manchester so their children were still using childcare up there. As personnel relocated to South Manchester, use of the nursery by employees steadily increased. In all it took two years for our plans to come to full effect. (That still leaves the question, of course, of what we can do about the non-Refuge children in the neighbourhood whose needs are not being met.)

We have since had feedback from Refuge that the nursery's 'impact on the working day has been nothing but good'. The Refuge employees are fortunate that their company was far-sighted enough to get involved in childcare in the days when the word 'demographics' had everyone reaching for their dictionaries and the headlines were all about rising unemployment. We also consider ourselves fortunate to have met with a supportive management team at Refuge, people who perhaps recognised our determination, enthusiasm and dedication to quality care for children.

The management of a nursery requires careful planning and organisation of day-to-day routines. When only one nursery is involved, most of this is the responsibility of the manager who, in the case of the traditional English private nursery, is the owner. Much of the procedure is informal, not documented, relying on the response of the manager to situations as they evolve.

When nursery facilities are expanded into two, three or more locations, however, the parameters change: the functioning of the nursery then requires a different approach; the systems need clear definition so that the staff are fully aware of their duties and the company's philosophies. The chance to operate three nurseries within a reasonably tight geographical area gave us the opportunity to evolve and test these systems. We found that we could not only maintain standards, but also even enhance them because of our removal from the direct firing line of day-to-day administration, giving us the chance to stand back, observe, criticise and modify. We could do better when we were not quite so bogged down in nappies and building blocks ourselves.

In our first nursery, Clairmont, parents still expected to find Jean on reception, responding to their enquiries, helping with problems and generally providing that important communicative link which smoothes over any difficulty. We took great care in selecting and training managers for our other nurseries and were delighted that the parents who brought their children there also developed a good bond with the staff. Under the lead of our first regional manager, Jenny Haywood, who had become a partner in the business, each nursery started to develop its own character, giving parents some choice.

As we took on more staff, training became the major area to require resources. Even though we allow for personality and individual skills, we need to ensure that our basic philosophies and practices are followed. This applies to any nursery, whether it be autonomous or part of a group. Any nursery proprietor or manager is faced with the problem of having to bring new staff into the fold from time to time and therefore having to make sure that training takes place in an organised way.

That is not to say that training is confined to new recruits, or just to unqualified staff. Nursery nurses generally qualify at eighteen. They all will have been placed in nurseries and schools during their two-year training, and some may have significant experience with children in their own families or those of their neighbours. However, they are beginners as far as working on a regular basis goes and therefore require support, assistance and further training. Even the more highly qualified recruit will need to be familiarised with the specific routines of the nursery, and will need regular assessment to ensure that standards are understood and maintained. There is also the miserable business of having to let staff go if they are not up to it, but it has to be done or they can create a difficult atmosphere and ruin the reputation of the whole nursery.

Any nursery worth its salt will have a continuing input of new ideas and techniques and therefore never stops training. The world of childcare is in its infancy (excuse the pun!), and we have much to learn from abroad, from the experiences of experts and others in the field.

We are gradually pulling the UK into the twentieth century where nursery education is concerned. Its historic position is one of unco-ordinated childcare, relying on volunteers and low-paid workers, or on enthusiastic and well-meaning but perhaps amateurish nursery owners. I am not implying that these people have not, in many cases, done an excellent job, and many adults now look back with affection on their nursery school and playgroup days. But with better financial resources, training, accommodation and equipment, so much more can be achieved.

The factors stimulating this development are nothing to do with childcare or education. The forthcoming shortage of skilled personnel and new recruits, and the economic necessity (no company can exist without staff) of providing childcare to enable women to make that decision to work even while the family is young, are driving us forward.

Our success so far has given us confidence that our investment in training programmes and assessment systems, large for such a small company, are worthwhile. We set about formalising our programmes in 1987 when the Refuge nursery opened, and are making good progress towards a complete training package which will lead to a recognised qualification in childcare. Demographic factors will affect the childcare industry over the next decade, as they will all others. We are pre-empting this by enhancing our capacity to recruit and train.

The expansion of childcare in the UK will have a positive effect on the status of the child-carer. Historically, private nurseries have been poor payers with the owner taking the top salary, making the possibilities for promotion very limited. The few jobs available with the Social Services, hospitals and schools pay significantly better.

We are faced with a dilemma in the UK. Nurseries, both private and within companies, need to be affordable. To keep down the price charged to parents, the only variable which is significantly flexible is the salary bill. This also makes up the largest single item on the list of nursery expenses. Therefore the problem has to be solved of how to satisfy the demand for nurseries while retaining the economic benefits for the company/employer, yet simultaneously improving the status of nursery workers and teachers.

We have been criticised for stating that raw market pressures are a force for good in this circumstance. Beyond the moral issues of minimum wages and good career structure, we can capitalise on the supply/demand scenario which enables 'Kids' to go into any location in the UK and compete with all sectors for staff, including the teaching profession, and offer the chance for career enhancement as the company expands.

Let us persuade companies, the government, parents and local authorities that good-quality childcare is worth paying for. And – a note to the Cabinet. We appreciate the proposed allowance against tax of the nursery costs. This is a major step forward. It will offer greater incentive towards setting up nurseries and will put more money into the industry, enabling us to assist the lower paid parents. The debate over who should pay the fees is, and will be, ongoing: the worker, the employer or the Inland Revenue? The fundamental point for discussion relates to who benefits – the child, the parent, the employer or the country. I believe that investment in our children is vital for the future of the UK; therefore the government should be in part contributing, and the balance should be shared between parent and employer. As far as nurseries are concerned this is now possible.

In early 1988, now with three extremely successful nurseries running, we decided that we should venture further afield. The Refuge was successful and the feedback positive, so why should other companies not require our services? We tried telephoning a few personnel managers.

The climate at the time was very different from today's. Most companies we know have a thick file of letters and documentation from would-be nursery operators and 'consultants', most of whom have no educational and childcare background but simply think it's a good idea. The responses were generally favourable, but some were irritating. We believe strongly in equality of opportunity and apply this throughout our company. Women do not have this equality of opportunity if they unlike men are responsible for their children! Surprisingly, some of the most biased responses we received were from women officials: 'If we provide nurseries, then we'll have to provide hairdressers and dentists'; 'If we provide this for the women, then what about the men?'; 'I don't have any children: will you also subsidise the cost of kennel fees for the dog?'. In many cases middle management were sympathetic, only to find the proposals shot down at board level: 'Women should be in the kitchen . . . at home . . . having babies.' (We still hear this from politicians too – mostly male, mostly older, but not always.)

It became obvious that the North West was not too receptive at that time. Unemployment was still high, so there was little economic pressure for employers to provide childcare facilities. We had heard that things were different in the South East where we were not known, so we set about making our paperwork look more professional by investing in photographs and a brochure. The day this arrived on our desk, the newspaper headlines read: 'Demographic trends indicate shortage of school leavers.'

Almost overnight the story had changed from how we should get used to massive levels of unemployment and how we should organise our leisure time, because we would have lots of it, to companies not able to recruit enough school leavers, staff having one job in the morning and getting a new one by lunchtime, and companies relocating from the South East to Scotland in order to obtain staff. We don't know how we managed to time it so well! We claim it was good judgement on our part. All in all, having all of our systems in place, having our plan of action decided and our paperwork ready gave us the springboard from which to lift ourselves to our current position, recognised market leaders and innovators. Now we are even advisers to the Cabinet Office and speak at seminars organised by government ministers.

We knew we had the formula not only for a successful business, but also to achieve wider and more lasting benefits for at least a proportion of the country's children. There had been similar drives in the past, based also on women being required in the workforce. The northern mills which employed women behind the machinery once provided basic nurseries. During the war, when men were away, their nursery provision was said to be good for the child, but it was amazing how, at the end of the war, children were suddenly better off in the home. As soon as the economic factors changed, the nurseries disappeared. We are sometimes asked whether the same will happen in the twenty-first century, when the demographic hiccup has passed, but I don't think it will. In America, Europe and Scandinavia modern families demand and get good childcare and educational facilities. The UK, although slow off the mark (as usual), is now catching on. I am convinced that good childcare is here to stay for the foreseeable future, and that the only nurseries which will close down when the demographics swing back will be the poor-quality ones.

The next company to make a positive decision to proceed was Body Shop. We had spent many days travelling down to London, talking to companies, hospitals and government departments. Our experience of the speed of most organisations' decision-making processes shows why the UK has a reputation for missing the boat when it comes to developing good ideas. The lightning response of the Body Shop was a breath of fresh air. Of course, the Midland Bank had gone to press saying that it was opening three pilot schemes, but we heard that they had run into problems. Our relationship with the Midland Bank was to come later.

Within two weeks of our meeting with Sue Belgrade at the Body Shop offices in central London, the confirmation came through that we had been chosen to set up a twenty-four place nursery in a house in Littlehampton adjacent to the firm's manufacturing and warehousing base offices. This property then fell foul of the neighbours who made objections. A quick change of plan gave us the go-ahead for a brand-new forty-place nursery, which within what seemed like a very short space of time became a forty-eight place establishment. Fortunately we had already gone through the design procedures with our architects and had ready a basic layout which suited our style and operation. This was duly passed over to the Body Shop's architects who designed the building from the layout.

The building, shaped like an inverted V, has been constructed to the highest specification, with triple glazing and solar panels. The four home bases link into the 'play street' which runs down the centre of the building. The rooms can annex part of the play street by opening their sliding screens, or can close these down for more homely activities. Each room has its own fixed storage units, designed to take the specific equipment, paper, paints and sleeping mats, and has child-height sinks or, in the case of the baby room, a nappy-changing area. Toilets, kitchens, staff room and laundry room are easily accessible. The design is very simple and we haven't needed to change it since its conception.

The Midland Bank's doors opened to us in February 1989. Their three pilots had by then grown to twenty to thirty nurseries and now their aim is 300 nurseries. As we write, most are still in the planning stage. Unfortunately, even such a large and powerful organisation had initially come off second best when face to face with planners and Social Services. We were needed to get the project up and running.

A project manager had been appointed to drive it forward. We met him several times during the winter of 1988 and early 1989 and, after our second meeting, were engaged to set up and manage the bank's first two nurseries in Sheffield and Leeds. Woodville Lodge, the house where the Sheffield nursery was to be sited, was fairly run-down. It had been used as a school for female plasterers. I won't comment on the plastering, a consequence of its having been a school rather than on the gender of the pupils! The architects estimated that the house could not be made ready before January 1990. We all reacted to this with one voice – it was too slow: August 1989 was required. The Midland had to have its first nursery open rapidly. The only option, said the architects, was 'fast track' – that is, there would be no time for tenders but only negotiations on price. The fact that the Sheffield nursery opened its doors on 11 September 1989, only three weeks behind the original target, is a credit to all involved – architects, builders and our staff.

The Leeds nursery opened one week before Sheffield. We took over the unit on the afternoon of Friday, 1 September, and opened on the following Monday. The nurseries are very different in terms of their buildings, Leeds being in a business centre within a very large office complex. Both, however, are working well for the children and parents and we look like having lively parent/staff committees to develop the links between all parties concerned and to organise events, fund-raising activities and so on.

We are now advising and working with many companies and see a steady growth over the next decade. Unfortunately, our success has worked against us in certain contexts. It is clear to us that each nursery is as valuable as the next, and we ensure that each child gets the care and attention he/she deserves. But we were saddened by the reaction of one company manager in our part of the world who stated that he thought we had become 'too high-powered' and that the 'working-class children' of his workforce did not need our approach. We wondered if he had asked the parents – or the children, who were thoroughly enjoying themselves.

We strongly believe that a larger company, if tightly controlled and well-organised, can through its capacity to recruit expertise, make more progress in all areas than a small, local one. The 'Jack of all trades' requirement of the small operator must dilute resources.

'Kids' is much better at all aspects of running a nursery than we were when we started seven years ago.

We sincerely hope that resources are put into the Social Services under-fives departments so that they can respond to the growth of nurseries in the private sector, and than an accreditation scheme is set up to ensure that the public knows that there are companies who are interested in controlling standards. Such a scheme must be organised by an independent body and is surely worthy of government backing.

We believe that the 1990s will be the decade in which the potential of the under-fives is realised. Their capacity to learn is greater than at any later time of life. A certain amount of 'education' of young children may happen by chance, but in a world of ever-increasing complexity the framework must be formulated at an early age. Children have the capacity of coping with explanation through curiosity: a capacity they lose for good as they get older.

We are nurturing the next generation, and no one will deny that it must be done as well as we can possibly manage. At the same time, women must have the right and the opportunity to make decisions regarding their future. Providing good-quality nursery childcare can only benefit everyone.

Thanks to:
 Our parents for believing in us
 Our staff for their continued loyalty
 Simon and Sadie, who inspire us
 Jenny, for being there

8
Getting the Government to Pay

by Hunada Nouss,
Arthur Andersen & Co.

Employers who pay more than lip service to the problems of attracting women to work recognise that, to succeed in swelling the workforce, they must be imaginative in structuring the reward offered in return for women's skills. Providing or assisting with childcare may be the key. A recent joint report by the Institute of Manpower Studies and the Equal Opportunities Commission suggested that up to one million women could be attracted into the workforce if they were offered proper childcare facilities and better job prospects.

For mothers who work, or wish to return to work, the problems of providing childcare are two-fold: availability and cost. There is little publicly funded childcare in the UK. The provision of childcare in the private sector, while growing, remains relatively limited. Mothers cannot be certain of finding nursery places or a child minder close to home. Nursery facilities are not sufficiently flexible to adapt to the long working hours some employers demand. In addition, the cost of childcare is high, particularly when mothers are obliged to engage private home care to meet their child's needs.

Despite initiatives from government, for example, assisting in the funding a national body, The Childcare Association, to advise working parents and employers on the availability of private nurseries and local childcare and in encouraging schools to allow children to stay on after hours, there is widespread conviction that more should be done. The debate has centred around the demand for tax relief for the cost of providing childcare. Until recently, legislation governing the taxation of income in the UK provided no specific reliefs in relation to childcare. Tax relief for the cost of providing a variety of forms of childcare, could, and still may be secured within the framework of the general tax system. However, in response to the urgent economic demand to attract women to work, and to the perceived lack of government support in this area, the Chancellor of the Exchequer introduced legislation in his 1990 Budget designed specifically to encourage the introduction of nurseries funded wholly or partly by employers.

Combing the existing legislation and the new provisions, employers must recognise the opportunities which, until now, have remained virtually unexploited.

Taking Advantage

There is no single approach to any problem. The key to successful planning is adapting the ideas presented to meet the circumstances. If a business's requirements do not fall within the new nursery rules it should explore the other possibilities for relief on payment for nannies and for assistance with home-based childcare.

The underlying strategy focuses on two objectives:
1   To reduce the net cost to the mother of care for her child.
2   To provide tax relief to employers who help, for example by establishing workplace nurseries, thereby increasing and tailoring the availability of childcare facilities.

The initiative lies with employers; the tools at their disposal are the skilful application of tax legislation. This may be achieved through a better understanding of the basic principles and, where appropriate, seeking professional advice.

Establishing the Ground Rules

For working mothers, meeting the cost of childcare out of after-tax earnings is an expensive exercise, and can indeed be too costly. A mother earning £8,000 per annum (£154 per week) in 1990/91 will take home, after tax and national insurance, just £6,199. Out of this she may need to meet the costs of getting to work and contribute towards the mortgage and household expenses, as well as meeting the cost of providing care for her children.

Where an employer meets the cost of a nursery place, childminder or nanny directly on behalf of the mother, an absolute cost saving can be secured.

The ability to secure relief arises from the application of a number of detailed tax provisions which either individually, or together reduce the burden of tax on childcare. Broadly these are:

i no income tax on certain benefits provided to employees earning less than £8,500.
ii specific relief from income tax on the provision of a work-place nursery.
iii no national insurance contributions for employers or employees on the provision of certain non-cash benefits.
iv the availability of tax deductions against the profits of the business for some or all of the costs of providing childcare for employees.

Understanding how the tax system works is a full-time occupation and certainly beyond the scope of this chapter! A brief summary of relevant sections of the legislation is, however, necessary to enable a better appreciation of the issues involved.

Income Tax

For income tax purposes, employees are taxable on total 'emoluments' – that is, wages, salary, bonus, cash allowances and vouchers. In addition, emoluments may also include non-cash benefits provided by an employer, such as a free nursery place.

The Taxes Act draws a distinction between employees earning less than £8,500 a year (£163 per week), and those earning £8,500 or more. The threshold is quite arbitrary: it was introduced to distinguish between higher-paid and lower-paid employees and has not been raised since the Budget of 1979/80. With the average annual earnings for women close to £8,500, this distinction can no longer be sustained. However, the threshold remains important in determining the taxability of certain benefits provided by an employer.

Where an employer provides a benefit to an employee, or meets a personal cost on her behalf, the employee is normally taxable on the provision of that benefit, but *only if she earns £8,500 or more.* In determining whether this threshold has been reached, the total of actual earnings and the cost to the employer of providing the benefit, must be taken into account. Therefore an employee earning £6,500 per year, for whom her employer also contributes £2,000 to childcare for her child, will be taxable on the £2,000 because together they take her up to the £8,500 limit. A similar employee earning £6,000, however, will not be so taxable. Such a contribution from the employer must be a considerable assistance for lower-paid and part-time staff, including those who are job sharing. There is one significant improvement to these broad rules in relation to the provision of childcare. The Finance Act 1990 introduces an exemption from income tax on a benefit in kind where it is a place for the child of an employee in a workplace nursery or a nursery partially funded by an employer, in partnership with others. The nursery does not have to be on the employer's premises. The same applies to partial childcare for school age children after school and in school holidays.

National Insurance Contributions

Class I National Insurance contributions are payable by both the employer and employee on earnings from employment. For the employee 'primary' contributions (not contracted out) are approximately 9 per cent, at the time of writing, on earnings up to a limit of £18,200 per annum (£350 per week). For these purposes, earnings do not include the value of certain non-cash benefits. For the employer 'secondary' contributions rise from 5 per cent to 10.45 per cent on total earnings, dependent upon the level of those earnings.

Corporation Tax

For the employer, the cost of meeting salary and related employment costs, including benefits in kind and National Insurance, should be deductible against the profits of the business in determining the company's liability to corporation tax (or income tax in the case of an unincorporated business). Expenses must be of a 'revenue nature, incurred wholly and exclusively for the purposes of the trade'. These conditions will normally be met in the case of most employment costs. Tax relief is also available for capital costs incurred for business purposes. That means the business can pay childcare costs for its employees and claim them against tax. Furthermore the company does not have to pay National Insurance contributions on the amount, so there *is* a subsidy.

The Workplace Nursery

In 1989 there were about a hundred workplace nurseries in the UK. The main providers are local authorities and health authorities, with only a few in the private sector. That position is changing. Notable companies, such as Midland Bank plc, British Airways plc and Grand Metropolitan plc have set the inevitable trend towards the introduction of more extensive crèche facilities in the workplace. The trend is much welcomed. Workplace nurseries are neither the best nor the only solution to the problem of inadequate childcare. The prospect of taking young children through rush-hour traffic and crowds is not a pleasant one. However, despite such drawbacks, a nursery at work does make the provision of childcare much more accessible to women. It can also tie employees to the company for some years, an advantage at a time of scarcity. The business may also be seen as a responsible and caring employer which may also help recruitment.

Weighing up the costs and benefits of introducing a workplace nursery is by no means simple. On the one hand, the costs are tangible and incurred today; on the other, the benefits intangible. The real rewards may not be seen for some years to come.

Tax relief is just one factor in the cost benefit analysis. On the costs side, tax relief may be secured for a substantial part of the expenses incurred in establishing and running a workplace nursery, by way of a deduction against profits for corporation tax purposes. The tax relief falls into three broad categories:

1   Capital expenditure incurred in constructing or acquiring a building or part of a building for the workplace nursery may be eligible for *industrial buildings* allowance (IBA), representing a deduction against profit of 4 per cent of the relevant cost each year. To qualify for the allowance the employer must be carrying on a *trade* in a *factory* or similar industrial premises: this does not apply to a service activity such as banking. For businesses operating in an enterprise zone 100 per cent IBAs may be available on the cost of the buildings.

2   Capital expenditure incurred in equipping the nursery, including the provision of tables, chairs, durable toys, kitchen equipment and so on should also be deductible on a 25 per cent reducing balance basis.

3   The day-to-day cost of running the nursery, including the cost of professional child-carers, is deductible against trading profits of the company as it is incurred.

As a result, a company may secure relief of 35 per cent (at current rates of tax) of the cost of establishing a workplace nursery.

Despite the availability of tax relief to employers for the costs of providing childcare facilities, there remained a perceived obstacle to the provision of good quality work place nurseries; the income tax charge on employees earning £8,500 or more on the cost of providing the benefit.

This obstacle was removed under proposals outlined by the Chancellor of the Exchequer in his Budget Statement on 20 March 1990.

The changes apply not only to a workplace nursery or crèche on site but also to provision of places in certain employer-funded facilities, which could be anywhere.

It is interesting to note that the relief is designed to promote the creation of additional high quality childcare facilities by employers. This is consistent with the government's frequently stated view that business must respond to the economic challenges of the 1990's, and address directly the problems of attracting women to work. Accordingly the provision of cash allowances or vouchers to meet the cost of a private nursery, child minder or nanny does not currently attract the same favourable treatment.

This said, the provisions have been drawn quite widely to maximise the take-up. The exemption applies to nurseries run at the work place or elsewhere by the employer. In addition, it extends to nurseries run by employers jointly, either with other employers, voluntary bodies or local authorities. The conditions require that the employer is wholly or partly responsible for financing and managing the provision of care. The provisions also apply to out of school facilities for older children. Such childcare facilities will, of course, be required to comply with any legal requirements for registration by the appropriate local authority.

At the time of writing, Parliament is in the final stages of the Finance Bill 1990. Practical considerations covering the extent of employer involvement in the establishment of nurseries have still to be addressed fully. These issues will ultimately determine the form and pace of growth of childcare facilities in the UK. It is therefore advisable that employers should agree the form of schemes with the Inland Revenue before commencement.

The additional advantage in structuring childcare in this way is that the benefit will not attract any National Insurance contributions.

Planning: Benefits in Kind

The availability of specific exemption from taxation for the provision of childcare applies only to employer funded nurseries. Numerous

other forms of childcare support and assistance remain, not covered
by this exemption. If employer-funded nurseries are not appropriate,
tax relief may be secured through thoughtful structuring of earnings.
This is illustrated by the case of Janc on page 158, showing a series
of examples.

Jane earns £8,500 per year. She receives net income after tax and
National Insurance of about £6,530 (Example A), out of which she
must pay for a nursery place for her daughter, Susie. For Jane's
employer, the salary and employer's National Insurance contributions are set against profits chargeable to tax. In this example
corporation tax relief is taken at 35 per cent, resulting in a net cost
to the company of £6,022.

Where the company meets the cost of the nursery place, *at no
additional cost to itself,* Jane's net disposable income increases by
£289 (Example B). This is attributable primarily to the saving of
employee's and employer's National Insurance on the benefit in
kind. Income tax is, however, still payable on the combined value
of the salary and benefits in kind.

The full potential of the situation has yet to be exploited. In
practice it may take immense skills of persuasion to convince Jane
that a reduction in salary to £6,400 plus the provision of a nursery
place for her Susie, costing £2,000, can result in an *increase* in net
disposal income. However, Example C illustrates how relatively
simple tax planning can generate an increase in Jane's net income
by £614 over what she would earn without planning. This is
achieved because Jane is no longer treated as a 'higher-paid' employee. The cost of providing childcare becomes tax-free to the
mother, but remains tax deductible to the company.

It is important to note that these calculations are done for the tax
year 1990/91 ending 5 April 1991. They can be reworked for any tax
year, the principles being the same. It must be emphasised at this
point that proper structuring of the arrangements is essential to secure
relief. To ensure that the benefit is not taxable, for a 'lower-paid'
employee, it must not be offered in terms of a salary sacrifice. Similarly, the arrangements should not provide for a cash option in the
event that the childcare benefit is no longer required. Following a
principle established in the leading tax case of Heaton *v* Bell, if the
employee is given a cash payment that is treated as salary; if the
employee receives a benefit in kind combined with a cut in salary
such that the full salary can be restored if the benefit is given up, then
the Inland Revenue will treat the benefit as if it were salary and tax it

Jane's Gain: How a Cut Becomes a Benefit

Example A: Employer pays Jane £8,500 p.a. (£163 p.w.) out of which she meets the cost of Susie's nursery place of £2,000 p.a.

JANE'S INCOME		COST TO EMPLOYER	
Salary	£ 8,500.00	Salary	£ 8,500.00
Income tax	(1,373.75)	Employer's NI (9%)	765.00
Employee's NI	(597.56)		£ 9,265.00
	£ 6,528.69	Corporation tax relief	(3,242.75)
Nursery place	(2,000.00)	Total cost	£ 6,022.25
Net income	£ 4,528.69		

Example B: Employer pays reduced salary to Jane of £6,665.14 p.a. (£128 p.w.) and meets the cost of the nursery place.

JANE'S INCOME		COST TO EMPLOYER	
Salary	£ 6,665.14	Salary	£ 6,665.14
Income tax	(1,415.04)	Nursery place	2,000.00
Employee's NI	(432.42)	Employer's NI (9%)	599.86
Net Income	£ 4,817.68		£ 9,265.00
		Corporation tax relief	(3,242.75)
		Total cost	£ 6,022.25

Net increase £ 288.99 attributable to NI saving.

Example C: Employer pays reduced salary to Jane of £6,400 p.a. (£123 p.w) and meets the cost of the nursery place.

JANE'S INCOME		COST TO EMPLOYER	
Salary	£ 6,400.00	Salary	£ 6,400.00
Income tax	(848.75)	Nursery place	2,000.00
Employee's NI	(408.56)	Employer's NI (7%)	448.00
Net income	£ 5,142.69		£ 8,848.00
		Corporation tax relief	(3,096.80)
		Total cost	£ 5,751.20

Net increase £ 614.00 attributable to NI and tax saving.

accordingly. For National Insurance purposes, payments in kind are excluded from earnings only if they meet two conditions:

1   They must be provided to the employee under a contract between the employer and the supplier of services. If the employer merely hands over cash to discharge the liability of the employee, Class I National Insurance contributions are payable.

2   The items must be incapable of encashment by mere surrender.

For the system to be effective therefore, the employer must contract directly with the nursery, child minder or nanny. This is less easy to achieve where the employer proposes to contribute in part only to the childcare costs. In such circumstances it may be appropriate for the employer to contract directly with the carer, but arrange for the mother to contribute towards the cost paid by the employer by way of deduction from her salary. If in doubt, the company should discuss the matter with the Inland Revenue, in advance of commencement of any scheme; this will avoid disputes later.

In addition, where packages are to be structured to take advantage of tax reliefs available, consideration must also be given to the non-tax implications. Payment in kind may affect pensions entitlement while the reduction in National Insurance contributions may restrict eligibility for benefits. It is therefore advisable to seek professional advice before agreeing to such a package.

Planning: the Voucher Scheme

A new initiative in the childcare area is the introduction of the childcare voucher. The scheme is designed to allow the employer flexibility in determining how much assistance it offers to employees, and allows employees flexibility in choosing childcare facilities to meet the needs of their child.

In one scheme (described in Chapter 9) the vouchers are supplied by Luncheon Vouchers Limited to employers. Employers award the vouchers to employees, who use them to meet the costs of childcare. The carer, who will become affiliated to the scheme, then redeems the voucher from Childcare Vouchers for cash within five working days.

From a tax perspective, vouchers awarded by an employer to an employee represent a benefit in kind, whether or not the employee's emoluments are above the £8,500 threshold. They are therefore taxable on the employee, at 25 per cent (or 40 per cent if earnings are greater than £20,700). There is, however, no liability to national insurance contribution (neither employer's nor employee's) on the value of the voucher. The government is effectively helping by this amount.

Take, by way of example, an employer recognising the need to assist employees in the provision of childcare. The company offers a cash allowance of £500 to eligible employees. The cost to the company of such an allowance, taking into account national insurance and tax relief, is £354. Childcare vouchers provided at the same cost to the company may result in an increase of £409 in the net disposable income of the employee. Thus the employee retains more than four fifths of the value of the benefit. This is illustrated in the example of Molly on page 161.

In practice the introduction of a new benefit scheme brings with it the problems of establishing eligibility. Companies may be required by equal opportunities legislation to make such vouchers available to all employees (both male and famale) with children, where both parents work, or where it is necessary to provide childcare, but this is not an Inland Revenue requirement. This draws the net fairly wide, and may reduce the take-up of the opportunity such a scheme affords. The attractions not only for working mothers but also for employee motivation as a whole should not be overlooked. The scheme is flexible in so far as employers may contribute as much or as little as they wish. In addition the scheme caters for the provision of childcare in a number of ways – registered child minders, private nurseries, nannies and *au pairs*, recognised out-of-school schemes, and even relatives – with the minimum of administration on the part of the employer. This is in sharp contrast with a direct-subsidy arrangement where the employer is required to contract with the carer to ensure that no liability to national insurance arises. The scheme is, however, less tax-efficient than a direct subsidy for lower-paid employees, as in the latter case they are not liable to income tax at all on the value of the subsidy. In cash terms there may not be much to choose between a voucher and a straightforward contracted payment or the provision of an on-site facility. Ease of administration and employee preferences may be the determining factors.

Molly's Dream: Voucher Scheme

Example A: Employer pays Molly £6,500 p.a. (£125 p.w.) Her daughter's child-minder costs £1,000 p.a.

MOLLY'S INCOME		COST TO EMPLOYER	
Salary	£ 6,500.00	Salary	£ 6,500.00
Income tax	(873.75)	Employer's NI (9%)	585.00
Employee's NI	(417.56)		£7,085.00
	£ 5,208.69	Corporation tax relief	(2,479.95)
Child-minder	(1,000.00)	Total cost	£ 4,605.25
Net income	£ 4,208.69		

Example B: Employer pays Molly £6,500 p.a. (£125 p.w.) plus £500 cash allowance

MOLLY'S INCOME		COST TO EMPLOYER	
Salary	£ 6,500.00	Salary	£ 6,500.00
Allowance	500.00	Allowance	500.00
Income tax	(998.75)	Employer's NI (9%)	630.00
Employee's NI	(462.56)		£ 7,630.00
Child-minder	(1,000.00)	Corporation tax relief	(2,670.50)
Net income	£ 4,538.69	Total cost	£ 4,959.50

Example C: Employer pays Molly £6,500 p.a. (£125 p.w.) plus childcare vouchers to the value of £545.

MOLLY'S INCOME		COST TO EMPLOYER	
Salary	£ 6,500.00	Salary	£ 6,500.00
Vouchers	545.00	Vouchers	545.00
Income tax	(1,010.00)	Employer's NI (9%)	585.00
Employee's NI	(417.56)		£ 7,630.00
Child minder	(1,000.00)	Corporation tax relief	(2,670.50)
Net income	£ 4,617.44	Total cost	£ 4,959.50
Net increase	£ 408.75	Net cost to company	£ 354.25

Planning: Employing a Nanny

For many mothers wishing to return to work, the only practical solution to the problem of securing adequate childcare is employing a nanny. The cost of doing so is high. The nanny's salary and benefits, including for example the provision of living accommodation and subsistence, or the cost of a car, is met out of after-tax income. In addition, as the nanny is treated as an employee, the parent must pay employer's National Insurance on the nanny's salary. Thus a nanny earning a gross salary of £7,200 p.a. (£138 p.w.) will cost the family £7,848 out of after-tax income. This represents gross earnings to the mother in the region of £10,500. The net income receivable by the nanny will be in the region of £5,670. Therefore, out of gross earnings of £10,500, 46 per cent is paid over to the authorities in the form of tax and National Insurance. If the mother is a top-rate taxpayer, the government takes in the region of 57 per cent. The numbers make uncomfortable reading.

On a more positive note, living accommodation provided to a nanny free of charge should not normally be treated as a benefit in kind. Specific exemption is given where the provision of such accommodation is necessary for the proper performance of the duties, or usual for the better performance of such duties. However, other benefits, such as subsistence or the provision of a car for private use, may be taxable, depending on total earnings taking into account the benefits provided. We are hitting the total £8,500 barrier again. A salary of £6,000 p.a. (£115 p.w.) plus a small car should not render the private use of the car taxable. Alternatively, where the nanny requires transport – for example, to take children to school – it may be sufficient to provide the nanny with the use of a car for the performance of her duties but not for personal use, in which case no question of benefit should arise.

The introduction of the community charge may impose an additional cost on the family who employs a live-in nanny. The Inland Revenue has recently confirmed its interpretation that the community charge is a personal liability. A nanny, who previously would have had no obligation to pay rates, must now pay the poll tax out of after-tax income. If the mother pays the charge on behalf of the nanny, this is treated as a benefit in kind chargeable to tax and national insurance.

In addition, the tax system imposes on the parent employing a nanny the administrative burden it imposes on all businesses of acting as unpaid collector of taxes for the Inland Revenue. The parent is required to deduct income tax and employee's National Insurance from the nanny's salary and pay these, together with the employer's National Insurance contribution, to the Inland Revenue weekly or monthly on the PAYE system.

Little direction or assistance is given by the Inland Revenue on the administrative aspects of the system; it is not complex, but care must be taken to operate it properly. Failure to account to the Inland Revenue correctly for tax and National Insurance due on the nanny's pay will result in a liability on the parent, not the nanny. A guide to the reporting obligations is given in the Appendix on page 165.

Employers can assist in relieving the financial and administrative cost of employing a nanny by engaging the nanny directly, and providing her services to the parent. The principle is identical to that shown earlier in the chapter for Jane on the taxation of payments in kind. The mother in this example, Sarah (see page 164), is £1,196 better off for giving up part, even a substantial part (over £7,100), of her salary. She also has fewer administrative headaches and legal responsibilities. Life can be even simpler if the company pays a nanny agency. The effect can be quite marked, as illustrated. Structuring arrangements in this way reduces the National Insurance cost to both employer and employee. In addition, the arrangements relieve the parent of the PAYE (pay as you earn) reporting and accounting obligations as the nanny is now an employee of the company.

The Way Ahead

Few employers can afford the luxury of ignoring the issues which concern women at work. Failure to invest in the future of women can only result in failure to invest in their own businesses.

The analysis in this chapter demonstrates clearly that the investment can be achieved, at least in part, at little or no additional cost to the employer. Even where costs are incurred, the tax system can be applied effectively to reduce the cash outlay.

That said, more can and should be done to enhance the tax reliefs for the costs of childcare. As Britain moves towards closer

Sarah's System: Employing a Nanny

Example A: Employer pays Sarah £17,000 p.a. (£326.92 p.w.) and Sarah pays nanny £7,200 p.a. (£138.46 p.w.).

SARAH'S INCOME		*COST TO EMPLOYER*	
Salary	£ 17,000.00	Salary	£ 17,000.00
Income tax	(3,498.75)	Employer's NI	1,776.50
Employee's NI	(1,362.56)	(10.45%)	
	£ 12,138.69		£ 18,776.50
Nanny's salary	7,200.00	Corporation tax relief	(6,571.78)
Employer's NI	(648.00)	Total cost	£ 12,204.72
Net income	£ 4,290.69		

Example B: Employer pays Sarah reduced salary of £9,894.52 p.a. and pays nanny direct.

SARAH'S INCOME		*COST TO EMPLOYER*	
Salary	£ 9,894.52	Salary	£ 9,894.52
Income tax	(3,684.38)	Nanny's salary	7,200.00
Employee's NI	(723.07)	Employer's NI	
Net Income	£ 5,487.07	– mother (10.45%)	1,033.98
		– nanny (9%)	648.00
			£ 18,776.50
Net increase	£1,196.38	Corporation tax relief	(6,571.78)
		Total cost	£ 12,204.72

integration into the European Community, it might take a leaf from the book of its Community partners. In France, Belgium and Italy over 85 per cent of under-fives are in publicly-funded childcare facilities. In Britain the comparable figure is 44 per cent, with only 2 per cent of children under two years of age. In addition, a substantial number of countries provide specific tax reliefs for children. The Fre..ch tax system provides a credit for tax purposes of up to FF3,250 (approximately £325) per child against the cost of providing care for children under the age of seven where both parents work. Germany offers a similar system of relief for one-parent families, as well as basic child allowances for all families. In the Netherlands proposed legislation introduces tax relief for employers providing childcare facilities of 175 per cent of the costs incurred.

Further afield, in the United States, the cost of childcare services borne by an employer are not taxable on the individual up to a value of $5,000. In addition, a tax credit may be secured for childcare costs borne personally. Oddly enough, despite the weaker tax incentives in this country, a far higher proportion of women work than in any other European Community nation but Denmark.

There are opportunities to offer similar reliefs in the UK – for example, by exempting childcare costs from the benefits-in-kind rules, or by returning to the former system of child allowances. For the present such changes are not forthcoming. Pressure groups will continue to lobby for reform. In the meantime employers must act to take advantage of the opportunities which are available now.

Appendix: Employing a Nanny – Sarah's Reporting Obligations

Sarah is required to notify the Inland Revenue that she is employing a nanny by completing form P223. The request for the form should be made to the tax office closest to Sarah's home address; it is this office, and not, for example, her own tax office, that will handle PAYE reporting. If the nanny has been in previous employment, she should have a form P45; she should complete part 3 of the form and send it to the Inland Revenue.

The tax office should provide tables for income tax (P16) and National Insurance (CF7), deduction cards and payslip booklets (P30BC(Z)). It is normal in such circumstances for the Inland Revenue to provide 'simplified' tax tables. The Inland Revenue should also notify Sarah of the amount of 'tax-free' pay due each month. This, together with the tables should allow her to determine the amount of tax and National Insurance to withhold from salary payments and work out the employer's National Insurance payable. She should also provide the nanny with a payslip showing gross pay and the amount of tax and national insurance deducted.

Sarah must complete the deduction cards on a weekly or monthly basis, as appropriate, and account for the tax and National Insurance to the Inland Revenue within fourteen days of the end of each tax quarter (5 July, 5 October, 5 January, 5 April). She must make an annual declaration (P37) at the end of each tax year summarising salary payments and tax and National Insurance, and return the deduction cards.

When the nanny leaves her employment, Sarah should complete a form P45 on behalf of the nanny. She must forward part 1 of the form to the Inspector of Taxes, while the nanny keeps parts 2 and 3.

Life is a lot easier if all this is done by Sarah's company, treating the nanny as just one more employee!

9

Childcare Vouchers

by Sue Harvey
Managing Director, Luncheon Vouchers Ltd

Fifty years ago Britain's male workforce was snatched from the factory floor and mobilised to Europe's battleground. Overnight there mushroomed a boom industry in local council day nurseries, workplace nurseries and private nannies as women – many of them raw to paid work – took up the mantle in business and industry. But as suddenly as it had grown, the childcare industry collapsed with the surrender of Germany when demobbed troops returned to civilian work.

Now the tide looks set to turn again. If CBI projections are correct – and early trends are already supporting the forecast – a return of women to work in numbers never seen since the 1940s is about to happen. Four out of five new jobs created by 1995 will be filled by women. Women already account for 44 per cent of Britain's workforce. There is a pool of more than one and a half million women with young children who could immediately add to this number. But will they? Can they? What encouragement is there for them to do so? What do these women want?

Luncheon Vouchers Ltd is the staff-benefits specialist of the French Accor group of companies. Inspired partly by the remark of Joanna Foster, Chair of the Equal Opportunities Commission, that childcare facilities would 'replace the company car as the benefit for the 1990s', we studied the market, researched the childcare industry and polled the views of scores of non-salaried young mothers.

What we established was not unexpected, but nevertheless alarming. There can be no doubt that factories and offices alike are changing their work patterns to accommodate the flexible needs of female employees. Larger numbers of part-time workers are being recruited, flexible working-hour schemes introduced; the practice of job-sharing is becoming more widespread and termtime-only employment is gaining increased ground.

On the other hand, more liberal social and moral welfare attitudes towards unmarried motherhood have bitten deep into what had previously been considered by employers to be a dependable pool of available single women. The rapid rise in numbers of single-parent families, so many of them caused by a record national divorce rate now affecting one in three marriages, and the disappearance of Victorian attitudes to illegitimacy has thwarted whatever innovation was developed in work-hour flexibility. The single women who used to be available to work are now changing nappies and collecting child benefit. Put simply and in practical terms, there are fewer 'in-laws' available to look after the children while the mother goes to work; less shared income to cover the cost of childcare. Fewer than half of all working mothers say they can call on the assistance of relatives.

But despite the difficulties, do these work-pattern changes address what young mothers – married or single – actually want? We concluded that they do not.

Luncheon Vouchers Ltd has a formidable track record in the staff-benefits industry dating back to 1955. Through our existing Luncheon Vouchers client base, we established that the burning issue with young mothers – many of whom had left salaried employment to raise their young – was the cost of professional and trustworthy child minding. Apart from the cost, for many in large cities the logistics of transporting their toddlers by tube and bus to company-subsidised nurseries was and remains unattractive.

Playgroups are not an alternative for working mothers as their hours are too limited. Local authority nurseries are as rare as gold dust and often available only to children and families with particular needs. We established that because the fees and enrolment expenses of private nurseries and nannies were often out of the reach of the lower-paid, a phenomenal 47 per cent of all working mothers in England and Wales call on the support of relatives for the childcare of under-fives. This compares with 4 per cent who use registered child minders; 13 per cent who use playschools; 0.9 per cent who use local authority day nurseries; 0.8 per cent who use private day nurseries and 0.8 per cent who have nannies and/or *au pairs*. So barely one mother in a hundred uses nurseries or nannies; nearly half use a relation instead.

In terms of expense – at 1990 rates – the average weekly costs of childcare facilities were as follows: local authority nurseries – free or up to £20 per child, according to financial circumstances; registered child minders – £35-85 per child; workplace nurseries – £100-150, but with the company normally paying two thirds of the cost; private nursery schools – £60-120; and nannies/*au pairs* – £60-80 per week plus live-in costs. Although for most mothers financial considerations dictated their choice of childcare, for some the convenience and flexibility of personal choice of child minder (either close relative or easily accessible registered carer) was paramount in their thinking.

Already convinced that Britain flounders far behind its European neighbours in providing either encouragement or childcare benefit to its women workforce, Luncheon Vouchers Ltd decided to look at its American Childcare Voucher programme before proceeding further in the UK. The American government, unlike that in Britain, operates a 'Dependent Care Tax Credit' system. Under Sections 125 and 129 of the Internal Revenue Code it allows employees to set aside a certain portion of their pre-tax salaries for dependent care, such as that of children, elderly or physically or mentally handicapped dependents. This pre-tax allowance can be claimed in three ways: annually on the tax return; by the receipt system where the employee pays and claims costs back from her company on evidence of a receipt; or, most recently, through the Childcare Voucher scheme.

What appealed to American employers and employees alike about the Childcare Voucher scheme was that it would provide a simply executed 'middle man' between the child-carer (invoice point) and tax authority (rebate). Whatever the method, however, the whole system is regarded as a public purse responsibility. This is not so in the UK. Our 'tax on employee benefits' attitude has done little to provide inducement to work. Luncheon Vouchers, for instance, were introduced in Britain in 1955 as a result of a demand by business wanting to take advantage of a post-war tax allowance to feed employees of companies unable to justify the burdens of subsidized staff canteens. Despite lobbying ever since, the tax-free allowance has remained the same in the UK at 15p per day. What could be bought for 15p in 1955 and what little, if anything, can be bought for this amount today do not merit comparison; if the amount were updated to today's values, it would be £2.20. However, meal vouchers alone have a £2 billion per annum value.

Nevertheless, from what we learned from our sister company in

America and what we had researched in Britain, Luncheon
Vouchers felt certain that it had got closer than most to establishing
what work-eligible women wanted. In the autumn of 1989 – three
years after the launch of Childcare Vouchers in America – we
decided to introduce a similar scheme in Britain.

Women wanted the security of mind to place their children in
safe child-caring hands while at the same time not being too much
out of pocket. They need to feel it is financially worthwhile to work.
They wanted to choose their childcare themselves, not feel obliged
to accept 'nursery or nothing'. Even before its official press launch
in October 1989, the response from companies large and small was
overwhelming.

So what is our product – this answer to what women want? In
its simplest form it is a financial-value voucher which a company
can provide to its staff and which they can use to pay for childcare
for their children. The company gives the voucher to the mother,
who uses it to pay the child's carer, who sends it in to Childcare
Vouchers Ltd, which pays her and bills the company plus a fee.
Money changes hands only between the company and Childcare
Vouchers Ltd and between CCV and the carer. A typical voucher
is £20 per week; the minimum service charge payable to CCV Ltd
is £30.00 and varies between 4.5 and 6 per cent thereafter, depending on the volume of business.

The success of the scheme hangs on its total flexibility: flexibility
of choice for the mother to select the preferred child-carer for the
child; flexibility for the employer to decide who should receive the
benefit and how much the company should contribute. Childcare
Vouchers can be accepted by: registered child minders; registered
nurseries/day-care centres/community nurseries; workplace nurser-
ies/partnership workplace nurseries; local authority centres; nannies
in the employee's own home; close relatives (full or half-blood);
recognised out-of-school schemes; and nanny-share schemes.

The most obvious benefit for the employer is attracting and
thereafter retaining valuable women employees. The scheme provides the employer also with various benefits, including the knowledge that the vouchers cannot be exchanged for cash or for any
other service other than childcare (and therefore cannot be misused).
The voucher is also a visible sign and regular reminder of the
company's commitment to staff. A further advantage to the business
is that the 'perk' – if it is perceived as such – is not 'lumped in' with
a salary and therefore less of an enviable upset to those workers

not on the scheme. In addition, since they are neither cash nor exchangeable for cash by the employee, the vouchers are free from National Insurance loading for both the company and the employee and thus become a more cost-effective means of providing specific staff support than paying the workers extra to buy their own childcare. Their cost can be offset against corporation tax. There is no capital expenditure; no additional employees to take on, no premises to find, no extra insurance as would be necessary for a company crèche.

The single largest drawback remains the government's view that Childcare vouchers should, in common with other non-contributory schemes, be deemed to be 'benefits in kind' and therefore taxable. Likewise the childcarers – those redeeming the vouchers – will have to declare the weekly income received from Luncheon Vouchers Ltd to the authorities, although it must be said that family carers having only one child on contract would probably come under the current personal allowance ceiling (£3,005 per annum at the time of writing) so would not be taxable.

The system is now up and running. Its success lies in its simplicity and in the fact that it is made so attractive to women employees and, indeed, single working fathers.

However, sometimes archaic management attitudes still have to be overcome. The realisation that the demographic timebomb is now on a short fuse has failed to penetrate a large number of corporate and public-service manpower planners. Others, who have become aware of the seriousness of forecasts for the 1990s, are cautious of the impact which adoption of the scheme could have on non-eligible staff – for instance, workers of equal grade and scale who have either no children or whose children are over the age of fourteen (the age at which children can be lawfully left unattended).

Aside from employer misconceptions, we have also had to address ourselves to the reluctance of some sections of the Social Services departments to accept that the private sector has a contribution to make. There is without doubt an element of mistrust of our motive. Some Social Services agencies have difficulty in believing that companies like Childcare Vouchers have a real interest in the problem. Particularly at local level they could offer more co-operation to our 'Hotline' phone service which exists to provide working mothers with, among other things, the names of registered child minders. There is even a misconceived suspicion that the private sector does not have the same commitment to the plight of working mothers as do public services.

Of more immediate concern, though, is the delay in the screening and registering of child-carer applicants. Depending on the region, the all-important police Criminal Records Office checks can take an inordinate period of time to process. There is currently a long backlog of child minders and private day nurseries waiting to be registered. New legislation due to be enforced in 1991 – and which we fully support – is to tighten up even further the registration of child minders as detailed in the Nurseries and Child Minders Regulation Act of 1948 and other statutes. Currently it is a criminal offence for unregistered child minders to care for children under the age of five (unless supervision is at the child's own home). This age limit is to be extended to eight in 1991. Even more child minders will join the long waiting list for official registration before that time. The irony is that the Departments of Health and of Social Security and, collectively, the local authorities of England and Wales are the three single largest employers of women in England and Wales. The whole process of police clearance and registration – obviously very necessary – has to be made more efficient if Britain's working women are to be encouraged to place their children in the care of professionals and our scheme is to become 100 per cent effective.

So much for the downside. Luncheon Vouchers Ltd has been around for long enough to understand that new concepts take time to develop. The positive side of the Childcare Voucher scheme is that it has, for the first time in recent employment history, brought real encouragement to young mothers anxious to begin careers or return to work after childbirth.

For the registered child minders – for so many decades a relatively unrecognised service industry – the scheme offers the following benefits. They can be sure of being paid, and promptly. Working with participating employers gives them increased status and better opportunities for further business and increasing their earnings. The scheme offers them support-lines to professional agencies and to Childcare Vouchers' 'Hotline'.

In my view our system, simple in concept and even simpler in administration, not only answers working mothers' needs, but also provides solutions for forward-planning employers. The benefits to childcarers have already been mentioned.

It goes without saying that Luncheon Vouchers Ltd, keen to

protect its international image and high reputation for professionalism, went to great lengths to ensure that the scheme was not open to tax abuse, fraud or any other statutory or moral corruption. Childcare Vouchers commissioned extensive research and opinion from financial advisers Price Waterhouse; we looked at the legal aspects and incorporated the full recommendations of legal advisors into our contract terms and conditions. Finally, we sought the opinion of the Equal Opportunities Commission.

It was from this final consultation that we received less than positive guidance, even though the EOC could not have been more helpful in volunteering support. In broad terms, where childcare assistance or benefit are on offer, it is unlawful to refuse them to a person on the grounds of sex or on the grounds that they are married (or unmarried as the case may be).

Taking the general ground-rule further, we put a series of questions to the EOC. Here are a few of their responses:

Q Could a company give childcare assistance only to female employees?

A No. This would amount to unlawful direct sex discrimination. As distinct from indirect, direct discrimination may not be justified. In any case, an invariable rule of this kind is simply not good management practice. It reinforces the idea that only women have childcare responsibility and excludes men who care for their children whether as a result of choice, divorce, spouse–illness or bereavement. Childcare Vouchers should therefore be available to both employee sexes.

Q Could a company give childcare assistance only to single parents?

A This is open to challenge on two grounds. First, it would threaten to discriminate directly against married people (unlawful marriage discrimination), and second it could discriminate indirectly against single males as opposed to single females.

Q Could a company give childcare assistance only to a limited group of employees – for example, secretarial/administration staff – where there is a recruitment and/or retention problem?

A The range of possible circumstances makes it difficult to speculate on the potential discrimination. It would very much depend on

individual circumstances in particular industries and localities. The
main pitfall here appears to be that certain classifications and
disciplines of labour fall also into male or female domains; for
example, secretaries, catering staff, nurses, primary teachers and so
on tend to be female and therefore there would be fair ground
for complaint from male industrial/business sections, for instance
shop-floor, middle managers, security departments and so on. The
EOC would take a common sense view on this issue.

Q Could a company limit its expenditure by giving childcare
assistance only to employees below a certain salary level or grade?

A For similar problems of grouping disciplines (above), it would
much depend on the type of business being carried out. In companies such as those in the oil and gas exploration and production
industry, the lower grades tend to be female-loaded (for example,
high numbers of administration clerks, secretaries, receptionists,
catering, typists and so on), where the higher grades or pay-scales are
filled by engineers, geologists, draughtsmen and so on, traditionally
recruited from the male gender.

In summary to our research questionnaire responses, the EOC
stressed: 'We appreciate that the legal requirements are complex
but, in essence, we believe that the issue is one of need and fairness
to individuals, not of giving benefits to persons of one sex or the
other or according to marital status.'
However, the vagaries of 'equal opportunities' are high on the
minds of today's legislation-fearing personnel director. Unlike other
employee-related statutes where definite lines of fair and unfair play
are laid down for all to observe, rules pertaining to equal opportunity
in the place of work are seldom defined until an employee grievance
has been lodged and the process of official arbitration – or worse,
resort to the courts – has begun. It is for this reason that we welcome
the EOC's offer to provide case-by-case advice to those companies
considering use of Childcare Vouchers.
From our further research of some 500 UK companies and
organisations employing, variously, between eighty and 36,000
staff, it appears obvious that there cannot be hard-and-fast rules on
the adoption of Childcare Vouchers. High-street retail stores, for
instance, employ a male-to-female ratio of 15:85; county councils
in England and Wales tend to employ male-to-female ratios of
30:70; building societies and high-street banks 40:60.

But need there be a feeling of unfair play by those not eligible for Childcare Vouchers? Our questioning of all groups of employees (not only working mothers) suggests that so long as the Vouchers cannot be misused or turned into direct cash benefits for the employee (and our system protects against such fraud), there should be little or no colleague envy. Most adult working women sympathise with the lot of the working mother. It was pleasing to receive returns from the males polled who generally responded to the question whether they would feel resentful, with a 'So what?' nod of indifference or approval. For those who did feel left out, perhaps a word in their wives' employers' ears would help!

Luncheon Vouchers Ltd sees Childcare Vouchers as just the start of a new method of employee relations in the UK. With a world-leading reputation in the staff-benefits industry (operating now in South America, the USA and throughout Europe), we are already planning for the years to come when vouchers for career development training, further education and career-related programmes can be added to our list of services. Those who have to balance career and family could enjoy equal opportunity with everyone else, male and female.

For the moment, however, Childcare Vouchers have brought a simple solution to what women want. They also provide part of the answer to what employers want. At their launch in October 1989 Angela Rumbold MP, Minister of State for Education, Vice-chair of the Ministerial Group on Women's Issues and Co-chair of the Women's National Commission, said of Childcare Vouchers: 'There are many talented women with family responsibilities who are needed in the workforce. Some firms are already taking a lead in attracting women back to work. I hope this private sector scheme will encourage more companies to follow their example.'

With the number of school leavers declining by 25 per cent between 1989 and 1995 and a further loss of one million from the top end of employment resource, we hope to have provided that encouragement. It's certainly something that women want.

SECTION THREE

Employers:
The Buck Stops Here

'Employers must look to women and not discount them as second-class citizens. Women will account for 80 per cent of the total increase in the labour force in the period to 1995,' said Norman Fowler, the Secretary of State for Employment, speaking at Cambridge on 18 November 1988, a year before leaving the government.

Fourteen months later his successor, Michael Howard, was extending the time scale. In answer to a question from Maureen Hicks, the member for Wolverhampton North-East, on 13 February 1990, he said, 'It is estimated that women will take up 90 per cent of the additional jobs that will be created between now and the year 2000. Employers will need increasingly to ensure that their work arrangements meet the needs of women.'

Maureen is a pal, a hard working lively Tory, just the sort we need more of in the Commons. In my first Parliament (1983–7) I was the only woman member with both young children and a seat outside the London area. For four years, dealing with the children's crises on the phone, I felt like a freak and often wondered if I had done the right thing. It was a relief to be joined in June 1987 by Maureen, who also has school-age children, and we now have another Midlander, Labour's Joan Whalley from Stoke-on-Trent, in a similar position.

I listened with delight to that exchange. This was no heat-of-the-moment comment from a minister under pressure. Maureen's question was first on the order paper, so Michael Howard was producing a reasoned response, stating policy and carrying it forward: employers will need to know what women want, and change their employment policies accordingly.

It ain't quite that simple. The chapters that follow are intended to cover some of the main areas where women can be expected to find employment in the busy years ahead. The employers who have contributed the chapters are already doing their best yet finding progress tough going. High-street banks and building societies, the insurance companies, indeed all the modern service industries are heavy users of female labour – though not traditionally, as Diana Balsdon of NatWest shows. Once all bank clerks and cashiers were men – as, of course, were all the customers. Today bank employees are likely to be predominantly female, in a ratio of three women to two men. Local councils and health authorities will probably have two women staff to every one man, with women predominating on the care side, working as, for instance, home helps or nurses or in catering. Retailing is likely to employ an even higher ratio of female staff, perhaps three to every one man; Chapter 5, on Marks and Spencer, has some points to make here too.

Organisations like these are huge users of women. There has already been some adaptation to what women want over the years, with a preponderance of part-time and flexitime working. In some firms the tradition is paternalistic anyway, in others flexible working has been the result of a casual attitude to women's careers, letting them work part-time if they want provided they give up all thought of career advancement and further responsibility until the children are grown up and the women are willing to come back full-time. A few of them might just make it to supervisor before they retire.

It has dawned on some employers, whether from necessity or out of conviction, that this won't do for much longer. With the demographic timebomb looming, it is clearly crazy to spend a lot of money training up young women only to lose them, possibly for good, when they wish to start a family. The Japanese try very hard to create company loyalty among their (male) workforce, a tactic which pays off in higher productivity; why shouldn't other businesses do the same with their women employees? In this section of the book are examples of how some businesses are trying, though it has to be said that there is as yet little experience of how the new improved policies will work, while the number of women employees who are really benefiting from improved practice is still very small.

If they find, as well they might, that the majority of women still prefer to clear off when the baby is due and come back five years later, these companies may just have to try a little harder to attract them back earlier. This may well mean an increase in the current handful of workplace nurseries, aided by tax relief; it may mean *moving more locations outside the main cities of the south, to avoid the misery of the 'commuter baby'. It may mean more outwork, more electronic links with home, more 'funny' shifts. It could mean more contracting out, more use of sub-contractors, women working for themselves or from home. As John Naisbitt and Patricia Aburdene, authors of* Megatrends 2000 *put it, coming to the same conclusions from a different direction:*

'New technologies have changed the importance of scale and location and extended the power of individuals . . . linked by telephones, fax machines, couriers and computers, a new breed of worker is reorganising the landscape of America today, and Europe tomorrow. Free to live almost anywhere, more and more individuals are deciding to live in small cities and towns and rural areas. This megatrend of the next millenium is laying the groundwork for the decline of cities.'

Margaret Jackson's chapter on BP reveals a very different background. A major international producer and manufacturer which traditionally has employed women only in smallish numbers in clerical and lab assistant positions, BP now finds that pressure both from within the ranks and without – the national shortages of scientists and technologists – obliges it to change its long-standing male culture. Senior management has been very supportive of the proposed change and clearly understands all the issues covered in this book. Real progress will be made, however, when the board of directors responds with enthusiasm to the increasingly persistent query at shareholders' meetings, 'When are you going to have a woman on the board?'

Companies like these are trying very hard and have good reputation as enlightened employers; that's why I asked for their contributions. They find it difficult to make progress. How much harder the future will be for businesses which aren't trying at all!

10

The National Health Service

by Barbara Young
General Manager, Parkside Health Authority

Three quarters of the National Health Service's million employees are female. It is the largest single employer of women in Europe. What's more, nearly one-third of the nation's annual crop of well-qualified young women (with five or more GCSE/'O' levels or their equivalent) enter health service careers.

That's the good news. Now for the bad news. In spite of generations of women employees passing through its hands, the NHS has progressed only a little beyond the terms and conditions it operated in the days of Florence Nightingale, who, I understand, might have been a little confused about her gender anyway.

The picture of women's employment in the NHS until recently was typified by features familiar from other employment fields:

1 Despite their greater numbers, women have had far less chance of being promoted to the more senior posts in the NHS. For example, in 1987, only 17 per cent of unit general managers (bosses of hospital or community services) were women. In nursing, the pattern is that 37 per cent of senior nursing posts are held by men in spite of men making up only 8 per cent of the nursing workforce. The nurse with the highest public profile since Florence Nightingale, Trevor Clay, who led the Royal College of Nursing with so much flair, was, at the end of the day, a man leading an organisation whose membership was predominantly female.

2 Though equal pay for equal work has been the norm in the NHS for many years, women's generally poorer performance in the promotion stakes means that men in the NHS are far more likely to earn higher incomes.

3 The normal pattern of work for men is unbroken full-time work. Women's working life, shaped by the need to care for dependents,

tends to include breaks in paid employment and periods of part-time work. Women who do not work full-time without any breaks in their working life are penalised by losing prospects of promotion.

My own career in the NHS, where I've tended to be the most senior woman around, might seem to break the mould but in reality simply confirms much of the traditional pattern. Though I've hit the higher spots on the promotion ladder, I'm flagrantly single and childless (a fact for which the human race ought to be duly thankful – passing on workaholic genes like mine would be rank cruelty to both my children and the world!). My appointments have often been openly noted as being against the grain. Ten years ago, when I was offered a senior post at the Westminster Hospital, the phone call making the offer was accompanied by a 'Strange really, y'know, the Westminster doesn't take women.' And my much loved chairman in Haringey was very apologetic in offering me a job as the youngest ever female district administrator and as almost the youngest district administrator of either sex, when he blushingly muttered he hadn't really envisaged the post going to someone 'quite so young and quite so female'.

One of the features of the NHS that has given me a lot of kicks over the years is the way in which its workforce spans every socio-economic grouping, from cleaning persons up or down (depending on how you look at it) to consultant medical staff. Each grouping varies in the problems it faces, yet in many cases the necessary solutions are in common.

Let's look at two groups which between them account for 70 per cent of the NHS workforce: doctors and nurses.

Half of all students entering medical training are now female. In the profession as a whole only 26 per cent of medical staff are women and at consultant level that percentage drops even further. In some specialities, often the elitist ones, women are very few and far between and there is no doubt that until very recently, and possibly even still, a male chauvinist lobby existed. Surgeons generally tend towards the more macho and chauvinistic end of the scale – it's something to do with wanting to spend your life cutting people open. Only 2 per cent of consultant surgeons are women. Of the three women surgeons whom I know personally, all three are as tough as old boots and two of the three are childless. The third is entirely aberrant, having four children. Closer examination reveals, however, that with each pregnancy she worked on until either labour, or an inability to reach the operating table because of the bulge, intervened. She then took six weeks' annual leave to deliver, recover and settle the baby with the nanny before returning to work. To all intents and purposes her work pattern was that of an honorary man. In many cases women take up consultant posts in less glamorous specialities where competition is less severe or where working hours are less erratic, and there is a clustering of women in the diagnostic specialities, such as pathology and radiology, in psychiatry and care of the elderly, in paediatrics and in general practice.

The pattern of medical training makes it a wonder that anyone survives, far less women with or without children. A long five-year undergraduate course is followed by periods of greater and lesser hell working as a junior doctor, often living in the hospital with long unsocial hours. Competition in many specialities is so intense that no concessions are given to domestic circumstances. Schemes exist to keep women doctors in touch during career breaks and to offer part-time work in training grades on return, but the reality is that a career break is incompatible with the current male-defined model of successful progression through training and the part-time work schemes are almost impossible to make happen in practice.

In response, women doctors are adopting coping strategies which in themselves are pretty bizarre. The normal pattern is for women doctors to concentrate on their career through undergraduate education and junior doctor training. By busting a gut, they speed up the promotion ladder as quickly as possible and attain the coveted consultant status at around thirty-five. This brings with it two boons. It is almost invariably a job for life with considerably autonomy, answerable (in the minds of some consultants) mainly to that great doctor in the sky and certainly not requiring one ever again to be dependent for a job on a reference from one's boss. It also means that after fifteen years of being on a rota every third night for getting out of your bed to see to patients, you can inflict that exquisite joy on your junior staff and get up only infrequently when they have run out of ideas and are panicking.

Freed from disapproving bosses and debilitating and trying on-call work, these women consultants rapidly get pregnant and have two or three kids in quick succession, supported heavily by nannies, housekeepers and the other accoutrements that their consultant salary will now support. Health service bureaucrats like me are resigned to appointing new female consultants, then immediately shelling out for expensive locums for what seems like years on end while they produce their kids. We try not to drop into the mould of the dinner-party guest who remarked to the most recently appointed of my female consultant acquaintances, 'Congratulations on your new job, Jane. Pregnant now, are we?' The phenomenon is, of course, contributing to the rise in elderly primagravida mums, or 'elderly prims' as they are known in the trade, though this to me has always conjured up images of dried-up old spinsters rather than bouncing, fecund thirtysomethings.

The pattern of employment of the second group of employees, nurses, who are the major employment group in the NHS, is very different. There are more than 400,000 nurses employed in health care in Britain. Mainly they enter the profession at the age of eighteen with a minimum of five 'O' levels. The system has been compared to running a bath with the plug out. Each year x new recruits to nurse training are poured into the bath but each year y leave nursing. Mammoth investment in training takes place simply to keep a reasonable level of nurses available in the bath. Now a sensible person would say, why can't we put the plug in? Which only goes to show how simplistic questions from sensible people can be rather annoying!

It used to be thought that part of the problem was the young female nature of the traditional nursing workforce, and it is true that a common career path is to train straight from school, then, once family commitments come along, to leave practising nursing at least for a period. Nursing is a strenuous, stressful occupation involving shift work and unsocial hours and may, for some, not combine easily with family responsibilities. Low pay was also assumed to contribute to the loss from nursing. Only when staffing crises hit the NHS and the inadvisability, if not impossibility, of continuing to fill the bath with the plug out became apparent did we probe behind the previously accepted reasons for thousands leaving nursing each year.

Some of the real reasons for the exodus were predictable, some wildly unexpected. Most were an indictment of the nursing profession and of the NHS as an employer. Studies were undertaken both of nurses leaving the NHS and also of stayers to find out what made people leave and what made people stay. Nurses, it seems, stay in the NHS because they like the ethic of service to people. They leave the NHS for a variety of reasons. Pay, though important, is not the major consideration. Family responsibilities are an important cause, though other factors figure as highly, particularly poor staffing levels – and it is clear that nurses feel very pressurised and stressed in their work. Self-determination, being valued by the system and not being a pawn at the whim of the rigid hierarchical nurse management system also registered as very important.

My director of personnel, a man and a chauvinist to boot no doubt, has a spurious, deeply offensive but pretty plausible rationale for the rigidity of nurse management. His theory goes that of this large annual intake of young women to nursing, pretty soon the attractive proportion get into relationships and leave to have kids, while the bright dynamic ones get fed up with rigid conditions and of being the doctors' handmaidens and use their get-up-and-go to get up and go. What stays behind and goes up the management hierarchy is what's left, and it is not therefore surprising that the image of senior nurses as formidable dragon-ladies ruling with a rod of iron is not yet as outdated as it might be!

The standard of work facilities are also important. In a public service like health care it is a huge temptation for bureaucrats like me to spend scarce money on patient services rather than staff facilities, and as a result staff are expected, through a sense of vocation, to put up with cold changing rooms last painted in the time of Edith Cavell, no rest rooms, lousy food, inadequate meal breaks and residential accommodation of a sort now no longer accepted for penal establishments. Christine Hancock, at the time of writing general secretary of the Royal College of Nursing but then health service manager, deliberately shamed a number of senior health service managers by inviting them to take part in a conference and booking them overnight accommodation in a nurses' residential home. I know the horrors of that night because I lived through it. The room had been institutional cream when it was last painted twenty years before. There was no carpet and the curtains were dirty and fell off the wall when I attempted to close them. Only an acrobat could have switched off the light from the bed. The furniture, a delightful 1951 utility design, was pitted with cigarette burns. There was a strong sweet odour which I concluded must emanate from a previous resident who had self-immolated in desperation. Twenty residents shared the bathroom which had been blessed with fine Victorian cast ironware in its youth. Alas, the Victorian enamel had worn through some time around the retreat from Moscow, though the consequent abrasive surface proved an interesting new remedy in my constant fight against cellulite. Many health service staff owe Christine a debt of gratitude for that night.

Bleary-eyed, I rushed off next day and instituted a £2 million investment programme in staff facilities in my own district!

London suffers especially from difficulty in recruitment and high turnover amongst the nurse workforce. Nurses on low pay cannot afford to live in London or can have an improved standard of living elsewhere. When they start families they often cannot afford or do not want to remain living in the capital and leave at that time. Traditionally London attracts young nursing staff who move off after two or three years to follow partners' jobs, to bring up families in a more conducive environment, to pursue further qualifications or experience elsewhere or to go abroad.

So there it is – a picture of an organisation whose workforce is primarily female but in which women have to struggle for promotion, which many leave after expensive training and whose turnover in many staff groups is high.

Until recently the impetus for change was not great. Generally the NHS could recruit as many doctors as it needed. Indeed, the competition for medical school places was intense. And the service could keep attracting enough young people to pour into the unplugged bath of nurses. Not any more however, for the demographic timebomb is ticking which will mean that employment patterns in the NHS will have to alter radically if adequate health care is to be provided for the people of this country over the next ten years. The approaching crisis is the same as that affecting all other employments and particularly the professions: the diminishing number of eighteen-year-olds, that traditional recruitment ground for healthcare professionals. It has been estimated that even to maintain recruitment to nursing at present levels, the health service would need to be netting 50 per cent of the eighteen-year-olds with five 'O' levels. This is an impossible target, especially when, in an increasingly service-based economy, there is growing pressure from other employers competing for the same recruits and almost always able to offer greater financial incentives. Simultaneously health services are facing rising demand as the numbers of elderly people grow and increased ranges of effective medical care are available yearly. The health service's ability to respond to this double demographic challenge is more crucial to health care in this country than any other single factor.

The demographic time bomb will not explode with expanding forces: it will implode, shrinking everything we can do, creating a great black hole of unmet need. So how can we cope with the rapidly yawning manpower (peoplepower?) black hole? It needs to be approached from two directions: what can we do about the supply of staff, both recruitment and retention, and what can we do about the demand for staff?

Health care is inevitably a primarily personal service. The scope for automation to reduce the requirement for staff is therefore limited, though information technology can make a contribution to reducing demand for staff, particularly in important clerical departments such as medical records. The health service is also planning to change the pattern of skills needed to reduce reliance on the most highly trained nurses and supplement their skills with support from differently trained health care assistants. If you look at the way nurses work, you see that they spend time on tasks that don't require the skills of scarce trained nurses. Nurses on wards will spend as much time finding out where the drug delivery has gone and why Mrs Jones's pathology report hasn't come back and on dispensing TLC (tender loving care for those not in the business – a talent which, incidentally, is not exclusive to those with five 'O' levels and three years' training) as they do on skilled nursing procedures. Health care assistants, directed by fewer highly trained nursing staff, can expand the effectiveness of the trained staff. But generally health care will continue to be highly labour intensive.

So the primary thrust in health care must be to maintain recruitment and improve retention, particularly to put the plug in the nurse manpower bath. We are slightly behind Sweden in the demographic timebomb's ticks, and when visiting hospitals in Stockholm in 1989 I noted that Sweden's health service spending crisis had passed. Swedish hospitals now have enough money because they can't recruit enough staff to pay it to. This is a sombre lesson for the UK.

Recruitment of health professionals in Britain has become a much slicker business, with glossier national advertising campaigns comparing the variety and importance of a nurse's job and a secretary's (though until recently the secretary was usually paid more). Local recruitment has become more market-specific with health authorities reaching out to local communities through local advertising, open days, links with schools, work experience schemes and through YTS and Compact schemes.

Some progress has been made but much more needs to be done and done quickly. Of the most importance is the overall image of the health service and of its careers. The NHS is rather like the map of Europe in 1918 – every political and ideological war known to man rages backwards and forwards across it and these battles, fought out in the media, while alerting the public to concerns about funding, pay and standards of care, must leave potential recruits with the idea that the health service is a run-down, cash-starved organisation rent by frequent industrial unrest where staff are poorly paid and morale is low. The image issue is clearly in play on the graduate recruitment milk round, though perhaps with a silver lining. For example, the graduate management training scheme recruitment round fails to net the brightest male graduates, who see the health service as some sort of woolly liberal organisation or as an undesirable big public bureaucracy. Instead they head off for industry or more likely now, the consultancies, the accountancy firms and the City. The NHS does, however, recruit the top-rank female graduates attracted to management with a social purpose, though it must come as a terrible shock to them when they arrive and find NHS management just as hard-nosed as, and far more complex than, anything industry can throw at them. Improved rates of pay and greater local flexibility to set rates more according to the market place have also helped recruitment, though more remains to be done in both these areas. The inevitable move will be towards individually tailored remuneration packages; which raises the question of perks for NHS staff.

The public sector has traditionally been rather po-faced about non-pay benefits, regarding them as not quite nice. As a result non-pay benefits have until very recently been limited to superannuation schemes (admittedly with that wonderful boon index-linking), subsidised accommodation for some groups, help with removal expenses and the facility to jump NHS queues for their hernia operation (this latter not to be sneezed at, though perhaps one ought not to dwell on the prospect of sneezing with a hernia). Now the need to compete with other employers for the diminishing pool of entrants and to promote the image of a progressive and caring employer has brought a rash of goodies: lease cars, cheap holidays and insurance, low-start mortgages, health checks, fitness clubs. In a moment of chauvinist despair we did think of offering a free junior doctor to every nurse recruited, but the nurses told us they'd rather have a discount scheme on conveyancing at the local solicitors. O tempora, O mores!

However, all the blandishments in the world won't magic up enough recruits from the diminishing pool of eighteen-year-olds and so we have had to widen our sights and target less traditional recruitment areas. The predominant image is that the caring professions are women's work. Efforts nationally and locally to promote these jobs as equally suitable for men and women are having some limited success and, apart from improving recruitment, 'deghettoize' caring jobs as purely women's roles and make improvement of conditions and earnings more likely and more rapid. (Sticks in the throat, doesn't it?) A second major new recruitment target is the mature entrant, primarily the woman who, less tied by the most pressing family commitments, could return to paid employment or even take it up for the first time. Attraction of this group requires very particular marketing, offering access schemes to allow an easier pathway to formal training programmes; refresher programmes to boost confidence and bring skills back up to date; and part-time and flexible work to fit with residual domestic commitments.

But the major employment feature in the NHS is the plugless bath effect. Even the most successful recruitment scheme has to be backed with a considerable effort to retain female staff, for whom a health service career may currently last for less then five years after training, many of whom will never return to the environment in which they trained. The NHS has made some progress in introducing thoughtful strategies to improve retention but the sheer seriousness of the black hole facing it means that time is running out for effective action.

The key to it all is enabling flexibility of work to allow women to fit together work and domestic commitments in a way which doesn't make a choice of one or the other necessary, or doesn't produce a continuing conflict between the two, with guilt, inadequacy and exhaustion the overridingly prevalent emotions. Progressive health authorities are now offering more part-time work, picking up on any hours women with scarce skills have to offer, no matter how few or sporadic. 'Part-time' can mean 'school term only', which fits well with school nursing and health visiting. Flexitime operated at ward or department level by staff groups themselves is popular. As a twenty-four-hours-a-day, seven-days-a-week service, the NHS is particularly well placed to foster job sharing, though progress is still slow. I have seen successful job sharing even at very senior levels. A pair of job-sharing consultant psychiatrists who broke through the medical mafioso selection process have survived and prospered in spite of appalling jokes about job shares, psychiatrists and schizophrenia. A superbly successful pair of general managers ran community and priority health care services in South London and confounded critics who said job sharing at that level wouldn't work. They were helped by both being called Sue! I knew they would work well together right from the beginning of the interview. The panel members were more nervous than the candidates: they didn't quite know how to interview for a job share. The two Sues put them at their ease, handed the questions back and forward skilfully and showed perfect teamwork. The male candidates paled by comparison. The panel fell upon the two Sues' necks – and with special gratitude for having rescued them from embarrassment.

Flexibility is vastly enhanced by the availability of adequate childcare provision. A number of health authorities are providing workplace nurseries, though these can be pretty bizarre institutions as they have to cope with childcare over seven days and with early-shift starts and late finishes. Why have so few authorities set up nurseries so far? They are expensive for staff unless subsidised and then they are expensive for impoverished health authorities which (unlike business) can't claim tax relief or run costs through into prices. The Institute of Personnel Management quotes £75,000 – 125,000 as the annual operating cost of a nursery with thirty or forty places. The current national rule is against subsidy, though sensible authorities seem to have lost the bit of paper enshrining the rule! The subsidy can be reduced by selling places to neighbouring private sector employers, though most NHS nurseries, once established, can be filled with NHS staff several times over.

Incomprehension on the part of the predominantly male managerial hierarchy doesn't help. The most successful initiators of workplace nurseries are female managers with childcare problems of their own. London is peppered with nurseries established for wonderfully selfish reasons by one woman manager whose successive pregnancies occurred in different jobs under different authorities. The process has been a monument to the concept of a product champion. In another age she most probably would have been beatified. In London commuting employees means 'commuter babies' so workplace nurseries are not the whole answer by any means. Many women would prefer to have an adequate salary and tax relief on childcare payments to allow them to shop around for the most flexible solution.

The higher-paid can just about afford the dreaded nanny syndrome. Everyone knows that even the conservatives (with a small 'c') in the NHS are really a bunch of woolly liberal pale pinkos, and it breaks my heart to see friends, who ten years ago wouldn't miss a CND march, now surreptitiously buying copies of the *Lady* to scan the nanny columns. Many women do, however, want to spend time with children in their pre-school years or beyond and this is where the work-break schemes are essential: they enable women to keep in touch during the break, ensure a smooth return to work and offer retraining or refresher training. The NHS has developed the delightfully sexist Married Women's Retainer Scheme to keep female doctors in touch, though the rigidity of the rest of medical training and career development more than counteracts any benefit this may offer. Informal keeping-in-touch and re-entry schemes are available nationally for career-break managers such as the one operated by the Institute of Health Services Management. Most importantly, on return from a work break, women must be able to re-enter at the level of seniority at which they left and not be penalised by demotion.

Training, career development and promotion opportunities are important if the NHS is to make the most of the capabilities of women in the workforce and, less altruistically, lock women into continuing employment. It is almost impossible to combine medical training and family responsibilities in hospital medical specialities and little has been done to remedy this because of intense competition for posts and sufficient men coming forward to fill them. A recent study by the Policy Studies Institute, commissioned by the Department of Health, mapped all this out clearly, but recent changes in the general practice contract make it less acceptable rather than more for GPs to work part-time. I doubt if much will change until the demographic timebomb finally hits medicine and women lead the British Medical Association and the Royal Colleges. The signs are that applicants to medical schools are reducing and after a woman president of the Royal College of Pathologists, we now have a woman president of the Royal College of Physicians. Only a dozen or so male bastions to go!

In other NHS employer groups, access to training for part-timers and job sharers needs positive action. Training on a part-time or extended basis to attract women with children into nurse and other professional training has been successful in some places. In health care management, distance and open learning methods open up training programmes more flexibly. The current progressive introduction of individual annual performance review systems should mean that bosses are compelled to the discipline of thinking through career development needs at least once a year with individual employees. The guarantee of ongoing training and career progression is as powerful a recruitment and retention factor as any material perk.

The Hansard Society for Parliamentary Government recently reported that '80 per cent of new workers in the next five years will be women, most of whom will have major family responsibilities. . . . The best man for the job in the 1990s is a woman!' If you want the NHS to provide first-class health care, that had better be the case and we had better give women what they want.

11
The National Westminster Bank

by Diana Balsdon
National Westminster Bank plc

I joined a constituent bank of National Westminster straight from school in the 1960s. It seems quite extraordinary to reflect now that at the time I started work, a woman employee of the bank who married was no longer considered a permanent member of staff and was transferred instead to the temporary workforce.

I remember well my first leadership course in the early 1970s. The course syllabus included team building and leadership exercises. One exercise took place in the badminton hall of NatWest's beautiful training college set in the Oxfordshire countryside. Two teams had to build a bridge to cover a make-believe chasm and then the teams had to cross the chasm in competition with each other. I swung inelegantly, clawing my way along a piece of suspended rope. A second exercise took place in the 'field' – that is, outside the grounds. This time my role was running along a muddy path to pass messages to various members of the team. Unfortunately, my team ran out of time, not through lack of enthusiasm on our part but because a number of us became extremely bogged down by the mud that day, myself included. There were fifty participants on this particular course: one woman (me) and forty-nine men. We were chosen as we had all shown the performance and potential to reach junior manager level. It appeared strange to me as to why a military 'field exercise' – which would for example have ruled out anyone with a disability, however competent – should be regarded as the ideal vehicle for teaching management style. However, as I mentioned, this was some time ago but highlights the masculine style of management in banking at that time.

I started work at the largest branch of the then National Provincial Bank in the West End of London. I struggled as a machine operator,

which was the job I had been employed to do, so I was moved
to become a cashier. In those days all the cashiers were very
distinguished-looking gentlemen who were not at all sure about my
joining them! You must remember that this was the age of the mini
skirt – the first time around. I moved from that branch and travelled
around the country helping to introduce computers into various
branches and offices, as far away as Kingston-upon-Hull and
Hatherleigh in Devon.

At the end of this period I married and went to work in a local
office close to where my husband and I were living. It was then
that I started thinking about the future. I became interested in what
was happening around me in the office. In a smaller branch there
was the opportunity of getting involved in various aspects of banking.
I soon learnt about the lending function and went to work in two
more branches close by to gain further experience. It was about
this time that I started taking my banking examinations. The main
thing that spurred me to take them was that I was told that although
I was good, I would never progress from being a clerk as I had not
studied for the examinations.

I eventually moved into London and obtained my first assistant
manager post in the late 1970s. Since then I have worked predominantly within corporate finance, dealing with large international
companies. Before being appointed to my present role as Manager,
Equal Opportunities, for National Westminster Bank in 1988, I
was a manager within the shipping finance section.

A lot has changed since I joined the bank – for women in society
generally and, in particular, within banking. NatWest currently
employs over 41,000 women, comprising 56 per cent of its workforce. Taking into account the reducing number of school leavers
and the increasing number of women returning to the workplace,
this proportion is expected to rise in the next few years. How large
the rise will be depends very much on the economic situation, the
changing needs of the bank's customer base and the increased
sophistication of automated internal procedures. The aim of Nat-
West is to maximise the full potential of all staff, regardless of
gender.

Historically, banking has been a male-dominated industry. Even
today it is difficult to name any well-known female financier,
though there are several noted women journalists in the financial
field, such as Mary Goldring and the redoubtable Sarah Hogg.
Banking still has a powerfully masculine management culture.

Attitudes – society's expectations, employers' expectations, the self-image of a woman herself – have all acted in the past against the progression of female staff.

A hundred years ago there were no women in banking at all. The typical bank clerk was a man. To quote Jerome K Jerome, *Three Men in a Boat* (1889), 'George goes to sleep at a bank from ten to four each day, except Saturdays, when they wake him up and put him outside at two'. NatWest's archives first recorded women in 1907: that year there were just four women among a total of 3,000 employees of the London and Westminster Bank. With the outbreak of the First World War and the more general use of the typewriter, numbers increased dramatically and by 1919 women formed about 30 per cent of the workforce. During the following years there was a gradual decline to under 20 per cent by 1939, but with the outbreak of the Second World War there was once more a rapid increase. In the first half of this century women employees were clearly seen in the support role and during the war years as substitutes for men, taken on only out of necessity. As we discuss the demographic timebomb there is a distinct whiff of the same attitude in the 1990's!

After 1945 the number of women in the workforce continued to increase, particularly as a result of the expansion in banking in the 1950s and 1960s when mechanisation and automation changed the face of the industry. Despite these changes, the progress for women was slow. Until the mid-1960s little encouragement was given, job advertisements at the time would read:

A career in the bank
for ambitious young men
and there's scope for girls as well

or

He after obtaining excellent GCE results
wants a career that will bring reward and status

She wants a well paid job that she will enjoy.

The majority of women showed no inclination to make a career of banking. Most women had resigned by the age of twenty-one. However, during this time, there were opportunities for some women to make progress in the career stream. These opportunities fell mainly within the personnel function which was then seen as a caring/welfare unit and was considered as a path along which women might move forward into management positions. The first women managers, given the title of lady staff controllers, were appointed to look after the special needs of the women staff in the early 1960s. Now over 13 per cent of NatWest's management team are women.

For the last twenty years women have dominated the employment picture at NatWest, making up over 55 per cent of the workforce. During the 1970s the bank identified that this half of its workforce was not being utilised to the best of its ability. We started to look at why so few women had progressed into the assistant manager and management positions.

If the bank were to make the most of its human resources, it could not ignore:

● statutory requirements and social trends;
● the fact that the bank's policy at that time was failing to develop all its existing talent;
● the fact that the traditional source of future talent was about to decline. At that time the forecasts had already shown that the number of school leavers, both male and female would decline from 640,000 in 1981 to 480,000 in 1991, a drop of 25 per cent. This drop would coincide with an increase in demand from the growing white-collar and service industries;
● the belief that managerial talent is not a male prerogative;
● the recognition that a management team comprising both men and women is likely to be stronger than one comprising only the members of one sex.

In 1977 NatWest was approached by a research team from the London School of Economics to take part in an action research project on women in banking. The project was to take place in Britain, France and the United States, and was funded by the German Marshall Fund of Washington. The aim of the project was to improve opportunities for women in banking in Europe by pioneering changes in a major bank in Britain and France, drawing on experience encountered in the United States.

As a result of the original review and subsequent research that took place between 1978 and 1980 and encompassed all areas of equal opportunity affecting women, NatWest formed a Positive Action Programme. The programme, which followed the then Draft Code of Practice compiled by the Equal Opportunities Commission, was given the full commitment of the bank's general management.

The original Positive Action Programme is outlined below:

1 A career planning adviser, with special responsibility for equal opportunities, was appointed in March 1980.

2 The bank's policy was publicised to all staff, job applicants and outsiders through internal circulars, and directories, through statements contained in recruitment literature, the bank's annual report and accounts and staff diaries.

3 Regular meetings would take place with the trade unions specifically to discuss the bank's equal opportunities policy.

4 The careers of women who were identified as having the potential to move into management would be monitored centrally to ensure that they received the necessary development experience and promotion.

5 Statistics would be maintained on a quarterly basis to show the numbers of men and women in each grade, the percentage of female promotions in each grade and the recruitment split of men and women.

6 The bank was cautious in the setting of targets and did not wish to enter a numbers game. However, it was felt that targets could help awareness and they were originally set for the number of women in assistant management positions.

7 The numbers of women attending internal training courses were monitored, as were the number applying for and obtaining study leave for the Institute of Bankers examinations.

8 Formal annual audits were undertaken by the career planning adviser with the personnel function in each region and division to discuss all aspects of equal opportunities, including promotion targets, study leave, training and the career development of women under their control.

9 Training specifically designed for women was supported. The bank still sponsors the Managerial Effectiveness for Women course and has sent representatives on an internal Civil Service course, Developing Skills for Women in Middle Management. Women are also sent on special external development courses as considered necessary, in addition to the normal training facilities available.

10 The Re-entry/Reservist Scheme was introduced on an experimental basis in January 1981. This allowed selected members of staff, male or female, to take a break of up to five years in their career to raise children.

11 Consideration has, over the years, been given to the provision
of childcare facilities, and although it has been decided not to set
up these facilities at the present time, the position is constantly
under review.

At one of the early stages in formulating this programme, the
bank asked fifteen women employees with identified management
potential to a three-day 'think tank' at Heythrop Park, its management training establishment, to consider their role within the
organisation and the barriers they saw for the progression of women.
The group produced a comprehensive report on the situation of
women employees and the action that would help promote women's
career development.

NatWest acted. The comments of this group would by now sound
predictable, but then were a revelation to the company, and as a
direct result, the role of a career planning adviser for women was
established.

The support that these women found in talking to each other
spread beyond NatWest and was influential in the setting up of
'Women in Banking' in early 1980. The first meetings were held
in the London School of Economics, with word of mouth invitations
being extended to anyone in each of the four Big Banks and some
smaller ones. This was the first time a network for women had been
formed in the banking industry. Working for a large organisation
such as a clearing bank, one can become very insular and this
network gave the members the opportunity of discussing issues of
mutual interest in open forum. The group is still in place today
and I have listed below their current aims and objectives.

i   Women in Banking is an independent organisation that is run
by its members, for its members, and with the full recognition of
the financial community.

ii Promoting the professional image of women in the finance
industry has always been a priority for Women in Banking.

iii The group offers its members an opportunity to learn about new
and developing issues in finance, the chance to establish a valuable
network of business and social contacts and an ideal environment
in which to prepare for further professional achievement.

We meet on a regular basis in London and other parts of the
country. Contact can be made through the Membership Secretary,
Caroline Gaffney, NatWest, telephone number 071-485 7121.

The bank introduced a Career Break Scheme as part of the
original Positive Action Programme. The scheme was introduced

for a five-year experimental period in January 1981 to enable members of staff, male and female, to take a break in their career to care for young children. The scheme was originally known as the Re-entry/Reservist Scheme – referring to the two levels at which it operates. Since January 1989 the Career Break Scheme has been open to all staff who have completed two years' full-time service with NatWest. Those adopting young children may apply and there is no restriction on the age of participants.

The scheme is run on two levels to reflect the different needs and aspirations of staff. Under the re-entry arrangement, the bank will guarantee an offer of re-employment to individuals at the same level of appointment at which they left and will provide a training programme on their return designed to update their knowledge and competence. This is open to those who are seen to have the potential to reach senior management and who expect to return to work with their career commitment undiminished. Under the reservist arrangement, there is no commitment by the bank to re-employ an individual, but it will consider participants by placing them on a reserve list until a suitable vacancy arrives at the level of appointment or grade at which they left the bank.

The scheme runs for a period of up to five years from the beginning of state maternity leave, although the offer may be extended at the discretion of the bank. The essence of the scheme is to be flexible and arrangements can be made, if individuals prefer, to take the period away from the workplace in smaller tranches than the full five years. Participants on the scheme give an undertaking to provide a minimum of two weeks' paid relief work per year (although many actually undertake far more part-time work than this) and attend an annual one-day seminar. Throughout the period of absence, contact is maintained with the bank through regular information packs, local meetings and invitations to local social events. Participants are encouraged to continue to study the Chartered Institute of Bankers examinations, where appropriate.

When the scheme started in 1981, there were fewer than a dozen participants and, in fact, its momentum has been fairly slow. At the beginning of 1989 the number was 146, which by the time of writing, early in 1990, had risen to close on 400. The rate of growth in the last year has been tremendous and this must surely reflect the social changes that are taking place in this country.

NatWest's Positive Action Programme continues today, although it has been enhanced and improved as time moves on. The role of the career planning adviser for women has progressed now to manager, Equal Opportunities Unit and has responsibilities specifically for gender and race. In addition, guidance has been introduced to ensure that there is no intentional or inadvertent discrimination against women at interviews. Within each sector/division/region of the bank personnel managers have been trained and designated with a specific responsibility for equal opportunities issues. They are responsible for relaying and implementing the bank's policy to line management.

The original Management Development Course for Women has been enhanced to meet the changing needs of women and the workplace. The course is normally run for sixteen participants – eight from NatWest and eight from both the private and public sector, such as Bank of England, British Airways, Marks and Spencer and the Civil Service. During the 1980s a Management Development Programme was also introduced to ensure more objective selection of staff for development and more rapid advancement for those of greater ability, ensuring equal opportunities to progress. NatWest has also set up a computer-based training programme, Equal Opportunities at Work, covering the legal and practical aspects of equal opportunities. This is available on a nationwide basis to all staff. The results of the Positive Action Programme have been carefully monitored and the most pleasing element is the number of women who are now coming through into the management roles.

My role as manager, Equal Opportunities, for NatWest Bank developed from that of the Career Planning Adviser mentioned in the original Positive Action Programme. As the programme has developed, along with the changing needs of equal opportunities within the bank, so has my role. I am responsible for implementation of the bank's policy. As well as with my own team in the bank's head office, I work closely with the senior managers throughout the country who have responsibilities for equal opportunities on a local basis. A programme similar to the Positive Action Programme described above was developed to look specifically at race during the time when the bank first monitored the whole of its workforce for its ethnic background. I am responsible for maintaining these monitoring procedures and for the development of strategies to ensure that none of the talent in our workforce is overlooked. I work closely with the Commission for Racial Equality and the Equal Opportunities Commission.

Women have now been identified as the main contributors to the UK's workforce as we move into the 1990s. In the banking sector they are becoming increasingly important, both as employees and as customers. Gone are the days when family finances were solely run by the man.

So, what do women want; what do they need to move forward? I often hear women saying, 'I am only . . .' – 'I am only a cashier,' 'I am only a housewife.' Why do we always underrate ourselves? A more balanced management team incorporates the attributes that both men and women can bring to the workplace. Women with a successful home life are likely to be competent administrators and magnificent planners. Consider what goes on within the typical family home every day. Who ensures that there is food on the table and in the fridge? Who makes certain that clothes are clean and that all members of the family get to their meeting or to school on time? Who makes sure the bill is paid so that the phone isn't cut off? Who gets the vacuum cleaner repaired? Who takes the car to be serviced? It requires a great deal of organisation, considerable talent in planning, attributes that cannot be switched on or off at 5pm. Most women who go out to work have to continue after their return home in the evening, regarding it as their job to ensure that the washing-up is done and so on; and they start again first thing in the morning, making certain that something edible is on the breakfast table before going on to ensure that the report is on their boss's desk on time.

Isn't this a sexist approach? Possibly, but it is an accurate reflection of how a good number of us behave. To point out that women fail to appreciate the complexities of their life often boosts their confidence. It does not necessarily confirm them in this domestic role forever.

Within a large organisation such as NatWest you can change behavioural patterns through training, action programmes and various initiatives. However, it is very difficult to change deep-rooted attitudes and prejudices which still lie entrenched in certain regions in the country, not always those furthest removed from the capital. In fact, London is far from guiltless in this respect. As a country-wide organisation, the bank has to work in partnership with, and sometimes around, these regional attitudes. We can alter and influence in the workplace, but outside that environment it is far more difficult to bring change. Perhaps we can make progress, however, as we widen choice and opportunities at work.

Backward-looking attitudes and assumptions are sometimes found in the most unusual quarters, where more enlightenment and intelligence might be expected. I am constantly being asked by journalists to arrange for them to interview a woman bank manager and we are glad to oblige. Their preconceptions are often bizarre. There is great disappointment when we do not produce either a female Captain Mainwaring or a Mrs Thatcher clone. On one occasion a video film crew who were preparing for a current affairs programme wished to film a woman bank manager working through a normal day, from the moment she left home in the morning until the evening. An interview was set up with a woman manager who happened to be in her thirties, slightly built, with shoulder-length hair and a very keen mind. Before the interview took place the customers of the manager were approached and confirmed that they would be happy to be filmed. Having met the manager, however, the interviewer asked if I could find somebody older who 'looked more the part'. I questioned what the interviewer meant by this and was given a pen picture of a rather strident woman in her fifties. In the end the interview was cancelled by the film crew, despite all the trouble that had been taken to arrange it.

In the past perceptions have been mainly based around disbelief that women have the necessary skills and *gravitas* to be involved in the work of the lending function. I myself have suffered as a result of this narrow outlook.

One wet day back in 1976 I was obliged to stand soaking in the doorway of a NatWest branch on the outskirts of London, explaining that I had *not* come to work as a cashier, but as the assistant to the lending manager. The fact that I was well advanced on the banking qualifications ladder did not cut any ice with the staff. I am glad to report that today there are over 32,000 women members of the Chartered Institute of Bankers, of which 3,400 have attained the Association of Chartered Institute of Bankers qualification.

Again, experience has taught me never to sit at the end of a table if I am the only woman in the room conducting a meeting of six or more. I may be the most senior person in the room, but still the conversation will continue further down the table without me. Instead I always place myself in the middle of one of the sides of the table. And *never, never* sit near the coffee or teacups: all eyes will immediately turn to you to pour. It takes real nerve then to turn to a male contemporary and say sweetly, 'Will you be mother?'

Identifying that we can do our boss's job is something that does not come very easily to women. On a number of occasions managers have said to me, when reviewing their staff, that women are not comfortable with moving on or seeking new responsibilities until they have fully mastered every aspect of their present job, whereas men, who may not be ready for their new responsibilities, are far keener to move and have already got their eye on a position several grades higher.

The identification of potential within NatWest is now linked with behavioural measures drawn from the workplace. The Management Development Programme has ensured a more objective selection of staff for development. The system involves mentors, assessment centres and self-development programmes linked to competencies. Since this system was introduced, a greater number of women are now coming through than before as being seen to have senior management and executive potential. It is now believed that a few years ago some subjective assessments were made, in particular with regard to women.

We are very lucky in NatWest that *any* member of staff, irrespective of sex/age/race/educational background can apply for the Management Development Programme. This is achieved through an annual open invitation which allows individuals to self-nominate themselves. The programme is structured to allow individuals to move through at their own pace.

What do women want to enable them to draw from the opportunities that are now available? Firstly, I believe that women want choice. To be able to choose a satisfying life and to be treated seriously, whichever path they wish to tread, is the dream of many women I meet. Within the banking environment more women are now realising that they can achieve their boss's position. However, this does not suit everyone; and in a very large organisation it is possible to accept that fact and to help individuals to reach the potential that is most comfortable to both themselves and the organisation. There are large numbers of both men and women who do not seek managerial roles. They do wish, however, to be able to *choose* how far they may go with regard to status.

There are now more and more women opting to resume a career following a break for family commitments. They're looking for the flexibility that big organisations, like NatWest, can offer to help them achieve the balance between career needs and family needs. Not every mother chooses to come back to the workplace directly after maternity leave, but the idea of taking a break from a career is now becoming far more acceptable. We still have individuals deciding to join the bank's Career Break Scheme, however, who are, in fact, breaking from their own peer groups and at times, their own families' views on women committed to returning to work. This can be a cause of friction in some traditional communities for a time and the problems it can cause should not be ignored.

Childcare is another very important issue dealt with elsewhere in this book. We have read a lot recently about the setting up of workplace nurseries. But there is no one easy answer to childcare provision and, in fact, NatWest's understanding as a responsible employer is that parents, again, wish to choose. The form of childcare provision is a very personal decision. Parents need to select the type of care that they feel most comfortable with: very important for both the children and the parents, whatever campaigners may think. And the importance of childcare by other members of the family and the support mechanism within families, if it is available, should not be overlooked or underestimated.

A great deal has been written about how to support families with children of pre-school age. However, there appears to be very little provision or mention of care for school-age children. In fact, with the increasing number of mothers returning to work, out-of-school care must be one of the most important elements to be considered. On a national basis associations such as the National Out-of-School Alliance are particularly looking to standardise and improve out-of-school care in this country, specifically through the code of practice which they launched in autumn 1989. The Alliance, now relaunched as Kid's Clubs Network, can be contacted at 279-281 Whitechapel Road, London E11; telephone, 071 247 3009.

In addition to these family needs, women want to ensure that they can have a fulfilling and interesting career ahead of them, including, for the majority, a break at some time during that career. At NatWest an increasing number of assistant managers who definitely plan to return to continue their career, are now taking their career break. Having obtained that more elevated position, they are not interested in returning to a lesser, junior role within the organisation, even on a part-time basis, a fact which must be made clear to society as a whole. This was highlighted to me very recently by a banking friend who, on a routine out-patient visit to a hospital in the suburbs of London just before the birth of her little boy, was advised by the nurse not to consider going back to work once the baby was born. When my friend explained that she worked for a bank, the nurse (female) advised that that was all right: she could go and work for a couple of hours as a cashier. My friend had already been identified as having management potential and was, in fact, already an assistant manager several grades higher than a cashier. The trained nurse might well have taken umbrage at the equivalent suggestion that she return to work as an auxiliary!

What women want is to build a fulfilling career in an area where they feel most comfortable and happy. They also want to choose, at different times of their life, whether to concentrate on work or home, family or to balance both.

All people, men and women, in busy and interesting jobs such as banking need the support of those around them; it is very important to build alliances with our partners, with our families and with our work colleagues. Then our bosses, our colleagues and our staff will have confidence in what we are doing and understand our ambitions, as will our families, neighbours and friends.

12
British Petroleum

by Margaret Jackson
BP Oil

Joe was the staff geologist to whom one turned for career development advice. He puffed slowly and deliberately on his pipe, then
looked across the desk at me and said, 'Margaret, if you want to get
on, get out'. From the tone of our conversation and his measured
statement, I knew I had reached a watershed, and so did he. His
words were not spoken in anger but in quiet recognition that the
last three years I had spent working in BP's Geological Information
Branch had done little to further my career in geology.

I was in effect a 'paper geologist' (I never saw a bit of rock from
one day's end to the next!). To have a career in geology you needed
field experience, working on drilling rigs or being involved in
surveys of new territories – but for a woman that was out. My recent
trip to the Middle East, where I had spent a month in a site office
in Abu Dhabi and during which I had badgered my way to a brief
visit to an offshore rig, had done nothing to further my cause.

So I had to start all over again – from scratch. There seemed
little point in looking for geological jobs with other companies,
although I did try and had the inevitable response. From one
company came the curt reply that, despite my background and
qualifications, which were exactly in accordance with the job
specification, they were not taking my application any further as
they didn't employ women – full stop. I was, thankfully, warned
off another firm by their personnel officer, who assured me that I
would be stepping out of the frying pan into the fire – and he ought
to have known: he had left BP and lived to regret it.

Fortunately, all was not lost back at BP, and through the internal
placement system I was offered a job working with marketing
engineers, the logic being that if I could cope with geological and

petroleum engineering data, I could pick up the knowledge required to be a technical assistant to the engineers. It bought me time, so I took it. In fact, it turned out to hold the seeds of my future career, as it was not long before I began to run safety courses for operations engineers, and a year later I was invited over a drink in a bar to join central personnel.

That was twenty years ago. The total number of women in senior positions in BP is still low but improving, and, faced with bald statistics, it would be easy to be misled about the position of women in the company. It has to be borne in mind that the business comes from an unusual cultural background. Much of BP's activities were originally concentrated in exploration and production in the Middle East, an area closed to women in more ways than one. As a result we do not have any tradition of women working in large numbers as do, say, the banks, the media and the public sector.

More recently the volatility of oil prices and organisational changes have kept BP constantly changing and adapting to new challenges and opportunities, and hence more opportunities for women have arisen in the firm. As our advertising campaigns have highlighted, we are a company 'on the move' in the marketing place, working today 'for all our tomorrows'.

Over the past ten years, and particularly in the last five, more and more women have made it to the upper levels of the firm's management and have found that there is more than ever before a climate of co-operation and support from their male colleagues to help them achieve their full potential.

Women have traditionally been less well represented in the technical areas of the BP Group, partly because of the minority of female students in these disciplines, but also because there have been other hurdles put in our way. These hurdles are now considerably fewer than in my own days as a geologist, when there was no Sex Discrimination Act to call on for help.

Take the case of Helen as an example of how conditions for women have improved in BP. She joined the firm as an engineer.

'I was working in the project team for the development of a North Sea oilfield,' she recalled, 'and we had reached the stage where off-shore visits were necessary. My manager doubted that it would be possible to send me offshore as the facilities were not very sophisticated and "he would feel terrible if anything happened to me".

'I decided not to make a fuss, although I was very disappointed. However, the senior engineer in the team was setting up a rota system to ensure that work at the onshore, offshore and head office sites was covered. He thought that, as I was a member of the team, I should take my turn on the rota and included my name. When it was discussed with the manager, he ended up accepting it, mainly I think because the others in the team just took it for granted that I was going.

'I made several visits offshore over the next six months and everything worked out fine.'

Helen is now the administration manager at BP's Kwinana Refinery in Western Australia – the first woman to hold that post.

My second example is Kate, a drilling engineer with BP. She too faced the problem of the lack of facilities offshore. Her manager was not against her going, but would let her go only if she could have a room to herself – the rooms were four-berth, which meant that if the rig was full to capacity (which frequently occurred), he would have to send out one of her male colleagues instead. Kate didn't object. But in the hurly-burly of operations this special proviso was very quickly forgotten. She explained to the chief steward on board that she would be prepared to share with the men – though not with one on his own! It worked, she was the least embarrassed of the four, and she was accepted as a professional member of the team.

These stories are, ultimately, good news for women's equality, but they also simply illustrate the converse of what many men take for granted – that their career will be in line with their qualifications and ability to do the job, and that no one would dream of telling them they can't do a job because they are male.

What women want is to be given an even chance of career opportunities, and to be taken seriously; they do not want to be asked, 'When are your physiological urges going to get the better of you?'.

An important aspect of working in industry with which women have to come to terms is 'the system'. Every organisation has one operating at both formal and informal levels. In this day and age the formal systems are unlikely to be overtly hostile to women, yet women can still come up against the informal systems which may still seem 'user-unfriendly' or just plain different.

One example of an informal system is that of the role model. It is a matter of debate whether the relative lack of role models for women is a good or bad thing. In a recent survey I carried out in BP Oil, I was surprised to find how many of the women I spoke to found being a lone woman in a work area could be an advantage. While the men have always had role models to follow, this has almost become a constraint. For the women there was the feeling of freedom to do their own thing and to develop their own style of management.

Then there is the scapegoat problem. The rewards of success are obvious and visible. The downside, the price of failure, is a burden put on women whether they like it or not, and whether they accept it or not. As a trail-blazer, if you win, you help those coming behind. If you fail, there is the danger that it is not only your own personal failure that you carry, but for those who still hold to female stereotypes your failure can be carried over to other women coming behind you.

Networking – the old boys' network – has been one of the informal systems which excluded women, and which we have not always copied, perhaps because of a feeling that good work and potential should be recognised and rewarded without having to make a song and dance about it. Self-publicity and the deliberate forging of links with other usually more senior managers for too long went against the grain for many women. Fortunately, women have learned to be more confident and assertive, and networking with male and female colleagues in all parts of the company is now a recognised necessity.

It always helps to know that there are others in the same boat, and that is one of the reasons why Women in BP was formed. It is a network of women throughout the group who hold regular meetings on topics of interest and who have also co-operated on the production of two important brochures for the company – the *Maternity Advice Pack* and the *Career Advice Pack*, both full of advice and the experience of women in the group. Women in BP was formed with the full backing and co-operation of the company's management. Indeed, it has been given valuable input, not only in terms of cash resources, but also in the form of advice and support from senior managers and the group's equal opportunities advisor, Vicky Wisher.

The networking opportunities that Women in BP provides give women the chance to share their experiences. One particular example of this support is given by Jill, who attended one of the BP Group's development assessment boards. It can be quite an experience for any candidate, male or female, to live through one of these events at which a dozen or so high-potential staff are put through a series of tests, interviews and group discussions: three days under the microscope that can be daunting for anyone. It was not that Jill felt inferior to the men. She was, however, concerned that the effect of being the only woman could have made her a scapegoat for anything that went wrong in the highly competitive environment under which everyone was operating. Being able to share that experience with other women who had been in the same position helped her to see things more in perspective, and that gave her the confidence to do her best. As a result of her performance on that assessment event, Jill is now on the individual development programme.

Another piece of the formal system is the mapping out of an individual development programme (IDP). The careers planned for those employees who are deemed to have highest potential for development are subject to forward review by a committee of the most senior executives from different parts of the BP Group, thus ensuring the opportunity to acquire a broader base of knowledge and skills before the individual reaches the highest jobs in the group. All fair and square for men and women? Yes, but . . .

One of the problems that has had to be tackled in the last few years has been the timing of the selection for this programme. It usually happens after a person has been in the company for five years – in their mid-late twenties if they come in direct from higher education. It is around this time that women are likely to be making other important life decisions than those related to their job, such as marriage and/or a family. To be 'an IDP' might involve a step-change in career development, leading to a possible postpone-ment of family plans. Once an employee has been designated an IDP, the next few years are critical in career development terms. In order to get a breadth of experience across the BP Group in a number of functional areas, IDPs change jobs roughly every two years. To take leave to start a family, even no more than the statutory maternity period, might lose valuable time on the programme. BP quickly realised that if women were going to be encouraged to stay on, but at the same time enjoy having a family, something had to be done. It was largely as a result of women in BP Oil negotiating a new arrangement that all parts of the BP Group have now adopted the same policy – the career break scheme.

This scheme enables a woman to take time out over and beyond the statutory minimum, or negotiate some form of part-time work-ing, either in the office, or from home. At the time of writing three senior professional women in BP Oil were on career breaks. Each case was separately negotiated to suit individual needs. There was an assumption in the past that this would be a temporary arrangement and that full-time working in the office would be the norm. One of the exciting developments, however, has been the way in which this type of arrangement has caught on, and we are now entering a new phase of expanding the options available.

Under the scheme the working mother can negotiate: a complete break for up to two years; a return to part-time working in the office; a return to part-time working at home; a combination of home and office full-time working; job sharing. If there is one lesson that we have learned by hard experience, it is that there is need for vigilance to ensure that, having set up the career break, it continues to be the best means of maximising working arrangements for the individuals concerned as well as giving job satisfaction and career development opportunities.

Working part-time is a relatively new concept in BP Oil, and we are still learning how to make it work. 'Part-time' has in the past been equated with 'part-commitment' to a career, but this is strenuously denied by those who are involved in part-time working arrangements. When managers have expressed reservations about part-time work, I have occasionally asked them to compare their attitude to a part-time professionally qualified employee with that to an external consultant. In many areas of the company the use of consultants provides a flexible arrangement to cope with extra work loads which require specialist input. The task is outlined, the objectives and deadlines set, the price negotiated. Few would say that the external consultants were 'not committed' to their professional tasks, even though they are effectively working part-time for the company. Their other responsibilities and commitments are of little interest to the firm – the main concern is that the task for which they have been hired is achieved professionally to an agreed timetable and budget.

The difference between the part-time employee and the external consultant is one of attitude, and part of my job is to challenge these assumptions and encourage managers to be more flexible and creative in their use of part-time working, job sharing and other options.

Jane, a chemical engineer with BP, is an example of a woman employee who has been on two career breaks in the past five years and is currently working from home on a part-time basis. Because of her particular circumstances, she does not anticipate a return to full-time working for a little while to come. What had originally been seen by management as a temporary arrangement prior to returning full-time has become a more permanent arrangement because Jane is unable to contemplate a return to full-time working in the office in the foreseeable future. This has necessitated a rethink of how to progress the career of someone who is on a career break. In Jane's case she is a recognised expert in her field and is valued by managers both in the UK and overseas. Her role in the company is on the longer-term planning side but of considerable importance to BP Oil. In her office at home Jane has a computer terminal and a fax machine and can communicate with colleagues all over the world. To keep up with developments in other areas of the branch, she visits the company office at least once a fortnight. In this way she feels less isolated than if she was only communicating by phone.

While Jane enjoys the work she is doing, she may well want to look for wider experience in the future to broaden her horizons. To facilitate this BP Oil has now set up an internal consultancy project to co-ordinate project work that can be done by people like Jane either from home or with occasional visits to the office.

The need for special arrangements has been recognised for all levels of employees at BP, not only for senior professional women. An innovative approach has been taken by the group's secretarial training school to help women return to temporary employment with the company, if they wish to keep the flexibility that 'temping' offers but within a firm that they already know. The benefit is thus two-ways: the individual feels at home in the office and the employer gains a motivated employee who has a knowledge of the working environment and systems that is by no means guaranteed when using employees from the usual 'temp' agencies. This flexibility enables a woman to have employment at times that suit her. If she has school-age children, she can take holidays at the same time as the schools. The company can plan ahead for this and, by setting up job sharing, can get the best of both worlds for itself and its women employees.

Such an innovative approach has also been employed in BP Oil's UK operations at Hemel Hempstead. A senior secretary has been given the flexibility of working during term-time only, to enable her to look after her children during the school holidays. During that time, her job is covered by a temp.

A desire to exercise control over their career is a key feature that emerged from a survey I conducted among women in BP oil towards the end of 1989. To prevent career development becoming a casualty in the career break scheme, BP Oil has introduced a system of 'mentoring' for women on maternity breaks or career breaks. Under the mentoring scheme, a senior line manager is assigned to each woman with the brief to keep in touch on a regular basis and to make sure that he/she knows the career aspirations of the individual, so that when discussions take place in the staff development committees, someone is well briefed on the woman's situation and can make recommendations on her behalf.

Maternity absence is an invaluable time for personal stock-taking. After the birth of the child, a woman can change her view on what she wants out of life. If she does decide that she wants to combine a career and a family, it will almost certainly have been only after she has fully investigated all the options and seen the downside as well as the advantages. If she is willing to pay out a major part of her salary in childcare arrangements, this should be seen by management as a far more positive indication of her commitment than is frequently the case.

It therefore makes far more sense to see the maternity absence/career break as a positive time for career planning. BP Oil has put into place a system of counselling which will encourage women to consider some form of relevant training or qualification while away. Not only does it give the woman a feeling that she has not been forgotten by the company, but, more significantly, it can also make good use of time away from the office and equip her for different areas of work on her return.

The training might be a short course on a business topic, learning a language or, if she feels able to take on the time commitment, a master's degree in business by distance learning or part-time study. Whatever is agreed, it is important to help the woman balance her commitments, and help her to benefit most fully from the time at her disposal.

Frances is currently on maternity leave following the birth of her child a few months ago. We have kept in touch over that time, and in passing Frances mentioned that she would love to be involved with the graduate recruitment programme, interviewing candidates. It was agreed that she should attend the same advanced interviewing skills course as all the other interviewers, and with skilful planning and occasional breaks to breastfeed her baby, Frances was able to participate in the programme.

A number of interviews are carried out in the office, which is not too far from Frances's home. This gives her the flexibility to come in for three or four hours a day to conduct the interviews, while still being able to manage her home commitments. She has had the opportunity to increase her interviewing skills and practice, and it has also been an excellent way of keeping in touch with what is going on in the office. The benefit has been two-way, as the company has also gained from her valuable input.

It has long been the practice in our refineries and shipping fleet to carry out 'preventative maintenance' – the idea being that it is better to maintain equipment on a regular basis rather than be faced with a crisis or, worse, an accident, if some piece of equipment fails. It is now becoming a part of the thinking towards our other great asset, people, to plan and maintain careers on a positive approach rather than from the reactive stance of the past. Time will tell whether we have made the right decision.

What women want is to be involved positively with the discussions and decisions on their future – to feel that there is a positive 'Let's see what we can do' approach, rather than a reactive 'Why must you be different?'

A fundamental objective of the personnel function is to attract and retain staff. What I have written about so far has been largely in the area of retention of staff, although I am not denying that the reputation a company builds up with regard to how it treats its staff is also a significant factor in the recruitment or attraction process.

Never have graduates 'had it so good' – the demographic changes are ensuring that they are now seen as a scarce resource, and companies are spending considerable sums in marketing their job opportunities, targeting both students and their parents. But if that is all employers are doing, which in itself will merely lead to a spiral in salaries as companies compete, the underlying problem of a shortage of skilled labour will not be solved. A longer-term perspective has to be taken.

While one aspect of my work is to look at ways of improving the opportunities and working arrangements for women, it is also part of my role to examine the contribution of BP Oil in the field of educational liaison, as part of the BP Group policy. Long before it became fashionable, the BP Group was involved in schools liaison, providing links between industry and education as well as materials for use in schools. Nowadays the brief has widened and BP is involved in educational liaison at all levels – schools, further and higher education. There are still far too few women available who are qualified to compete in the more technical areas and this is one reason why BP as a group is solidly behind initiatives like WISE (Women into Science and Engineering).

Over the past few years BP has given direct financial support to the Women's Engineering Society by sponsoring the Verena Holmes Lectures and a Women Returners' Fellowship at Kent University to create a post for a woman scientist to return to work after raising a family. In addition, there has been support for various conferences and literature.

Since 1980 BP has been supporting women's training roadshows – exhibitions and training events at locations close to BP sites. The sites provide materials and personnel. BP's contribution has been to encourage women to work in industry, with special emphasis on science and engineering.

This support is taken seriously at the most senior level in the company – Basil Butler (a Managing Director of the BP Group) is a patron of the Ninth International Conference for Women Engineers and Scientists to be held in July 1991.

But the encouragement of women engineers and scientists is necessary at as early a stage as possible in the education process. While the new national curriculum will go some way towards preventing the disastrous early choice away from science subjects, much more needs to be done in schools to make science and engineering subjects attractive and seen as worthwhile. So what are we doing about encouraging young people to become interested in science and technology subjects while still at a stage when they can make decisions on their longer-term education?

BP's educational relations unit has been building links with schools for over twenty years. Today more than 200 schools close to the main BP sites, ranging from Shetland to South Wales, are linked to the company, enabling the direct involvement of BP staff with teachers and young people. A BP staff member (link officer) and a link teacher from the school act as a communications channel and arrange activities, which can span the whole curriculum. The scheme forms the basis for all BP's work with education, and its main objectives are:

● to create a better understanding of BP and industry generally by students and teachers;

- to increase the number of industrial experiences available to students and teachers;
- to create a better understanding of education by BP staff.

In addition the Project support programme has as its main objectives the better learning of maths, science and technology, increased economic and industrial understanding and the development of more confident and motivated young people with better capabilities and transferable skills relevant for working life.

For some, however, the die is cast and, whether by choice or constraint, they land up at university or polytechnic reading for an arts degree. If I had a penny for every time I have been asked at careers fairs whether BP is interested in history, languages or other non-vocational subjects, I would be rich! One of the most rewarding things I have experienced in my time in BP Oil has been to see graduates from wide cross-section of degree disciplines settling into a commercial career with the company. Some have the opportunity to put some of their acquired knowledge into practice, either as linguists, computer scientists or chemical engineers. More often it is the personal skills that a graduate has gained that are most useful – the analytical skills of an historian, the communications skills of an arts graduate.

Careers guidance is crucial to decisions both at school and in higher education. As part of an industry/government exchange programme, I spent a year working in the Department of Education and Science, largely pre-occupied with a project which started with the unlikely title of Computer Aided Careers Guidance System (CACGS), now known as PROSPECT, which was designed to assist undergraduates in making reasoned choices through an understanding of their personal profile – likes, dislikes and attributes and the careers for which these would be best suited. In many universities and polytechnics the work of careers advisors has been severely curtailed through lack of finance, and a wealth of expertise and help is being under-utilised as a result.

One of the initiatives which I have undertaken with a small number of careers services is a project to enable them to test and train undergraduates in numeracy. A short test lasting fifteen minutes has been devised with a group of occupational psychologists. The test is easily marked and the careers service staff can then concentrate on feedback and remedial work where necessary to enable those less familiar or confident with figures to understand the type of numeracy skills which a company like ours requires of its graduates. It is by no means obvious to many students who would like to explore opportunities in marketing or international oil trading that numeracy is essential. The glitz and hype of the advertising world and 'marketing' is skin-deep. (As most of the professionals admit, it's 90 per cent perspiration and 10 per cent inspiration.) Detailed market analysis needs a head for figures! The test is being piloted by five campuses in 1990, and the Association of Graduate Careers Advisory Services (AGCAS), is looking at the potential use of the test on a nationwide basis.

It is a regrettable fact that many girls are frightened off maths and the sciences at school and instead choose arts subjects to study at university. By enabling testing and any remedial training on numeracy to be done while these students are still in higher education, we hope to attract even more women candidates into BP Oil.

There are other initiatives that BP helps by sponsorship which have been set up to assist students in developing the skills they need, but which they may not have developed through their course at college. PEGASUS is an example: it consists of a series of learning modules such as presentation skills, developing communication skills, developing assertiveness, managing change.

At the heart of it lies our concern to keep choice open, because that, after all is what women want.

13

Take a Good Look At Yourself

by Anita Higginson
Brook Street

There are two main problems encountered by women wanting to return to work in Britain. One is the lack of confidence of the women themselves, the other is the intransigent attitude of employers. Over the past eighteen months we at Brook Street have been trying to tackle both in the most constructive way possible.

Firstly, women across the country have to realise they are increasingly needed as the skills shortage becomes acute. For those thinking of coming back to work, there has never been a better time and it is a real case of 'your country needs you'! Demographic statistics show a long-term shift in our population balance, with a growing proportion of older people. By 1995 there will be a million fewer school leavers and 900,000 new jobs, of which an estimated four out of five will be filled by women, particularly women returning to work after a career break. So they are desperately needed if the wheels of industry are to be prevented from grinding to a halt.

Secondly, there is the question of whether or not firms are really ready and, indeed, willing to take an older women returning to work. Changing entrenched attitudes involves a long, uphill struggle but, thankfully, many companies are beginning to adapt their recruitment and training policies to accommodate women with childcare problems, low self-esteem and poor confidence levels. The big banks like Midland and companies in the retail sector like Boots and B & Q have been especially helpful in setting up schemes to help women return to work. Other major companies are also thinking about these issues. Smaller businesses, on the other hand, will probably always find it harder to adapt; they feel they cannot afford to take risks and they may be doubtful of the permanence of change.

Two years ago, Brook Street carried out a survey of the obstacles – both real and perceived – facing women thinking of resuming a career. What clearly emerged was that women are desperate to go back to work, for a huge variety of reasons. For some it was simple economics: the problems of coping on one salary, with increasingly high mortgage costs forced them to think about supplementing the family income. Others felt strongly that they should be seen as individuals in their own right, rather than as somebody's mother or wife. Added to this, many women felt the need for social interaction with other adults, claiming that, after years confined to the home with small children, they feel they lacked stimulation and challenge.

The survey also demonstrated that many were frightened to take even the first steps toward getting a job. A chronic lack of confidence was the main cause, often irrespective of how long they had been away from work. They frequently wondered whether they really had very much to offer, despite having spent years overseeing the family budget, chairing the local school's parent/teacher association, organising a never-ending succession of children's parties, running a scout troop. . . .

As a part of our programme for women returners, we point out that a tremendous number of social, interpersonal and crisis management skills are developed while running a family, not to mention attributes like managing a household budget, acting as a mediator and negotiator, taxi driver and social secretary. It is a tremendous feat of administration.

Many women have all these skills without realising it. A middle-aged woman who came into one of our branches for help and advice on returning to work was asked what she had done over the past twelve months. At first she could think of nothing of any significance, but later mentioned that, when her daughter got married recently, she had masterminded both the wedding and a reception for 200 guests. Apart from making the bride's and bridesmaid's dresses, she had organised the caterers, made all the bookings and done all the liaison work, between the customer (her daughter) and the producers (musicians, transport, flowers, the bar, the church, and so on).

If you told that woman that your secretary had just organised a conference for 170 people, she wouldn't be able to see the analogy between the two events. Once gently pointed out, the same woman who thought she was fairly worthless begins to see that she does have the kind of skills an employer would value. Other women, who say they have done 'nothing' since their children were born, may have chaired the parish council, organised charity events and produced highly-popular local theatrical performances – all skills acquired at home that are discounted because they do not constitute paid work. An employer would pay a woman for using those same skills in a job, and quite rightly so.

Childcare is another stumbling block on the path back to a job and Brook Street's 100 branches, while not in a position to provide the ultimate expertise, ensure they are equipped with a broad range of information about what is available in each area across the country. Just knowing what is available gives them a head start. We find this helps women over the first hurdle, when their confidence may be at its lowest. We also provide details of training courses, often run especially for women returners to enable them to not only brush up on job skills but also to meet other women in a similar situation.

So, two years ago, we set about trying to get the message across that women must regard themselves as individuals and value the experience they can bring to a job, because employers desperately need them.

The company organised a nationwide series of seminars open to the public. To our amazement, thousands of women attended. We assured them that we sympathised with their lack of confidence but were keen that they realised they were not alone. We were able to change their attitudes by helping them to value their work and to appreciate that competence and skills achieved while at home looking after a family were easily and readily transferable to the work place.

We have discovered that the first step in building self-assurance often comes after the advice sessions at this sort of seminar, when women start talking to each other and realise that their fears are mutually shared and can be easily overcome. Sometimes people benefit just as much from this personal interaction as from the practical instruction. You can almost hear a sigh of relief when other women echo their anxieties. I believe that absolutely anyone, man or woman, young or old, irrespective of how long they've been out of the work place, will feel exactly the same.

One of the greatest concerns about getting back into the modern-day work force is fear of modern technology. Those of us in offices are often guilty of making the word processor or personal computer sound as if it's something that launches spaceships. In fact, just about anyone who can operate a microwave or a video machine at home can use a computer at work.

At our seminars, we introduce a highly-sophisticated but remarkably easy-to-use computer system which utilises a training package called Audition. This system evaluates and develops existing skills to take into account the demands of modern technology. Without interfering or advising, we encourage women to experiment so that, within a few minutes, their confidence has begun to return and they start to feel that they have something really positive to offer.

Older women also feel threatened by their perception of more attractive and younger colleagues. For example, they believe youthful, better-looking secretaries are more acceptable to an employer. I strongly question this perception and a gratifyingly increasing number of employers do too. After all, if a company takes on a 'dolly bird' to do a secretarial job and she can't type adequately, she is more than useless. She costs the company money and fails to deliver; that can lose business very quickly. It is personal ability and commitment to do a job that counts in the end, not personal appearance.

Of course, many would-be returners simply apply for a job advertised in a local newspaper, or contact an old employer. Modern employment agencies, however, now offer far more than vacancy listings. Using an employment service when job-hunting takes away a lot of the pressure and the daunting problems that go with it. It helps women re-evaluate themselves, prepares them for interviews, gets them in the right frame of mind and can help match them to a job with which they can cope.

We open doors that even the best written CV can fail to penetrate. In many firms, women are still sifted out, on paper, if they are over forty and don't have current or recent work experience. An agency with a good reputation can overcome that rejection by telling an employer with whom the agency has a strong rapport why a particular woman fits the bill.

Any person, young or old, in any new job has a learning curve. Older women coming back into the jobs market have skills that can be swiftly upgraded and a work ethic that is often stronger than that of younger people. More mature people often give 105 per cent instead of 95, dragging themselves into work even when they are ill and devoting their entire day to the job at hand, with fewer social diversions. Companies who have tried taking on mature people are usually quickly converted.

One employer I know, who took on a 43-year-old woman return-ing to work after some years, told me, 'I just know that the commitment and loyalty I will get from Mrs X will be higher than I'd get from a younger person. Okay, when it's sports day she'll want an afternoon off, or, when the kids are ill, she'll need even more time away from the office, but I also know that, whatever days I give her, she'll give back twofold.' Discussing these examples with both employers and women returning to work helps overcome the psychological hurdles.

An employment service may help women to build on the expertise they already have, rather than assuming they must throw it away and start afresh. For example, if ten years ago you were a nurse, your medical knowledge might be outdated, but how about writing down the other, human skills, that were vital in that job? A new job that requires those abilities, even if it's not a return to full-time hospital nursing, could be found very easily. Likewise, if you have always been really good with figures, you never lose that intuitive skill; it is like riding a bicycle. Instinct with figures is more valauble to an employer than up-to-date knowledge of new technology or accounting programmes, which can be taught very quickly.

Feeling good about your appearance is crucial to making others feel good about you. It really doesn't matter how old or dowdy you are! Improvement is usually easy with a little professional help. If you have been at home for a while, you may not have had the inclination, or the money, to spend on new clothes. By returning to work, you are entering a different environment, so you should analyse your intended job and dress accordingly. You don't have to invest a fortune to make yourself look competent. It is crucial to look as if you are working in the Nineties and not the Sixties, but at the same time, it is a mistake to try and appear young and trendy if that's not how you really are. If you hike up the skirt, apply too much make-up and gel your hair unnecessarily, you will not be comfortable and won't perform well at an interview or – moreover – in a job.

An employment agency will also give help with interviews, with advice for people who have not faced this kind of situation recently. For example, by taking your coat off when you arrive at an interview, you already look as if you belong whereas, if you leave it on, the impression is that you are an interloper. It is also wise to do some research about the company beforehand, so you can talk intelligently about why you would fit the job. When applying, you should concentrate on positive points, not on the reasons why you think you could be unsuitable. Instead emphasise your past experience, stress that you have become familiar with new technology and mention your reliable childcare arrangements.

So the world of work needs you. You have more to offer than you think and retraining today is easy. I have concentrated on office skills, but all service industries – retailing, finance and caring – are searching for older people, particularly women, wanting to return to work. Whether you live in John O'Groats or Mayfair, the problems are the same, and so are the solutions. My message is: remember that women have a choice, employers do not. There has never been a better time – go for it!

SECTION FOUR

Second Thoughts

Right now the debate is about childcare and getting more women into top jobs. Pretty soon, if the feeling in my bones is right, it is going to move on. This section will provide some flesh for those bones, some food for thought. It won't be quite so easy to fulfil everyone's dreams, to meet every need, in the 1990s as the pressure on women increases.

Women have always been guilty creatures. Since time immemorial we have done what was expected of us: marry without question, in most ages and still in most countries today; seek and accept a lower status than men, often subservient; see yourself and all your worldly goods transferred to your husband on marriage, so that for many generations, even in Britain, a wife was regarded as her husband's chattel. Till this year, indeed, her income was not her own; for tax purposes it was lumped together with her husband's and she had no right to privacy, while he could and often did conceal his financial position from her. The support for child benefit as 'the only income a woman has in her own right' is a legacy from those days, and in my view less appropriate now that three quarters of all women are working, a majority of mothers too.

Today not all is enlightenment either. Until very recently the active and determined discrimination in law against married women created strong incentives to stay unmarried. The single person, male or female, was treated much the same, and the single woman had far more rights than her married sister, so many couples just didn't bother with a marriage certificate at all. Widows still suffer this type of discrimination: if they remarry, bang goes the pension. If, as my following chapter suggests, you wish to marry, the law on taxation, pensions and property is now far more on your side; the law on rape isn't, at least in England, but we hope to see that changed before too long.

My guess is that women no longer feel guilty about such discrimi-

nation, about such forced and limited choices, but angry about it. Perhaps that's the big change in the 1990s. Challenge a roomful of working mothers with feelings of guilt and they will laugh at you. The guilt now, it appears, has come full circle. It is the women at home who feel they have to justify themselves, not their sisters and mothers pulling in a pay packet. My preference would be that no one feels guilty; in a free society no one should feel pressurised into a direction she does not want to follow. The anger persists and must be addressed.

Meanwhile intelligent government ministers, encouraged by their thoughtful wives (more than one of whom works in the House of Commons library's research section, and understands this stuff better than I do), are saying that outdated laws which discriminate against women and against marriage are intolerable, and are taking steps to change them. But there will be opposition. Just as there are people around who advocate cigarette smoking on the grounds of freedom, or who opposed (and continue to oppose) the law on car seatbelts, so there are those who will take the view that women should be barefoot, pregnant and in the kitchen and like it.

Not only men are guilty of this outlook; there is the faintest whiff of such unreconstructed attitudes in John Whelan's chapter, as he carefully points out that what men want must be taken into account too. I know John and his family well – I've been out canvassing with them on hot summer days in hopeless seats, worked professionally with both him and his wife, like and admire them both, envy them their friendly and co-operative lifestyle. In fact, he is no male chauvinist pig but a good supporter of the ideas in this book. Nevertheless, tongue in cheek or otherwise, he warns us that it is wise to be aware of the teasing and the innuendo that will be directed at any woman, particularly any wife, who starts talking about equality. As Gordon Heald pointed out in Chapter One, barely half the people of Britain in 1987 were in favour of complete equality at home.

It is a legitimate viewpoint, even though I, who stopped working when my first daughter was born and was bored to tears and fighting for something more to do within three months, find it a struggle to come to terms with those who would advocate that I should love washing dishes and making the perfect casserole. They forget two things, in my view.

First, that the choice of staying at home is only a real choice if the alternatives are available. The majority of women stuck at home with small children plan to get back to work (not necessarily the job they left, of course) as soon as possible. A very large proportion of those at home are single parents – about a million of them. Two thirds of single parents exist on state benefit, half of them not ever having married and many receiving no financial help from a partner. Almost half the single mothers would happily return to work tomorrow, given a chance and some help with childcare. So the 'barefoot in the kitchen' brigade is way out of line.

Then there's the little question of how long we live. The answer is ages – the life expectancy of a little girl born in this country today is approaching eighty years. In historical terms that's an astonishing figure. At the turn of the fifteenth century Lucrezia Borgia was married at fourteen, on her third husband at twenty-one and after eleven pregnancies was dead of old age at thirty-nine. She spent the whole of her short but spectacular life being married and having children. Even at the beginning of this century life expectancy still hovered around forty. At fourteen today, a girl is starting her GCSEs; at twenty-one she's buying a car; at thirty-nine she's worrying about the mortgage. And in the years between the odds are she is working, just as she expects to work for several decades after the children have gone to school. The period in womens' lives when that 'MCP' attitude is just about applicable is now a tiny proportion of the years available to us. Barefoot in the kitchen? You must be joking! What may just be OK in the childbearing years sounds pretty stupid flung at a competent fifty-year-old woman lawyer or a forty-year-old woman truck driver or a thirtysomething lady doctor.

Perhaps in the circumstances we should not be surprised that one marriage in three ends in divorce in Britain, the highest divorce rate in the European community: match it with the highest activity rate (apart from Denmark) for women in the EC too, and with the least official childcare help. Barefoot in the kitchen, trying to do everything, leaving all the finances to the husband can sound pretty hollow in the aftermath of a messy divorce. Then women have to stand on their own two feet. Often they wish only that they had done so earlier.

As I read John's chapter, particularly his comment, 'As the professional woman moves up the ladder, so does her requirement for staff on the home front . . . ,' a bell rang. Is he really saying that what such women (like me) want is a wife?

Oh, for a wife . . . I looked up again the famous remark of 'Red Ellen' Wilkinson, that fierce spinster lady elected as a Labour MP *over sixty years ago. She had just collected her letters from the House of Commons post office and was looking at them forlornly when new MP Edith Summerskill commiserated. 'Oh, for a wife . . . ,' Ellen said. 'If I had a wife, she might have collected these, drafted answers and finally typed them. She would help with the women's section, give a hand with the bazaar and, when I get home fagged out, have a delicious meal ready for me.'*

According to Melville Currell in Political Women, *published in 1974, at least two other women MPs have gone on record as lamenting the lack of a wife. Shirley Williams spoke from the heart in an interview in the* New York Times, *back in the years when she was a Cabinet Minister:*

> *Absolutely no concessions are made for the special problems of being two things at once. . . . I can see the argument: why should women ask for concessions when they want equality? But it's no good pretending, if you're the person who's supposed to take the kids to see the dentist or get the meat at weekends, that you're in the same position as someone who has a wife to do all these things for them.*

The pressures, both in marriage and after it, can take a terrible toll on women's health. Each of us feels that we have to solve the problems alone: how to stay awake and sane and juggle home and kids and husband and boss, get to work on time, take the dog to the vet and grandma to the doctor's, grab the groceries, and tidy the flower-beds and still end up at the firm's annual dinner looking a million dollars. If you know the answer, I'd like to hear it too. Anthony Clare reminds us that women have always been regarded as the weaker sex, with our hormones to prove it. The Lancet's *rejection of female suffrage 120 years ago on the grounds that in women 'there is less physical vigour, and less fitness to encounter the obstacles of the world' does not sound so out of date: women parliamentary hopefuls, trying to convince a selection committee that here is just what they are looking for, encounter the same conviction every week. Many women struggling with the physical demands of having too much to do are tempted to believe it too, when instead the offer of a little help, and a lowering of impossible standards on their own and their family's part, might do wonders for their sagging morale and falling arches.*

What is more intriguing is that research shows that married men seem to do better psychologically than single men, whereas single women seem to do better than married women. Given that some of the studies on which these cautious conclusions are founded stretch back over thirty years or more, it can't just be a phenomenon of the 1990s. Perhaps marriage is a natural state for men but not for women? That would counter all our cultural conditioning, but it makes you think! Don't accept it too readily, though. It took a woman – Dr Rachel Jenkins, who used to be part of my team on women's health at the Department of Health and Social Security, as it then was – to suggest that the bulk of the demonstrated bias in psychological health was due to social rather than gender differences. Pick a really homogeneous group to study, such as a single grade in the Civil Service, and the differences between men and women disappear.

Perhaps the argument will come full circle one of these bright days. If women are more likely than men to show symptoms of illness typical of a lower social status, and if women are successful in improving themselves in the wake of the demographic timebomb, some of these symptoms might diminish. Perhaps work is good for us, ambition a healthy sign and promotion wizard for our psychological well-being? We shall see, but I doubt it, unless husbands start collecting the kids from school and ironing their own shirts at the same time.

What women want is choice, and respect, and time to enjoy both – just like the men, in fact. Perhaps in the decade to come, some of us, at least, will get closer to having it all. I hope so.

14

To Wed or not to Wed?

By Edwina Currie MP

Budget Day in the House of Commons is always an exciting affair. This is one of those days when being an MP matters – we will hear the Budget first, and only we will have a chance to speak and vote on it. Since before the First World War, budgets and financial matters have been the exclusive province of the House of Commons, the elected house; their lordships don't get a sniff at it. Earls and viscounts had taken one look at Lloyd George's budget of 1910 creating the first old-age pensions and thrown it out. Not until the King intervened, threatening to create 400 new peers at the stroke of the monarchical pen, did their lordships give in. From then on, only the Commons has a Finance Bill, only the green benches sit to hear the Chancellor intone the details of the taxes we would all have to pay in the year to come.

On Budget Day in 1988 I sat in the overspill galleries, up above Neil Kinnock's head, looking down on the front bench where Nigel Lawson was preparing himself. When the chamber was rebuilt after being bombed during the war, Churchill pointed out that most of the time MPs are being frightfully busy elsewhere, so a chamber big enough to hold them all would often be accusingly half-empty. Better, he said, to make it a bit smaller and put a few spare seats upstairs. As a minister I was entitled to sit on the bench behind Nigel, watching the back of his head, but I like to be up in the gods when there's a big occasion. It is less cramped, for a start; down there grown men sit red-faced and squashed together like badly-packed tomatoes. If we are delayed – as happened that year – I can yawn and stretch, even go to the loo. Best of all, I'm in striking distance of a phone, to ring my local radio station with delighted and adulatory comments before anyone else.

There was plenty for me to be pleased with that year. Sipping his water and wine, the Chancellor announced:

My first reform concerns the taxation of marriage. The present system for the taxation of married couples goes back 180 years. It taxes the income of a married woman as if it belonged to her husband. Quite simply, that is no longer acceptable. . . . I intend to introduce . . . a completely new system of independent taxation. Under this system, a husband and wife will be taxed independently, on income of all kinds. The tax system will continue to recognise marriage, as it should do. . . . But what matters is that, for the first time ever, married women will have the right to complete independence and privacy so far as tax is concerned.

The new system of independent taxation came in on 6 April 1990. Now both husband and wife are responsible separately for their own tax and all their income, including investment income and capital gains, just the same as if they were not married. So there is a big improvement for married women, compared with pre-1990; our main gain is privacy, and our money is not all lumped together with our husbands', shoving them into the higher tax bracket as used to be the case. That was some incentive to stay single.

The married couple will do even better if one partner pays a higher rate of tax than the other. For example, a married woman who is not working and is therefore a non-taxpayer should ensure that she receives any income from her savings gross. The building societies in these circumstances have been at a disadvantage for their interest has been paid net of (non-recoverable) tax. From April 1991, however, non-taxpayers can get the interest gross. Lots of retired married women will benefit if they know what to do. Tell your granny to put her share of the joint nest egg in tax-free National Savings or a Personal Equity Plan (PEP – also tax free) or shares or special savings accounts such as TESSA (Tax Exempt Special Savings Accounts). Best of all, get some proper financial advice on how to take advantage of the changes.

There is still some discrimination in favour of the husband and, surprisingly, in favour of the unmarried mother. A married woman will get a personal allowance against income tax. Her husband will get the same – and, in addition, a new married couple's allowance (MCA). It goes to him, not her. That means she may be earning the same as her husband but find she's paying more tax than he is. Some equality, huh?

The married couple receive the MCA whether or not they have children. An unmarried couple without children don't. They will each get the personal allowance, but nothing else. It is at last worth getting married these days. It is particularly good news for the married man, who is now smiling broadly, his extra allowances jingling in his pocket.

Only if a married man does not have enough income to use the MCA in full will he be able to transfer it to the wife to be used against her income – a recognition, perhaps, that there are many couples where the husband may have taken early retirement, and the wife is earning more than him (the personal allowances are not transferable). The allowances are much higher for people over pensionable age, so that merry widower may well be worth checking out.

If an unmarried couple have a child, an additional personal allowance (APA) is available to them. But this time, if the child is the woman's in circumstances where she and not he is responsible for its maintenance, she can claim the APA instead of her partner. So the married woman with a child has to depend on her husband's tax allowance, whereas the unmarried one depends on her own. It is an odd bit of discrimination in favour of the unwed mum as opposed to the married one, even though their expenses might be similar.

Let's add, for completeness, that a single woman is treated for tax purposes the same as a single man, claiming only a single personal allowance; it is expensive, living alone. If she has a child, she will get the APA as well. So will a single father. And since 1988 he can't claim the housekeeper or nanny any more than she can – here we have a little more equality, a lot more tax.

The Chancellor on that spring day in March 1988 made a further announcement: the ending of dual tax relief on mortgages as from August 1988. Strictly speaking, that tax relief was an individual matter, provided the people weren't wed. Any number of partners or friends, sexually involved or not, could claim relief on interest on loans up to £30,000 each. As I write, that is worth over £1,800 per year to a top-rate taxpayer or over £1,100 for standard rate. An unmarried couple could claim twice that, a married couple only once. You had to love the guy a lot to marry him in such circumstances!

The outcome of that announcement could have been predicted: a tremendous rush to buy property – almost any property – under the old rules before the August deadline. House and flat prices were already climbing. By August 1988 they had risen by 20 per cent compared with the previous January. A crash was inevitable. Many people found they had bought overvalued property in the rush; within weeks the market was dead and prices were falling, especially in London. The huge rise in house prices, the excess demand for new furnishings and more building fuelled inflation, to which the Chancellor's reaction was a painful but necessary series of hikes in interest rates – and mortgage costs followed suit.

It suddenly dawned on many of the unmarried partners that they now couldn't move at all or they would lose the additional tax relief. A mortgage is a loan secured on a particular property. A fresh mortgage would qualify for only one relief – one £30,000 – which meant that they would have to trade down, buying something a lot smaller or cheaper, to keep repayments at the same level. Poor souls, they're going to have the same standard of living in future as married people! For the moment they're stuck, and it will be some little time before the inevitable increments in earnings catch up with their predicament and release them.

From that point onward, it was clear that the Treasury was scrutinising proposals to ensure the elimination of any discrimination against marriage. Under the community charge (poll tax) legislation, for example, husband and wife are jointly and severally responsible for their payments. They pay one personal charge each and must ensure that the other pays his/her share. (Why? To stop anyone getting away with not paying, of course.) If they have savings, they are aggregated – as I write, £16,000 savings between them (not each) will disqualify them from rebate: not the same as the nice fair treatment under the tax laws, where savings could be split. An unmarried couple, living together as man and wife, will be treated exactly the same.

The rules for benefits are similar: most of the time a couple who live together will be treated exactly as if they were married. If the chap moves in, the single-parent status moves out. There is no room here to go through all the possibilities of the most complex system of social security in the world, but one famous case in 1985 involving a Mrs Jacqueline Drake pushed the then Department of Health and Social Security into changing the law for women carers.

Attendance allowance is payable at two different levels, depending on the degree of disability, to anyone who needs looking after – dressing, feeding, turning at night. Attached to it is a carer's allowance, the invalid care allowance (ICA). ICA is intended to compensate a carer who cannot work. From the start in 1975, therefore, it was payable only to people of working age – not pensioners – and not to married women living with their husbands, though it was available to married men. This, believe it or not, was the discriminatory brainchild of the last Labour government, so I feel no compulsion to defend it! The originators would say in mitigation that the new scheme would never have survived the eagle eyes of the International Monetary Fund, which was running our economy in those days, had it been more generous. I became a minister in the DHSS soon after Mrs Drake, a married carer, took her case to the European Court. In June 1986 as ministers heard a whisper that she had won, they gave in graciously: ICA was extended to married women and almost 100,000 of them now claim it.

The European Commission, and women's libbers in other European countries, make a big play on more equality for women in both tax and benefits. British women, married ones most of all, should be a little wary of some of their ideas, for in pensions we don't have equality – instead we have very favourable treatment indeed, which might disappear, disadvantaging over two million women, if true equality were enforced.

Ask your granny where she gets her pension. The answer is that she paid for it herself if, like many of the women who worked throughout the war, she paid a full national insurance stamp (that's a Category A pension). Ten years' contributions is enough – and if she has just a bit less, she can buy in the extra. One of my elderly constituents, armed with a well-thumbed copy of *Saga* magazine and a pocket calculator, took me through all this recently. Together we challenged the Department of Social Security and won her a handsome back payment. But if a woman doesn't have enough contributions in her own right, she can still get a reduced-rate pension on her husband's contributions (that's a Category B pension). When he dies, she gets widow's benefits, again on his payments, even if she has never worked.

This only applies, however, if they are wed. A married woman doesn't even have to be living with her husband; they may long since have parted, provided there has been no divorce. Girlfriends and mistresses, even if there's no wife around, don't get a bean. There is real *sex* equality – it applies in the rare case of a man claiming on a wife's contributions. Only if the girlfriend is looking after the man's child can she claim any money, and then solely for the child. For herself, it is social security. Want to check it all out? Try Ogus and Barendt, *The Law of Social Security* (third edition): this bit came from page 200. And the best of British luck!

If we women could have only the pensions we had paid for, a lot of us would be in the soup. Marriage in this country to a contributor confers considerable financial gain on the wife. That helps explain why state pensions look bigger in other European Community countries. Apart from in Britain, the wife/widow does not usually qualify for money in her own right based on her husband's contributions, so his single pension has to cover them both. In many cases, when he dies she is forced to claim social security or whatever system exists. Bear in mind that a true pension is payable as long as needed, whereas in many countries social security is by contrast time-limited.

In some jobs it doesn't help if you're single, male or female, either. George Newstead, a civil servant, took the Department of Transport and the Treasury to the European Court of Justice in 1985. He objected that he had to contribute 1.5 per cent of his salary to a widow's pension, while single women did not have to make a similar contribution to a widower's pension. On 3 December 1987 the court decided against him since survivors' benefits were excluded from European Community legislation. But the British government, on reflection, reckoned he was right in principle and changed the system. As a result thousands of single women civil servants and teachers are now required to contribute to a widowers' scheme. More than a few grumbled about it, yet that's what real equality means.

Occupational pension schemes follow the same ground rules as state pensions: not wed – can't claim. It's the same for the State Earnings Related Pension Scheme (SERPS) and for contracted-out schemes. The rules are getting more generous to the surviving spouse as time goes on, widening the gap between the widow and the cohabitee. From April 1989 personal pensions have had to provide a widow's or widower's pension by law, equal to half the pension in payment if the employee has already retired and is drawing his/her pension. If a man dies before retirement, his widow gets the lot – full rights. That is a big improvement. And in the latter circumstances, the employee who is divorced or single could nominate someone else to collect the pension on his death, so he could look after his girlfriend if he wanted to, provided he is not wed at the time. If you are living with someone and his health is shaky, just make sure he's nominated you to his pension scheme as the beneficiary. If he won't sign the papers, he doesn't really love you!

Many occupational pension schemes paying out to a widow will, however, take a dim view of her marrying again. The pension will stop. (That may also happen in the case of a widower claiming from his deceased wife's pension scheme, so watch it if your pensioned lover was once wed.) An unusual encouragement to living tally, perhaps? This was discussed in a debate on the Finance Bill in the House of Commons on 14 July 1987, when that lovely man, Sir Brandon Rhys Williams, took up the issue not long before he himself died. He said:

> I have often thought it a most disagreeable condition that where a wife remarries after her husband's death the scheme shuts off her benefit. It is a vindictive clause and the woman should not be expected to remain single after the husband has died in order to obtain the benefit of his assets. If the surviving annuitant does not go through a marriage ceremony to another party, but continues to live in the same house with that person, the scheme has to go on paying.

Yes, but . . . however odd that may be, as another MP, John Greenway pointed out:

> From an actuarial viewpoint the real issue is the provision of a pension for a member of the scheme – the person who is buying the pension policy. The more people and conditions one puts on the payment of benefit after the member's death, the less pension benefit the individual will obtain in his retirement.

What you pays for, you gets, and no more.

For much the same reasons, divorced women will find they can't claim a pension from their ex-husbands. It can be hard when the woman lived in circumstances where she couldn't work. Lady Ewart-Biggs, widow of a diplomat, pointed out in the House of Lords on 16 June 1988 that in other countries special arrangements are made for the divorcees of diplomats so that a proportion of the occupational pension goes to each wife! Handy when you are permitted several, I suppose, but it won't happen here. The Lord Chancellor issued a consultation document on the issue in 1985 (Occupational Pension Rights on Divorce), but no proposals for legislation have appeared and I wouldn't put my money on their doing so. You want a pension? Stay married, or pay for your own.

People decide to marry or not on many grounds – the legal and tax positions are seldom uppermost in their minds. In recent decades there has been official discrimination against marriage which has now all but disappeared. During that time living together without marriage became much more popular and socially acceptable in all social classes. By the late 1980s co-habiting was no longer a distress choice, where for example one of the partners was still married to someone else; it was, dare I say it, even trendy. A quarter of all the children born in these years were born out of wedlock, many of them lovingly registered by both parents. Perhaps now that the Chancellor has sorted out the main discouragements to the wedded, the trend will change back?

Or maybe not. I had tea with a woman friend who lives with her chap; they have one much loved child, and a failed marriage each behind them. No, they are not planning to get married – what for? Anyway, we can't afford to, she told me, for we would lose the additional tax relief on the mortgage. And aren't nannies expensive these days . . . ? Thinking about it as I drove home, I reflected on that ordering of priorities. If they can afford a nanny and a very big house and three colour televisions and two cars and . . . they can afford to get married. If they wanted to.

The only important benefit for the unmarried I can see under current law lies in an unpleasant field – the law on rape. Just as Queen Victoria would not allow the banning of lesbianism because she didn't believe it happened, so English legislation does not recognise that a married woman can be raped by her husband. Under guidelines first set down in 1736 it has long been held that marriage in itself constitutes consent to sexual intercourse. The law was reviewed by the Criminal Law Revision Committee which confirmed this position as recently as 1984. The Committee members concluded by a narrow majority that a change in the law was not desirable 'as it raised issues about the nature of marriage and about violence in the domestic context which went beyond the scope of the criminal law'.

In Scotland, however, the High Court ended husbands' legal immunity in 1989 when it ruled that a man could indeed be charged with raping his wife while the two of them were living together. The decision, which was widely welcomed, was upheld on appeal. At present in England the police can prosecute a husband for the lesser crime of indecent assault on his wife, and she will be protected if he causes her actual or grievous bodily harm – but he can't be charged with rape, which can carry a life sentence. He can, however, if she is not married to him. The evidence of rape has to be collected in the usual way and there seems no reason other than outmoded prejudice why the law is so written. On occasion I venture to disagree with one of my male Tory colleagues. Try this remark from Tony Marlow, the MP for Northampton North, in the Commons on 21 February 1990: 'How on earth do you prove that rape has occurred between cohabiting husband and wife? If the good lady has a headache, it could be inconsiderate for the husband to proceed. If she had a bad headache, would it be rape?'

In February 1990 John Patten, the Home Office Minister who chairs the inter-departmental Ministerial Group on Women's Issues, announced that the law was being sent for review by the Law Commission. It will be at least a year before their report will be received, with legislation possibly a year after that; meantime the law remains as now. I firmly hope that we get it changed.

The law on property has altered a great deal in recent years and now generally favours married women. Most of the time couples don't hassle about who owns what and there are no great differences between married and unmarried women. Only if the relationship breaks down, or when the partner dies, are women likely to discover that co-habitation is not such a great idea.

Under the Matrimonial Causes Act of 1973, the divorce courts have a wide discretion to decide how property should be disposed of. If a house is in the man's name, the wife may nevertheless lay a claim to it even if she has never paid a penny into the home; it is taken for granted that a wife makes a contribution just by being a wife. That is not true for a co-habitee, however: she has to prove that there was some kind of financial arrangement. The courts have no special powers for her. Disputes over ownership are then determined by applying the usual rules of law governing property, contract and trusts, as if the man and woman were and always had been strangers. Often a woman can prove she helped pay for a house, or that she was financially dependent on a man. There is no difficulty, usually, in a child proving dependence, but the courts often take the view that a normal single woman who has had a relationship which has broken up may be expected to provide for herself, and has no claim on the man. No palimony here: had he wanted her to have a claim on him, he would have married her.

The courts do have wide powers when there is a real divorce going on. In the celebrated divorce case of John Browne MP, he was able to prove that money in his ex-wife's name actually belonged to him – a matter which took her (not him) to the bankruptcy court.

There's no statutory co-ownership of a home, even though many married women believe there is. Such a tightening of the law in favour of married women (as opposed, of course, to married men) has been discussed on several occasions, and was recommended by the Law Commission in its Third Report on Family Property in 1978, but it has never been implemented.

The unwed might try having a legal contract, a method which is popular in the USA. All I can say is: don't rely on it. You would have to enforce such a contract in a dispute through the courts, where you might find it's not worth the paper it is written on. If you want a contract, the safest position in Britain is to use the marriage contract, backed up by the existence of stacks of case law which may settle any arguments forthwith and which on the whole has treated women very fairly.

What happens if your husband dies? On the death of one partner any jointly owned property will automatically go to the surviving joint owner, whether the partners were married or not. That is the sum total of equality under the current law; everything else favours the wife as against the mistress.

If the partner dies without making a will, for example, a surviving spouse takes everything (unless, under legislation dating from 1925, he has included certain other relatives, in which case there are special rules). A co-habitee is not entitled to such a share, but can apply to the courts. Then she will come under the same rules as if he has made a will leaving her out.

We can all make a will leaving property to whomsoever we wish. Provided it has been properly made, the courts will try to accede to the deceased's wishes, however bizarre. Lots of wills are challenged every year, but it is only worth trying if you were dependent on the dead man and can prove it under the Inheritance (Provision for Family and Dependants) Act 1975. Under that legislation, however, there are two rules, one for the wed, one for the unwed.

The court can order financial provision for spouses and any other person who immediately before the death of the deceased was being maintained wholly or partly by the deceased, where the will (or lack of a will) fails to make 'reasonable provision' for them. Spouses do not need to show that they require provision for their maintenance; they can simply apply for a greater share of the estate. Cohabitees are required by law to show their need. The court's powers are quite limited and the word 'immediately' catches people out too. If you never married him, but carried on working and then find he's left all the money to his mother, take some legal advice before you challenge the will. Good luck to you – it's a miserable business and any gain can be swallowed up in legal fees.

As Adelaide in *Guys and Dolls* says, 'Marry the man today' – and she did.

15

What Women Want . . . By A Man

by John Whelan

'With men he can be rational and unaffected, but when he has ladies to please, every feature works.'

Jane Austen.

What do men want? The novelist Jane Austen believed that a large income was the 'best recipe for happiness' but she described as a truth universally acknowledged 'that a single man in possession of a good fortune must be in want of a wife'. Had the early nineteenth-century author who with somewhat false modesty declared she was 'the most unlearned and uninformed female who ever dared to be an authoress' lived today, she might have been more circumspect. Instead of a wife, Mr Knightley in *Emma* would have sought a partner. Austen herself would have been less insecure and would have called herself an author, accepting like a shot an invitation to appear on the *Terry Wogan Show*. She would certainly never have said, 'One has no great hopes from Birmingham,' having once stood for the City Council.

To fulfil her true mission of making the ideal wife the Austen heroine would need far more than the leisurely pastimes of a gentlewoman: embroidery, drawing and conversation. There'd be a driving licence, Mercury pager, Oxbridge degree, budgetary skills, professional qualification, diploma from the Prue Leith School of Cookery, not forgetting squash lessons, swimming and a neighbourhood aerobics class to keep in shape.

There is one question every man has to duck. It is simply giving too much away to declare here and now what a man expects from a woman, apart from the common denominator of timeless womanly attributes – sex – appreciated by everyone from John

Knightley in *Emma* to any other bloke today. Making a partnership work in the 1990s is almost as exhausting and exhilarating as dealing with American executives, sulky managing directors or ungrateful editorial contributors. When one working day ends, another begins. Households daily become more like the workplace. Soon there will be a software package to manage domestic relationships, bleep when the children have to do their homework and sound the alarm if one partner is about to lose their temper. 'Symphony' would be a good name but that's already been bagged by the accountants for analysing their working papers.

Returning briefly to Austen, how do men make 'every feature work' when there are women to please? It is a challenge with its own no man's land and shibboleths. The best one can say is that the knack is never quite learned, like trying to repeat tricks from *The Paul Daniels' Magic Show*.

The workplace is, however, inexorably changing. During my career in newspapers stretching back twenty years to the days of hot metal typesetting, the proportion of woman colleagues to men has risen fourfold. Some of the men are arguably wimps, so perhaps don't count. Some of the professions are dominated by women, but how few of them get to the boardroom or when they do are taken seriously by their male colleagues. Issues like that, however, are dealt with elsewhere in this book. In recent years both I and my wife have worked from home. The problems and the possibilities are different.

Let's look at the working home. By the year 2000 many more people will work in home-based businesses. That is a different concept from the 'outworker' of recent years, regarded with deep suspicion by the Inland Revenue and VAT collector. A home-based office has a personal computer, fax machine, photocopier, tame accountant; the mobile businesswoman bristles with portable tele-phones in and out of the car and at least one Mercury pager. Yet working successfully at home, particularly if both husband and wife do it, requires iron discipline and control no Harvard Business School could ever teach. The man is often, nevertheless, the winner in this kind of arrangement. His work takes priority on the PC. Nobody plans it like that, of course, but it is often so. The lament is always, 'I'd have met the deadline if you hadn't decided to operate from here today'. If that happens, buy another PC and double up on the software. Then you'll be arguing about the printer when she changes it from pica to elite.

Likewise the telephone. Once the clients complain about not getting through, install a second line and qualify for low usage discount on one of them.

Most men profit from a spell of home work. Out go the lager and sandwiches for lunch. Site visits take place only when strictly necessary. The amount of time wasted in meetings is reduced, while the number of hours really spent inputting text or compiling figures, as opposed to thinking about it, increase. The 'end of day' unwind in the wine bar or pub which may now be a ninety minute journey away, is almost impossible.

There's the rub. Life can easily become an unequal job share on the home front: men can find themselves actually helping with the chores. Before long it is the twice daily school run, picking up the dry cleaning, buying pancetta at the Italian deli and taking the children swimming after violin class. The time manager course soon goes out of the window and vital calls are unanswered. Of course that is what most working women have to cope with too, but it comes as a big shock to a man, accustomed to assuming all these necessities just happen without his intervention, as he realises he is expected to muck in too. His objections will sound unreasonable. He is amazed that anyone should ask him to dissipate his time like that.

The right approach here is to preserve the differences. Careers can work in parallel but space in which both parties can operate is all important. If you are well-organised, it helps to discuss who-does-what, as a partnership, well in advance, and then stick to your side of the deal. If you are too disorganised, then accept a shambles and don't moan; your partner is busy and most emphatically is not your servant too.

Coping with an upwardly mobile partner means a lot of adjustment. It is important not to compete with each other, create internal jealousies within the relationship or fail to give support when required. Barbara and Ted Castle had that down to a tee if Sue Lawley's interview on *Desert Island Discs* is to be believed. For the sake of saving face, pretend that her press release is a worthy effort, even when every sentence is inverted and shapeless ideas are linked with the word 'and'. If possible, knock it into shape before it goes out on the fax; she'll think the editor did it. Both face and reputation are preserved.

If your *forte* is words and hers is numbers, you have the ideal partnership. MS-DOS is a total mystery to me but my wife sails effortlessly through computer manuals as if she'd imbibed it all with mother's milk.

What if the woman works for her man? The temptation to take her for granted, both as homemaker and office staff, is intensified. While forty-three-year-old Paul spends a week photographing camel racing in Abu Dhabi, followed by three days at home, then ten days in East Germany, twenty-five-year-old Sarah minds the six-week-old baby and runs the office. 'I went out and got her a Mothercare credit card and left her three blank cheques,' he says cheerfully over a cocktail in the Abu Dhabi Sheraton.

Back at home Sarah is bored. Instead of chasing payments from slovenly magazine accounts departments she's hankering after the freelance nursing job she left before child birth. It had a routine, an importance and is locked into the wider community as a whole. It meant she talked to adults who even sometimes said 'thank you'.

'But I've trained her to put up my lights and at least she wouldn't have left my adaptor plug behind at the last shoot,' says Paul.

Paul claims he will make sure Sarah doesn't remain a telephone-answering service and plans to involve her in the business, marketing pictures and keeping his clients happy. It doesn't occur to him that perhaps he is planning merely to extend her subservience and she may have other thoughts. He can show he regards her as an adult, to start with, by giving her joint signing powers on his bank account. It'll probably never be equal to night nursing at St George's (who'd think she'd ever miss that?) but it may do until Sarah is ready to return to work full or part-time. The point is, not to take the partner's acquiescence in your plans for her for granted. If she is seething underneath, you may find yourself heading for the divorce court straight from the airport.

The home-based workplace does, however, offer marvellous and unexpected opportunities. Age doesn't matter. When sixty-three-year-old Charles' Norfolk building company closed, he didn't get on his bike but stayed at home. Norman Tebbit's father Leonard would have approved although curiously when Mr Tebbit Senior got on his famous bicycle it was the building industry that gave him his job. Seven years after the family contracting company closed its gates, and thanks to *perestroika*, Charles has built a successful business as a freelance translator using the Russian he learned in the navy at the height of the Cold War.

His wife Mary, aged sixty, only recently gave up supply teaching to write educational books full-time from home. With the four children gone their different ways, two to London, one all of twenty miles away to Norwich and the last to Australia, it's a two PC, one dog family, with the only fax machine in the village. There is time to get involved with the heavies at the local parish church, jolly up the village conservation society and support local charities. The couple's only regret is that they didn't go it alone years before. If the wrinklies can do it, why not the younger generation?

Now let's turn to the community. Giving something back to the community is at the root of most motivation. Yet if we are to get more women school governors, councillors, magistrates and voluntary workers, men have to give ground – the high ground in public life. That means men putting women forward, suggesting their names for appointments, being willing to serve under them as chairholders without making silly comments. Public bodies must create frameworks in which women can operate without falling into the trap of legislating for quotas, as in the Norwegian cabinet. Men must take action to ensure that women can play a bigger role in the council chamber, in the staff room or in court administration. The sadness is that most men from Nicolae Ceausescu of Romania downwards find it difficult to surrender the reins of power. Most men are guilty of tokenism in advancing women's claims to play a bigger role in the community as a whole; one or two women are acceptable, but the hackles rise, the teeth are bared, if women get anywhere near equality of numbers.

Some women, too, are guilty of prejudice, which scarcely advances the cause of greater equality. Linda Bellos, the former Labour leader of Lambeth Council, once declared that being black and Tory was a contradiction in terms. She was scathing about Tory women, her gentlest epithet being that they're 'ugly', although few members of the current Labour leadership in South London would win a beauty competition. Bellos is, of course, unique in that she claims to represent at least four 'oppressed groups' in one – being black, Jewish, lesbian and female. Lambeth may have seen the last of her thanks to the Widdicombe reforms which prevent highly paid senior officers in one local authority (she works for a different Council) being a member in another.

Persuading women to stand for political office is a major headache for all the recognised parties apart, it seems, from Sarah Parkin's Greens (although she lives in France). It is not for want of trying by the main political parties. Women seem too easily discouraged; commitment sometimes appears to be lacking. What women often want is the quick fix rather than the long haul: if at first they don't succeed, too many women shout 'prejudice' and give up. It is, however, difficult for a man who has sailed through the selection procedure – or even the occasional outstanding woman who has done the same – to accept that a potential woman candidate has to be better to get to the same point as an average chap.

Appearances can also be deceptive. One young woman looked to us like a dream candidate: – blonde, training for a professional examination, going to regular exercise classes – until she organised a fund-raising event and laid on special 'scented cigarettes' in the garden. Not right for presiding over the local magistrates court, but at least she managed to make a profit on the event, although some guests walked home in a bit of a daze.

In politics, on the magistrates' bench, in the governing body, the pattern of evening meetings, week-end engagements and casework is inherently inimical to family life. Because of this there are relatively few women with young children in local government or on the bench. Those that are get shunted into women's slots – children's home committees, social services and fund raising. These committees are, of course, important but until more women come through the system they will continue to be seen as appropriate for the 'ladies' and so remain female ghettos.

Then there is the biggest paradox of all. Constituency executive committees which choose Parliamentary candidates often contain a majority of older women. Yet try to persuade them to go for a female candidate! Curiously, the more objectionable prejudice these days in politics seem to be that only boy or girl wonders, still wet behind the ears, can ever make it to the top. Surely it is not too late to make a comeback after the age of forty. It suggests some deeply held irrational views about what a proper MP should look like. After eleven years of Margaret Thatcher, it is no easier now for a fifty-year-old woman to be adopted for the first time than it was half a century ago.

In my household both husband and wife have enjoyed going into community work. So far this arrangement has proved of interest only to a local free newspaper. Our partnership will never be as famous as the Bottomleys', but at local level it is already effective. Two into one often goes.

Working together in politics means flexible and rapid response and two votes on most things instead of one, provided the pre-meeting meeting has been done properly. Communication can take place at any time of the day or night. Try thrashing out the council's education policy cuddled up in the duvet, or creating a strategy to defeat the South Circular Assessment Study while making the children's breakfast. You get to essentials fast, you can test out the best arguments, and rehearse the speech while washing up; if it sounds daft while waving a Brillo pad, it won't sound too bright in the council chamber either.

One danger is to allow domestic disagreements to spill over into the political arena. The sound of the telephone is, blissfully, often enough to halt an argument. By the time the constituent's housing benefit problem is resolved, the tiff with the wife has been forgotten. Discipline is required but resigning in a fit of pique is not on. Once community involvement begins, the partnership is involved for the long haul. That, believe it or not, is the hardest thing for some women. Men seem to find it easier to accept defeat, to shrug the shoulders and head for a different battle they can win. Women seem to feel everything more personally; there is the danger that 'Why don't you agree with my views on the location of the new Fire Station?' may turn into 'Why don't you love me anymore?' on too many occasions.

Local politics may never get you to the Palace of Westminster except for a fund raiser or tour of the Commons but other local goals and objectives can be just as satisfying. The pressures on the family are, however, very similar to the demands of other important and absorbing jobs, except that community work has to be fitted in *after* the job, and after the chores too. At least one day of the week, usually Sunday, should be a family day. Yet how are the leaflets to be folded, the deliveries done, canvassing completed and the noon drinks party to be attended? 'Never on a Friday' is the rule with one influential, God-fearing segment of the local community ('never on a Saturday' for others) which doesn't leave much time if Sunday is also knocked out.

Should we involve the children? It can be some compensation that children make good envelope stuffers, aged seven or more, but once they reach teenage years they become more erratic as political aides. Unless they're desperate for a secret drag in a no-smoking household you are better off trusting the more elderly helpers for a leaflet delivery. The only beneficiary of our teenage closet smoker is the West Highland terrier, who gets twice as many walks in school holidays when our eighteen-year-old sneaks out for a fag.

This brings me to the subject of domestic help. There are times,

I freely confess it, when I feel that what a woman really wants from a man is an unlimited amount of household skivvying. That applies even to those who fail to be fastidious when left to themselves – drawers never shut, teabags tossed in the sink and half eaten carrots everywhere. True liberation for a woman is knowing that the Sainsbury's shopping will be done (but why send a man? – he'll come back with liver pâté instead of potted meat paste), the coal fire will be laid, the rubbish bagged up and the cellar will neatly be cleared of jumble. And that's just Saturday mornings before 10 o'clock. As the professional woman moves up the ladder so does her requirement for staff on the home front. Soon it is outside caterers for the dinner party instead of getting up early like Mum used to do. Home baking is a thing of the past and even the Yorkshire puddings come from a packet. But peas do come from the deep freeze rather than the pod, don't they? Aren't Marks and Spencer wonderful these days –?

In a family where both partners (or either) enjoy housework, cooking, gardening, chauffering and the like, there is no problem. When both are working, there most definitely is, and daily. The simple solution, since Marks & Spencer has yet to market a convenient robot capable of doing all the housework, is to deploy a tried and tested solution – the *au pair*. In the 1960s this practice was already well established among the middle classes. The household gets five hours' much needed attention a day, although light duties only are permitted. One ruse is to split the *au pair*'s hours, making sure she is on duty for breakfast: that's a way of getting a lie-in.

Thanks to the European Community there is now an endless supply of young girls willing to spend a year in England with a family in return for £30 a week, board and lodgings and the chance to attend English classes at the local technical college. (Watch out though – they have to pay the community charge.)

The family which wants dependability rather than flair from her *au pair* is probably best advised to choose a German or a Scandinavian. Norwegians are to be recommended but are thin on the ground. A Latin (Italian or Spaniard) will be fun but, if experience among our friends is any guide, more likely to get into scrapes. Unlike the punctuality of the German or Scandinavian, expect more laid back attitudes. A word of warning, however. The Teutonic *Hausfrau* mum rarely gives her post Berlin Wall daughters much instruction in cooking or cleaning. They're mollycoddled at

home and the big adjustment in coming to Britain is how egalitarian we are with chores. So if good cooking is required go for the
Mediterranean where kitchen skills are learned from a tender age.
Be prepared, however, for a sulking fit if the children reject the
trippa alla Nepoletana in favour of tinned spaghetti rings.

Remember you are dealing with healthy young women. Cupid
can strike with amazing alacrity even in the urban wilderness of
South London, although love also entangles the more stolid
Northern Europeans. A local barrister was amazed when his Canary
Islands *au pair* announced she was pregnant and getting married
to a Mexican. She suddenly upped and left in a taxi one morning.
Even more alarming was when the girl's brothers arrived with a
shotgun looking for the father of the unborn child.

Our household started with Turkish girls, Osgay and Meral. The
first was quiet, reliable and much liked by the children. Before she
left number two was recommended as a successor. It turned out to
be a case of Jekyll and Hyde. The children were left in her care one
weekend and on return it became apparent that various 'uncles' had
been to stay the night, causing enough noise to alert the local
Neighbourhood Watch. That lady was clearly getting what she
wanted.

While the woman of the house is getting what she wants out of
the *au pair* – chamber maid, woman servant, confidante, friend,
translator, philosopher and guide, the man needs to keep his
distance. Any impropriety is definitely not on. It is best to cultivate
the expression of a Cardinal Hume about to conduct a funeral if
suddenly confronted with a semi-naked woman on her way to the
bathroom in the middle of the night. This can impose strain,
although the solution for the wife appears to be not to panic but to
pick an *au pair* for her looks. In a sensible family parts of the house
simply become no-go areas. A harem (forbidden area) quickly
establishes itself. Both propriety and dignity are thereby preserved.

It is, of course, possible to specify a no smoking *au pair* before
entering a contract of employment. It is less easy, however, to
predict other habits. A Croydon couple we know started childrearing
late in life. He was forty-three and she was thirty-eight when twins
were born, the equivalent of batting No 11 for England and scoring
a century. It is a relationship where she wears the trousers, heading
to exotic places like Bophuthatswana to sell movies to television
stations. From day one – she was back at work a week after the
double birth – they have had a Norland nanny but also employ a

cleaner with a weakness for a drop of the hard stuff. As a result the drinks cupboard has been moved to the boot of the family car and the bar is open only by special arrangement.

Au pairs are often guilty of telephone abuse. Enter Mercury. Itemised telephone billing may not be the complete answer but at least it gets home the message about what it costs to dial an 010 number at various times of the day and night. Special training is also needed for all helps, foreign or otherwise, in telephone answering and message taking. A conversation can go like this. 'Hello, is Mrs Whelan there?'

'No, she's out'.

'This is Mr Whelan'.

'No, he's out'.

'This *is* Mr Whelan'.

'No, he's at work.'

Part of the angst of course is having a stranger around the house, with all the feelings of invasion (mainly on the part of the male) this can entail; knowing that we need the stranger's efforts or the household will collapse only makes it worse. Feeling responsible for the stranger – a young foreigner and (another) woman to boot – can make for very fraught relationships indeed.

In time of crisis, of course, there is nothing like a British grandmother. She is the unsung heroine of many a successful working marriage, not in the Maureen Lipman sense but as hospital visitor, baby sitter, cook and occasional bank manager. It helps if a grandmother is young enough to play Wonder Woman at short notice, hitting the train at 6.00 am to take over the household for a day. Grandfathers matter as well but the adjutant is always a better ally than the company commander.

When both partners work outside the home, the children can sometimes suffer. That problem is well covered in discussions on women's expanding role. The converse is the dependency syndrome which builds up in children if one or both parents are always available. The temptation is to ask Mummy and Daddy – often, perhaps, as a means of attention-seeking. An element of benign neglect does wonders for children. They can develop enormous self confidence from discovering just how much they are capable of doing for themselves. Our seven year old is a dab hand at cooking delicious scrambled egg while writing letters to Breakfast TV and the four-year-old has a nice line in peanut butter sandwiches.

Just how harmful is it for a boy to grow up knowing that mother as well as father works, and that every member of the family has a part to play in the smooth running of the household? Will he look in later life for a similar arrangement, and treat his wife as an intelligent equal partner, or will he be driven instead to find a passive soul to wait on him? Women's attitudes have already changed; men's have some way to go, if we are being honest. Teenagers who have known no other but a two-working-partner household may well take it as the norm in future.

How then does the balance sheet square up on the working wife? What are the pluses and minuses? It's clearly best not to judge the contribution a second wage packet makes in strictly financial terms, despite steadily reducing rates of income tax and the ending of joint taxation of man and wife.

Once childminding costs are deducted and all the paraphernalia of home helps taken into account, many couples calculate that two wage packets make little sense. They lie back and plan a bigger family. Profit is, however, not the only motivation. Indeed a life plan will obviously fail if a woman's formative years are spent solely at home weighing up the pros and cons of different brands of disposable nappies. The quality of a relationship may falter if the man's career advances while the woman's only thought process revolves around the home. Some will always prefer this track (our mothers did if we're over forty) but they'll miss the main chance. Who will know of their excellence?

Two years ago Clare, aged thirty-four, a mother of two children under the age of seven, had never made a speech in public. She regretted losing out on a university education and saw herself as a glorified typist weighed down with responsibilities and having no street cred. Life's opportunities had, she felt, passed her by, despite her practical bent, attention to detail and grasp of mathematical concepts.

Now she confidently argues the case for a traffic management scheme instead of a cut-and-cover tunnel proposed by the Department of Transport. Dealing with local bureaucrats, the police, lobbyists and hecklers no longer holds any fears for her. Clare's working days are spent moving quickly around from town hall to old people's home, probing, investigating other people's business and being a reliable friend to those in need. To her, committee rooms are no longer a minefield set with traps for the unwary. There was no road to Damascus; just a steady progression from the known to the unknown, support from sympathetic male colleagues too experienced to patronise and a growing belief in self and rising esteem.

Her husband is proud of her and amazed at his own ability to adapt, keener than in any traditional one-breadwinner home to please her and make her life easier, to enable her, too, to fulfil her considerable potential. At least I know what that woman wants — she's my wife.

16
The Pain of Change

by Professor Anthony Clare

'The great question that has never been answered and which I have
not yet been able to answer, despite my thirty years of research into
the feminine soul,' declared Sigmund Freud, 'is "What does a
woman want?"' He addressed this puzzling question to Princess
Marie Bonaparte, one of his most devoted pupils.

Given the circumstances of her life, perhaps she appeared particularly well equipped to attempt an answer. A direct descendant of
Napoleon's brother, Lucien, as a young girl she had desperately
wanted to be a physician. Her father, a geographer and anthropol-
ogist, regarded such a career as quite unseemly for a female member
of the aristocracy and forbade it. Subsequently she married a brother
of the late King of Greece, but in her mid-forties she gave up
everything in order to learn about psychoanalysis at the knee of its
founder.

A glamorous and vivacious woman, 'the Princess', as she was
known to her fellow members of Freud's inner circle, exercised
considerable influence yet she was to remain vulnerable all her life
to the limiting facts that she was a woman and she lacked a medical
qualification. In addition, in the world in which she moved,
that of international aristocracy, she was suspect. Her maternal
grandfather had been the founder of the Monte Carlo gambling
casino. She could be, and often was, snubbed at the Athens court
on account of the 'tainted' money in her background. She had,
therefore, good reason to ponder not merely what it is that women
want but also a question Freud did not ask: namely, how do women
get it?

There is no record of how, or indeed whether, the Princess did
answer Freud's question. The subsequent controversy has thus
tended to concentrate on what it was that moved Freud to ask it in
the first place. It is difficult to believe that he was all that ignorant

of women's wants. He had grown up in an exceptionally feminine environment, the son of a doting and proud mother and the brother of five sisters. In his professional life he regularly analysed female patients in depth. Throughout his later years he was surrounded by a coterie of loyal, dedicated and sympathetic women which included Marie Bonaparte and his own daughter, Anna. As a result, some contemporary commentators suggest that Freud, in asking the question, was jesting or that he was merely stating in reverse Hermione Hushabye's impassioned (and also unanswered) question at the end of George Bernard Shaw's *Heartbreak House* (which had its first performance around the time of Freud's question): 'What do men want?'

An American psychiatrist has recently suggested that Freud acknowledged the genetic, hormonal, anatomical and psychological differences and similarities between the sexes and accepted that such differences and similarities had nothing to do with superiority and inferiority. The answer to Freud's famous question, James L Knoll suggests, was supplied by another glamorous woman, Marilyn Monroe, who, when asked what she really wanted, replied, 'What I want is – everything'. Which, concludes Knoll, is what all of us, men and women, really want.

I do not know whether Freud was puzzled or joking and perhaps it doesn't matter very much one way or the other. What does matter is that, eighty years on, the self-same question is still being hotly debated by women and men. If, as several contributors to this volume suggest, this is a man's world, then, whatever views may be held about man's pursuit of the elusive 'everything', woman's quest seems certain to take its toll. Does it? Consider the medical evidence.

Psychological Ill-health

One of the most consistent findings of epidemiological research is that women report symptoms of both physical and mental illness and utilise physicians and hospital services for these symptoms at higher rates than men. Such a finding stands in sharp contrast to the fact that the female life expectation exceeds that of males at every age. Before I take a closer look at these facts, I should point out that a long-standing explanation of such sex differences in ill-health is that which accounts for it by reference to the stresses and the strains supposedly associated with women's biological status. From the biological perspective, women are often seen as the products and the prisoners of their reproductive system. Such a view was held with a particular vigour of physicians in the nineteenth century, an age which still exercises a singular influence on contemporary thinking concerning the relations between the sexes. The female sex, as one physician explained in 1827,

> is far more sensitive and susceptible than the male, and extremely liable to those distressing affections which for want of some better term have been determined nervous, and which consist chiefly in painful affections of the head, heart, side, and indeed, of almost every part of the system.

The intimate and hypothetical link between ovaries, uterus and nervous system was the logical basis for the 'reflex irritation' model of disease causation so popular in nineteenth-century medical texts, and it was accepted that any imbalance, exhaustion, infection or other disorder of the reproductive system could cause pathological reactions in other parts of the body. As another physician of that period explained: 'These diseases will be found, on due investigation, to be in reality no diseases at all, but merely the sympathetic reaction of the symptoms of one disease, namely a disease of the womb.'

No organ, and certainly not the brain, was untouched by women's reproductive system and fluxes. The brains of women, in the view of one senior French scientist in the late 1880s, Gustav le Bon, resembled more closely those of gorillas than adult men. Yes, le Bon conceded, there were a few adult intelligent women in the world, some of whom were even superior to the average man; but it was a grudging admission, for he then went on to argue that such women were monstrosities, like a gorilla with two heads! In his classic text, *Functions of the Brain*, published in 1876, the celebrated British neurologist David Ferrier argued:

> As the reproductive organs in women form such a preponderant element in their bodily constitution, they must correspondingly be more largely represented in the cerebral hemispheres, a fact which is in accordance with the greater emotional excitability of women and the relatively larger development of the posterior lobes of the brain.

By the end of the last century it was being seriously suggested
that there was a male hemisphere and a female hemisphere in the
brain – the male being the left cerebral hemisphere and regarded
as more stable, verbal and intellectual, the female being the right
and viewed as more excitable, intuitive and more readily exhausted.
The medical historian Anne Harrington, commenting on such
ideas, observes somewhat wryly that once one has given the two
hemispheres gender identities, the idea of cerebral dominance,
whereby the left is characteristically seen to take precedence over
the right on account of its being the location of the speech centre,
'becomes a rather apt metaphorical encapsulation of the social and
economic relationship between the sexes in nineteenth-century
Europe'.

Theories of female insanity were specifically linked to the biological milestones of the female life cycle – puberty, pregnancy, childbirth and the menopause – during which the mind could be
weakened and the symptoms of psychological exhaustion and even
insanity could emerge. So worried had physicians become concerning the alleged impact of woman's 'periodical ordeal', (meaning
menstruation) for example, that they began to express warnings
regarding its effects on those women who had begun to invade
traditional bastions of male supremacy, such as medicine and
the medical school. 'One shudders to think,' wrote one horrified
physician in 1869, 'of the conclusions arrived at by female bacteri-
ologists or histologists at the period when their entire system, both
physical and mental, is so to speak "unstrung", to say nothing of
the terrible mistakes which a lady surgeon might make under similar
conditions.' God knows what he would have made of a female
Minister of Health! Rejecting John Stuart Mill's proposal for female
suffrage in 1867, the *Lancet* observed that a woman's place is in
the home; in support of this sturdy proposition, the journal pointed
to the fact that women's physical nature 'shows a comparative
delicacy, the conformation of structures and organs is less developed;
there is less strength and vigour, and less fitness to encounter the
obstacles of intercourse with the world'.

Doctors continually emphasised the dangers of needlessly court-
ing the competing demands of motherhood and intellect and the
exhausting effects of the combination of academic study and menstruation on the female physique. Henry Maudsley, perhaps the
foremost British psychiatrist of his day, pointed out in 1874 that
'when Nature spends in one direction, she must economise in

another'; while Auberon Herbert in 1888 argued in his protest against examinations that women's delicate health rendered examinations even more damaging to their education than to men's. There were, of course, doctors then, as there are today, who cautioned against too ready an acceptance of the notion of women as weak, but in general women patients were confirmed in their subordination by always seeming at a disadvantage as a sex, in the words of historian Brian Garrison, 'whether because of childbirth or because they sought abortions or because they had damaged their health by procuring abortions illegally, or because they were suffering from a "hysteria" which itself often reflected a social deprivation'.

Then, as now, women appeared trapped whichever way they moved. The traditional Victorian woman, constrained within an occupational role she neither accepted nor could find relief in and fearful of the outside world of which she was still unsure, languished in a state of constant nervousness, to judge from the records of physicians of the day. Because of the lack of diversification in women's work, they were seen to be the victims of 'habit fatigue'. A psychophysical change was said to occur which affected the centres of sensation in the brain and gave rise to feelings of lassitude and tension.

The radical woman wishing to break out of this unhealthy domestic 'hot-house' could not apparently avoid the vulnerability to neurasthenia which appeared to accompany the more traditional feminine role. Indeed, her very efforts to immerse herself in the outside world only exposed her innate weakness all the more. Because a woman used her brain 'but little and in trivial matters', as George Beard, the American psychiatrist who 'discovered' neurasthenia elegantly put it, and because the capacity of her brain was but nine tenths that of man, the efforts to change her life-style amounted to a futile challenge to her physical and mental constitution. Indeed, some went further and saw in a woman's efforts to alter her social role evidence of mental instability itself. In a letter to *The Times*, the prestigious bacteriologist Sir Almroth Wright alleged that 'there is mixed up with the women's movement much mental disorder', a view which echoed those in a number of *Times* leaders, most notably that of 16 March 1912 which, under the heading 'Insurgent Hysteria', described the 'regrettable by-products of our civilisation' whose lack of mental balance provided the suffragettes with their recruits. Earlier, in 1908, the Emeritus

Lecturer in Psychological Medicine at St Bartholemew's Hospital, T Claye Shaw, had likened suffragettes' interruptions of political meetings, adopted for political reasons, however mistaken, to 'the explosive fury of epileptics'.

Many of these self-same arguments, albeit couched in seemingly more scientific and detached terms, can be heard today. Women are prone to psychological and psycho-somatic complaints, so the argument goes, and this is due to their hormonal make-up, their innate excitability, their lack of stability. The historical debate closely foreshadowed the questions raised today. Is the excess of psychological ill-health in women more apparent than real? If real, is it due to innate biological factors or to social and environmental stresses and strains? In other words, is what women these days want – love, a relationship, a worthwhile and valued career, a public as well as a private role – too much for them and is it producing, as those nineteenth-century doctors and commentators so gloomily insisted, psychological dissatisfactions and disorders?

The Findings

At first sight, and indeed even when more detailed analysis is undertaken, it does indeed appear as if women are more psychologically vulnerable than men. It is during adult life, up until retirement, that differences in the illness experience of the two sexes seems most marked. During this period, women report more acute illness and make greater use of health services, whereas men are more likely to develop chronic illnesses and to die. These findings persist even when illness and disability associated with pregnancy are excluded from the comparison. Women exceed men when it comes to complaints of depression, anxiety and other neurotic symptoms, while men exceed women in relation to alcohol and drug abuse and disorders associated with serious personality abnormalities.

Scandinavian psychiatrists have been prominent in endeavouring to calculate the risk of a person developing a depressive illness in his or her lifetime. In one particularly cautious study by Essen Moller and Hagnell, the lifetime risk of such illness was estimated at 85 per 1,000 for males and nearly twice that risk rate, 177 per 1,000, for females. Such a risk rate is remarkably close to that provided by a British general practitioner, Watts, who over the course of ten years' observation reported seeing very similar rates of consultation.

Many studies, however, are based on the frequency with which the sexes contact services. There are biases in such an approach. For example, perhaps women are more likely than men to seek help with psychological problems. Perhaps doctors are more likely to identify such problems in women than in men. To avoid such problems, researchers have conducted community surveys such as that by Martin and her colleagues which studied 750 families in a Hertfordshire housing estate in 1957. Respondents were asked to rate their experience of a number of classic psychological symptoms and the results indicated a clear excess of self-reported depression, 'nerves' and sleep problems in the women.

One of the most extensive and intensive recent community studies is that undertaken by Paul Bebbington and his colleagues in Camberwell, South London. Eight hundred subjects were screened using well-established measures of psychological ill-health and a final prevalence of psychological disturbance was calculated at 6.1 per cent for men and 14.9 per cent for women. Women showed a higher prevalence of disorder in the age groups twenty-five to thirty-four and forty-five to fifty-four, whereas in men there was no significant association. This study did not find the association of depression with social class reported by sociologist George Brown in his classic 1978 study of depression in women. What it did show, however, was that while single men had very much higher rates of psychological ill-health than married men, single women had better levels of psychological health than married women.

In an even more extensive community survey of nearly 6,000 people representative of the population of West London, Joanna Murray and her colleagues explored the correlates of health and illness and found a clear sex difference in the frequency with which the sexes reported symptoms. Men were more likely than women to rate their psychological health as good or very good (66 per cent compared with 54 per cent) and this sex difference persisted across all age groups.

The link between sex and psychological ill-health, suggested by hospital outpatient statistics and research findings in general are confirmed in community-based studies. This somewhat dispels the argument that the discrepancy is due to doctors' labelling women as ill or to women's greater tendency to seek help. But there is still the problem that the samples within the community surveys are not homogeneous. One of the few early studies which attempted to diminish the bias introduced by the social and occupational differences working in the late 1950s with employees of the New York Telephone Company. The researchers examined the medical records for the preceding twenty years of a random sample of telephone operators and craftsmen who had been continuously employed by the company during those years. They found a prevalence of 141 general illness episodes in males and 237 illness episodes in females per hundred persons per year. In men there were 1.42 episodes of anxiety, tension and other psychological symptoms per year compared with 5.98 episodes of such symptoms in female per hundred persons per year.

However, the study illustrated some of the difficulties encountered when any attempt is made to establish a truly homogeneous sample. The report stated that the men and the women were comparable in terms of social and economic factors in the preceding twenty years, but in fact no account was given of the sex difference of individuals' grades within the company's hierarchy. Similarly, no account was given of the sex distribution within the telephone operators and the craftsmen, but it seems more than likely that the bulk of telephone operators were women and the craftsmen were men. Thus the population was almost certainly not homogeneous for occupation. In addition, the residual population that was studied, composed of 96 telephone operators and 116 craftsmen who had been continuously employed for the twenty years, represented 90 per cent of the original men employed twenty years previously but only 10 per cent of the original women, presumably because most women married and left to raise a family in the intervening years. Indeed, the sample of women studied contained a disproportionate number of single, widowed and divorced women, a group who are often reported to have higher rates of ill-health.

The great bulk of studies of homogeneous populations are of students and in general they do not show a significant sex difference when it comes to psychological ill-health. Gordon Parker in Sydney reported in 1979 on a study of 242 students undertaking the one-year postgraduate diploma of education at Sydney Teachers' College. The sexes did not differ in terms of their experience of psychological ill-health. A number of other studies involving students comfirm Parker's negative findings.

The problem is that student populations are somewhat atypical. The age range is not the one in which sex differences are usually reported anyway. Students themselves are exposed to special risks in that their suicide rates is many times that of the equivalent age group in the general population. It was to clarify the sex-difference issue while avoiding any such bias that Rachel Jenkins in London and Kay Wilhelm in Sydney decided to embark on more recent and more careful studies of their own.

Jenkins selected a sample of employed men and women drawn from a population of executive officers in the Home Office. The study used a number of tried-and-tested measures of psychological ill-health and social stress and involved 104 men and 80 women. The sample was chosen because Home Office executive officers, male and female, are comparable in terms of age, educational background and achievement, occupational and social environment and, indeed, occupational opportunities and prospects. She found that there was no sex difference in the prevalence of psychological ill-health or its outcome between the men and women in this group.

Wilhelm was similarly anxious to ensure that the men and the women she studied were comparable in terms of important social factors. Setting aside such dominant elements would help establish the extent to which biological factors do indeed play a crucial role in any excess of psychological morbidity in women. A sample of teacher trainees, 350 in number, was scrupulously assessed and then reassessed some five years later. The mean age of the group on entry into the study was twenty-three years (twenty-eight years at follow-up). There was no difference between the sexes in terms of their rates of consulting for help with psychological symptoms although, interestingly enough, women were more likely to have sought help from a friend for depression. Medication for 'nerves' had been taken by 11.9 per cent of the females and 7.1 per cent of the males in the previous year. Scores on depression and self-esteem scales were the same for males and females, but females scored significantly higher than males on measures of dependency and neuroticism.

What these two studies suggest is that the differences in rates of psychological ill-health between the sexes reported in a variety of studies are due more to social than to biological factors. Separate out or eliminate the influence of these social factors and the difference disappears. If this is a correct assumption, what might be the social factors? A number have been suggested.

The first to be considered is the possibility that women in general experience more stress than men. To date, the evidence is inconclusive. It may well be that women do experience more undesirable life events by virtue of their low social and economic status overall since there is much evidence that they still have less overall status than men, both at home and at work, and frequently earn less even when in comparable jobs. There is also some evidence that women do experience more chronic social stress than men.

A second hypothesis is that women have less social support than do men. It has been shown that casual, less intimate acquaintances as well as close, intimate friends can afford protection from developing illness and that psychological symptom levels may well vary with the levels of social support available. It has been suggested that men, by virtue of their exposure to colleagues, have more sophisticated support networks than their isolated, house-bound wives. Certain studies have reported more social integration for men than women, but there is some evidence that this superiority in terms of quantity is more than compensated for by a superior quality of social integration experienced by women.

At the present time much attention is being paid to the possibility that it is sex-role conflict that renders women more vulnerable to psychological ill-health. It has, for example, been suggested that sex differences in the early upbringing and social environment of men and women place a permanent stamp on the personality of the individual, thus affecting their vulnerability to psychiatric ill-health in later life. Evidence certainly exists to support the notion of sex stereotypic beliefs about male and female abilities. There is some evidence that these sterotypic beliefs, particularly as they relate to female abilities, encourage low self-esteem, but how far this phenomenon might account for the sex difference in illness rates reported remains to be assessed.

It has also been argued that if women are biologically more susceptible to mental illness than men, women should have higher rates of such illness in each marital category. In fact, the literature tends to suggest that while married women do indeed have higher rates of psychological ill-health than married men, single women, the divorced and the widowed do not have higher rates than their male equivalents. Indeed, this has led some to conclude that being married is a less stressful and more satisfying experience for men than for women in Western society. However, more searching studies, attending to other factors including social class, social isolation, poverty and the presence of children, have established that the relationship of marital status to psychological ill-health is complex and varies among groups of different educational attainments and social expectations. The argument, for example, that employment protects women, single and married, from psychological ill-health is likewise complex. Some studies have found clear health advantages in employed women *versus* unemployed women, while others have found that the relationship is complicated by other factors such as the duration of employment and the presence or absence of a strong, intimate, confiding relationship.

'Women are not healthy,' wrote Emily Davies in 1866. 'It is a rare thing to meet with a lady of any age, who does not suffer from headaches, languor, hysteria or some ailment showing a want of stamina.' Miss Davies saw the answer to this invalidism in higher education, although many medical men of her time believed that the root cause was embedded in the remorseless biological demands placed by nature upon womanhood. Today the argument continues, although headaches, languor and hysteria have given way to depression, anxiety and irritability and the biological and social explanations now include the female sex hormones, sex-role stereotyping and role conflict involving the competing demands and needs of marriage, family and occupation. The current evidence is still modest and frail but does suggest that when social factors are controlled for them, men and women have comparable records of psychological health and illness. But men and women are not normally socially comparable – men differentially occupy to a greater extent the power positions in society, in politics, the professions and the media, whereas women disproprotionately are to be found in low-status, low-paid positions. Indeed, it has been said that once a profession becomes identified with the female sex, its standing in society and its remuneration fall. The teaching and nursing professions are a case in point.

The issues of status and self-esteem, however, are crucial to any discussion of what it is that women want. At the present time women are in danger of being trapped between the frying pan of the traditional duties of wife and mother and the fire of work and social function outside the home. The woman who commits herself to the traditional role finds herself guiltily explaining why she is 'just' a housewife, a role that receives no remuneration, less and less taxation and benefit advantages and possesses little social clout in a society deeply ambivalent about childbearing and rearing. The woman who is in full-time employment has to justify why she has turned her back on the traditional domestic and maternal roles, has negated her femininity in the eyes of the traditionalists. The woman who tries to play both roles experiences a nagging doubt as to whether she is performing either role to her or anyone else's satisfaction. In such a socially ambivalent culture it is hardly surprising that women manifest so much psychological distress and dissatisfaction.

An interesting New Zealand study underscores the role of social esteem. Sarah Romans-Clarkson and her colleagues in Dunedin, Otago, studied psychological health in a random community sample of New Zealand women. To their surprise, they found that married and widowed women and mothers had *lower* rates of psychological ill-health than the never-married and childless women. Commentators on New Zealand society emphasise the highly gender-differentiated nature of social roles. The explanation is traced to the pioneer circumstances of the latter half of the nineteenth century where the numbers of men far exceeded those of women. As a result a male culture was established, while women developed their own parallel but separate society. Despite or perhaps because home and family, the arena of female activity, was unfamiliar to men, its importance was highly valued. Romans-Clarkson and her colleagues suggest: 'Women who were mothers were regarded as meeting the general social expectations and those who did not bear and raise children were deviant. The deviance of childlessness, whether voluntary or enforced, carried the cost of social opprobrium.'

These New Zealand researchers point out that one explanation for the more common finding of high rates of psychological ill-health in married women with small children is the hard work, the long hours, the lack of any financial reward, the low status and the poor recognition. Another explanation is the social isolation experienced by many young mothers with small children. In New Zealand, they suggest,

> children, rather than isolating their mother from society, facilitate contact at least with other mothers through pre-school and school activities. State schools depend heavily on voluntary fund-raising carried out by the parents, in particular women. Such co-operative community effort provides a sense of social connectedness.

While the evidence that social factors play the major role in determining the higher rates of psychological complaint in women seems convincing, the arguments in favour of a biological vulnerability, so prominently advanced in the nineteenth century, still have their advocates. Sometimes it almost appears as if being female is itself a disease. The medicalisation of the menstrual cycle is a case in point. While it is nearly sixty years since the American physician Robert Frank first drew attention to symptoms occurring in the few days before the appearance of the menstrual period, it has been only in the last twenty years that the syndrome has acquired widespread recognition. Until then there had been some tinkering with the definition of the syndrome but little progress, which was hardly surprising since there was little agreement as to what symptoms constituted the syndrome, whether they promptly disappeared with the onset of the period and what possible causes were involved.

By the mid-1970s, however, an observer might have been forgiven for believing that an epidemic of pre-menstrual disorder was under way. A growing number of experts insisted that in up to 90 per cent of women the five to seven days before the arrival of the menstrual period were a traumatic time marked by depression, tension, irritability, breast tenderness, headache, bloating and a variety of disturbed behaviours including suicide attempts, aggressive and anti-social activity, poor academic performance, increased attendance at medical clinics and accidents. Much of the energy behind the surge of interest could be traced to one individual, the persuasive London physician, Katharina Dalton. Indeed, so powerful a view has Dr Dalton's been that one commentator, Germaine Greer, in a characteristically astute essay written in 1981 but more recently published, suggested that it might be less confusing 'if we decided to follow the procedure usually adopted in such cases and named the syndrome after the woman who has devoted the last thirty years of her life to tracking it down and treating it, simply, the Dalton Syndrome'.

Such was the public impact that some influential voices called for the modification of the circumstances in which menstruating girls sat important examinations, others insisted that warnings be circulated to women concerning the need for special care while driving in the pre-menstrual phase and doubts were expressed regarding the suitability of women to occupy posts in which periodic attacks of irritability, clumsiness and depression might be a particular hazard, such as those of airline pilot and politician! The reported prevalence rates of the condition steadily rose until eventually it seemed that the really odd woman was the one whose periods caused her little concern. Of course, there were some demurring voices. The American sociologist Mary Ann Parlee, in a sober and balanced review, lamented the quality of much of the research, its uniformly negative approach to the whole subject of menstruation, the reliance on retrospective reporting, the lack of standardised measures of symptoms and behaviours and the marked variation in the definition of the syndrome employed.

While many of the methodological shortcomings have been addressed and overcome in the years that have passed, the original claims have remained remarkably persistent despite the frailty of the foundations on which they rest. Few laymen and laywomen seem to realise, for example, that the claims linking pre-menstrual disturbance with serious crime, poor examination performance, suicidal behaviour and road accidents have never been substantiated!

Take what is potentially one of the most damaging claims – that a woman's ability to function intellectually during the pre-menstrual phase is impaired. Katharina Dalton's study of the intellectual performance of English schoolgirls provides the main supporting plank. The study involved an assessment of the effect of the pre-menstrual and menstrual phases of the cycle on the weekly grades of schoolgirls in a boarding school. A fall in the standard of school work during the pre-menstrual phase was found in 37 per cent, no change was found in 50 per cent and an actual improvement was found in 17 per cent. No statistical validation of the data was provided, nor was the magnitude of any disimprovement revealed. In a different sample Dalton also reported that lower examination scores among English schoolgirls were noted during the pre-menstrual phase, but again no statistical data were reported.

Since these early studies there have been several quite detailed and careful attempts to establish this negative effect of the pre-menstrual phase with little success. In a particularly thorough effort an American group studied the examination results obtained by 344 female medical and paramedical students in all examinations taken during one year and utterly failed to show any significant menstrually related effect on academic performance. Nor could any effect be found in those students who possessed personality traits known to be associated with a proclivity for psychomotor disturbances nor in those women who did indeed complain of severe pre-menstrual symptoms.

The tired, resigned question 'What do women want?' often seems to imply that the wretches are hopelessly discontented and seriously neurotic. After all, they constantly complain of psychological distress and does not everyone know that around the time of their periods they are inordinately touchy, unpredictable and explosive? A superficial familiarity with the research findings might appear to support such a view. The cruder studies show women complaining of various psychological ailments more frequently than men and suggest that substantial numbers of women experience all manner of pathology during the pre-menstrual phase. But much more thorough study indicates a different state of affairs. In so far as there are indeed differences in the prevalence of psychological symptoms, these differences appear to reflect the very real discrepancy in social status, autonomy, responsibility and power between the sexes. As for the research into pre-menstrual psychopathology and physical symptoms, the better studies all point to a very much smaller proportion of women affected than appeared to be the case ten years ago and indicate that there is no scientific justification for excluding women from positions of authority, responsibility and power on account of their biological functions.

Conclusions

The history of medicine, and particularly the history of psychiatry, is a story which from time to time tells of attempts to establish a scientific justification for the lowly position in public life occupied by most women and of equally vigorous attempts to contest such a view. Today, as more and more women, and indeed many men, ponder the question 'What do women want?', there is a resurgence of interest in and study of the psychological health of women and the related issue of the impact of their biological functions on their intellectual functions. Women in the active adult phase of their life are confronted by the dual demands and opportunities of child-rearing and professional development. That same phase is characterised by high rates of psychological ill-health and impaired social function. It is also the phase of their lives in which the full biological effect of puberty, pregnancy and the monthly cycles of the menstruum is exercised.

Today, as a century ago, there are experts who insist that women are profoundly affected by their hormones. In the 1970s a prominent

Cambridge professor of medicine suggested that women who entered 'male' sectors of life, and who were forced to adopt masculine attitudes and behaviours to survive, actually developed excess hair and deep voices as a consequence of the hormonal changes. Others, however, prefer to emphasise the effect of the disparity between female aspirations and possibilities on the average woman's confidence and self-esteem. Nor surprisingly, given the complexity of the issues involved, the argument is not cut and dried, but such evidence as we have provides little comfort to those who insist that women are biologically flawed or that their proper role is as housewives and mothers.

What emerges is what emerges from other areas of public life which are subjected to scrutiny. Women are confronted by a very real role conflict, a conflict which most men have yet to face. In many spheres, such as the higher reaches of the medical or legal professions, women either become 'surrogate' males, denying those traits, attitudes and values which they very often embody and which are not commonly emphasised in all-male preserves, or they drop out and settle for a lower level of professional life. Those who opt for domestic life suffer the widely articulated opinion that such a 'career' is suffocating both personally and professionally.

Whatever it is that women want, it is difficult for them to get it and even more difficult for them to feel satisfied when they do. In such circumstances, it is hardly surprising that women express their dissatisfaction and distress. Nor is it surprising that when women have the opportunities and the supports enjoyed by many men, their health, their social functioning, their self-esteem and their performance do not appear to differ greatly from those of the more favoured sex. From the viewpoint of psychiatry and medicine, therefore, the physical and psychological health of women may well be as substantially improved by the kind of social and political changes discussed in other chapters in this book as by advances made in our understanding of their biological status.

Biographical Details

EDWINA CURRIE was born in Liverpool in 1946, and read philosophy, politics and economics (PPE) at Oxford University, and economic history at the London School of Economics. She married Ray in 1972 and they live with daughters aged fifteen and thirteen in a converted windmill in Derbyshire.

She was elected to the House of Commons as the member of Parliament for South Derbyshire at her first attempt in 1983. She was the first maiden speaker of the new parliament and served on the Select Committee on Social Services and on the BBC's General Advisory Council. During her first parliament she was the only woman member with small children and a seat away from London.

In December 1985 Edwina was appointed as parliamentary private secretary to Sir Keith Joseph, the Secretary of State for Education. In September 1986 she entered the government as Parliamentary Under-secretary of State (a junior minister) in the Department of Health and Social Security, where she became the first minister responsible for women's health in the UK. She continued in that position when the separate Department of Health was created in the summer of 1988. A poll in the *Economist* magazine at that time showed she was the best known politician in Britain after the Prime Minister. Edwina resigned in December 1988. Subsequently she wrote her first book *Life Lines* about her experiences in government.

In December 1988 she was voted runner up to Margaret Thatcher in the BBC Radio 4 *Today* programme 'Woman of the Year' poll, and came sixth in the same poll in 1989 between Mother Teresa and Raisa Gorbachev. She became the first President of 'Women into Business' in 1989 and was recently voted Speaker of the Year by the association of Speakers Clubs of Great Britain.

GORDON HEALD was born in 1941 in Bournemouth. He graduated in physics from London University, in economics from Cambridge and with an M.Phil from the London School of Economics, and was a Fellow of the London Business School before joining Gallup Poll, where he is now Managing Director.

Gordon has concentrated on social and political investigations and research on human values; he carried out presentations to the President of the United States of America at the White House in both 1987 and 1988, and is currently advising several emergent nations in Eastern Europe on polling public opinion in their own countries.

Gordon and Christine have three sons now aged twenty, eighteen and fourteen.

PATRICIA MANN is Vice President International, J Walter Thompson Company, with particular responsibility for European affairs. She is married to Pierre Walker, and they have one daughter.

Patricia has been a member of the Council of the Institute of Practitioners in Advertising for more than twenty years; she was also for fourteen years a council member of the Advertising Standards Authority and has been involved in self-regulation and the development of codes of practice in advertising. She is on the Board and Council of the European Association of Advertising Agencies.

Patricia is the editor of *Consumer Affairs*, a bulletin with subscribers throughout the world, a government appointee on the Gas Consumers' Council and occasionally broadcasts on consumer issues. She was appointed in 1986 by the government to the Food Advisory Committee which advises the Ministry of Agriculture, Fisheries and Food on aspects of domestic and European food policy.

SUE DICKS read English at London University and following post-graduate training went into teaching. She has worked at four different schools, taking a year out at one stage to do research into the teaching of the English language.

Now, after a mid-career change, she works at a part-time secretary and freelance writer, specialising on women's issues, education and gardens and conservation, though she will tackle 'any topic that is of interest'. In 1966 she moved to Cambridge 'for a year or two' and would now hate to live anywhere else.

JOANNA FOSTER was appointed by the government to the chair of the Equal Opportunities Commission in May 1988. She and her husband Jerome and their children aged eighteen and twenty live in Oxford.

After attending an all-girls school she became a secretary on *Vogue* magazine, working both in London and New York. Since then she has had a 'patchwork' of jobs including the setting up of a bi-lingual nursery school and an adult language school near Paris; public relations work involving travel with three Prime Ministers; editing two newspapers for an international business school; and Director of Education for the Western Psychiatric Institute and Clinic at Pittsburgh University. On her fortieth birthday she signed up to study for her first degree.

She returned to England after ten years abroad to head the Pepperell Unit, the equal opportunities division of the Industrial Society, where she helped organise a national campaign focussing employer attention on the need for better training for young people at work.

Joanna is now an honorary Fellow of St Hilda's College, Oxford and is a member of the European Commission's Advisory Committee on Equal Opportunities in Brussels, the Industrial Society Council and other public bodies.

CLARE BAGGOTT was born in Liverpool in 1954 but grew up in Lancashire. She took a joint honours degree from the University of Keele in French and History, followed by a PhD in Mediaeval Social and Economic History. She married in 1975; her husband is senior systems business manager for Avis and with their two small children they live on a modern estate in Wokingham, a town near 'Silicon Valley' with one of the largest population increases in the 1980s.

Clare undertook several jobs after university including editing, writing, teaching, translating and adult education until retraining in technical writing and writing for translation in 1986. She joined Digital Equipment in March 1987 where she is a computer specialist. Apart from her home and family, Clare plays bridge and is an active member of the Working Mothers' Association.

STEWART AND JEAN PICKERING are founder partners and directors of Kids Day Nursery in Wilmslow, Cheshire, now trading as Kids Unlimited. They are in their early forties and both come from the north of England, Stewart from Hull, with a degree in physics and electronics from Manchester University, and Jean from Wallasey in the Wirral. She has qualifications in both clothing technology and teaching.

Stewart worked for ICL and other electronics companies on leaving university then became a teacher. From 1979 he ran his own music and recording studios until eventually the nursery company took over his and Jean's lives. Jean originally ran her own clothing business, but soon began teaching dance and physical education and running workshops and displays. In 1977 she joined Parkside experimental school in Manchester where she was responsible for establishing learning programmes for children and teachers. In 1980 she became a part time lecturer in physical education. Jean and Stewart were married in 1973 and have two children born in 1979 and 1986

HUNADA NOUSS was born and brought up in Cheshire. She is a graduate of Oxford University and qualified as a chartered accountant with Arthur Andersen & Co in 1984 where she is now a senior tax manager with a substantial portfolio of UK and international clients.

Hunada now lives and works in central London and spends much of her spare time in the West end, enjoying in particular the theatre and ballet. She is an active member of City Women's Network, which she says she enjoys for the stimulation and the lively exchange of ideas and debate on a wide variety of business issues.

SUE HARVEY was born in 1951 and is Managing Director of Childcare Vouchers Ltd, a division of Luncheon Vouchers which was launched in the autumn of 1989

Sue joined Luncheon Vouchers Ltd as marketing director in 1985 following the takeover by the French company Accor. Her brief from the parent company was to relaunch the meal voucher brand as a serious staff benefit. She became sales and marketing director in 1987, was promoted to become managing director of Luncheon Vouchers as well on 1 January 1990 and has now been appointed to the Board of Accor's United States Childcare Voucher Corporation. She has been both the architect and driving force behind the first such scheme in the UK.

BARBARA YOUNG is general manager of Parkside Districk Health Authority, which was formed in April 1988 by the merger of Brent DHA and Paddington and North Kensington DHA.

She is a Scot and has spent all her career in the National Health Service, starting with the South-East Scotland Regional Hospital Board based in Edinburgh. She moved into hospital administration with the Greater Glasgow Health Board and the Forth Valley Health Board, where she undertook all aspects of hospital management and development.

She moved to London as director of planning and development at St Thomas's. In 1979 she became the deputy administrator for part of the Kensington, Chelsea and Westminster Area Health Authority; on the next reorganisation of the NHS in 1982 she went as District Administrator to Haringey, and came to the Paddington and North Kensington Health Authority in 1985. On its merger shortly after with a neighbouring authority she was put in charge.

She has been an active member of the Institute of Health Services Management for over eighteen years. She chaired the national council in 1986/7, and the following year was appointed as the first woman President. She gets very little spare time, but confesses to being an avid cinema goer.

DIANA BALSDON was born in 1946 in Prestatyn, North Wales but grew up in Wimbledon. Both she and her husband Richard work for the National Westminster Bank, where she is the equal opportunities manager, responsible for the continuing development of NatWest's policies on equality.

Diana joined NatWest from school and by the late 1970s had become an assistant manager. Her career has taken her across many areas of banking, including lending, training, planning and international corporate finance. She is an Associate of the Chartered Institute of Bankers. She represents NatWest Bank on the European Women's Management Development Network and on the United States-Based National Association of Bank Women, and is an active member of Women in Banking.

MARGARET JACKSON is now recruitment co-ordinator and equal opportunities adviser for BP Oil, the refining, trading and marketing ('downstream') business in the BP Group, She is forty-three years old, has a degree in Geology, and is a Member of the Institute of Personnel Management.

Margaret has had a varied career with BP, starting as a geologist, then moving to the technical side of marketing before going into personnel in London and in Harlow. She spent two years with Deutsche BP in Hamburg, and prior to her current position she took part in a joint industry/Civil Service exchange in which she spent a year in the Department of Education and Science.

Margaret is also ordained in the Church of England in a non-stipendiary capacity and is an examining chaplain to the Bishop of Southwark. She is an active supporter of proposed recent changes to the priesthood of the Church. She is an avid photographer, enjoys singing, tapestry and embroidery, gets to grips with being a golf widow, and looks after an eccentric cat.

ANITA HIGGINSON was born in 1946 and educated at Slough; she trained as a teacher in Doncaster and taught at Godolphin Primary School. Anita then went with her husband to New York, where she was sales correspondent for an American law publishing company, and then to New Zealand. She joined Brook Street in 1971, and was appointed national accounts manager in 1983 and promoted to director in 1987. She is now marketing and corporate development director of Brook Street, one of the country's largest agencies placing around half a million people in jobs every year.

Anita and her husband live in Kent near Faversham; she is a cat lover and enjoys travel, the theatre, music, gardening and badminton.

JOHN WHELAN was born in 1947 in Hull and educated at Stoneyhurst and Oxford University. He spent much of his childhood in Malaysia.

John has spent his entire career in journalism. From 1977 to 1989 he worked for the *Middle East Economic Digest* reporting on Africa and the Middle East. He has been a regular contributor to the *International Herald Tribune*, the *Wall Street Digest*, the *Economist*, the *Sunday Times* and other British and foreign newspapers. He has published several guides for business travellers, the latest being for the United Arab Emirates.

After a spell with Redwood Publishing, he is now entirely freelance and working from home.

John and Clare were married in 1980 and live in South London with their children, dog and *au pair*. They are both actively involved in local politics in Lambeth.

ANTHONY CLARE who was born in 1942, is the Clinical Professor of Psychiatry at Trinity College, Dublin, and is the Medical Director of St Patrick's Hospital, Dublin, where he trained more than twenty years ago. He was born in 1942 and educated in Dublin. He and his wife Jane have three sons and four daughters.

Professor Clare studied at Syracuse University, New York and later at the Maudsley Hospital in London. He was appointed Professor and Head of the Department of Psychological Medicine at St Batholomew's Hospital ('Bart's') in 1983.

A most distinguished practitioner, skilled and respected teacher, assiduous researcher and the author of major scholarly works, he is best known to the lay public through his two radio series for the BBC, *In the Psychiatrist's Chair* which has been running since 1982, and more recently, *All in the Mind* which seeks to explain the psychiatrist's work more widely. His recreations include tennis, broadcasting, theatre and family life.

Index